ANTHROPOLOGY AND

Other books by Ernest Gellner

Words and Things
Thought and Change
Saints of the Atlas
Contemporary Thought and Politics
The Devil in Modern Philosophy
Legitimation of Belief
Spectacles and Predicaments
Muslim Society
Relativism in the Social Sciences
The Psychoanalytic Movement
Nations and Nationalism
The Concept of Kinship and other Essays
Plough, Sword and Book
State and Society in Soviet Thought
Culture, Identity and Politics
Reason and Culture
Encounters with Nationalism

Anthropology and Politics
Revolutions in the Sacred Grove

Ernest Gellner

First published 1995

Reprinted 1996

Blackwell Publishers Ltd
108 Cowley Road
Oxford OX4 1JF, UK

Blackwell Publishers Inc.
238 Main Street
Cambridge, Massachusetts 02142, USA

British Library Cataloguing in Publication Data
A CIP catalogue record for this book is available from the British Library

Library of Congress Cataloging in Publication Data
Gellner, Ernest
Anthropology and politics : revolutions in the sacred grove / Ernest Gellner.
p. cm.
Includes bibliographical references and index.
ISBN 0–631–19917–9 — ISBN 0–631–19918–7 (Pbk)
1. Political anthropology. I. Title.
GN492.G45 1995 95–14738
306.2—dc20 CIP

Typeset in 11 on 13pt Plantin
by Graphicraft Typesetters Limited, Hong Kong
Printed and bound in Great Britain by T. J. Press Ltd, Padstow, Cornwall

This book is printed on acid-free paper

Contents

For Raymond and Rosemary Firth

Preface

Anthropology is inevitably political: it impinges on politics at a number of points. Theoretical anthropology cannot but imply a vision of what we are, what our society is and can be: the limits of possible forms of social organization constitute crucial evidence concerning sensible and absurd political aspirations. They tell us what is or is not within our reach.

Even if grand theorizing has been in abeyance, all important work in anthropology has implications for it, and the theorizing itself is bound to return, if indeed it has not already returned. Within Marxism, of course, theories of early man and early society had an important, indeed essential, place in the total system of ideas: without it, it would have been incomplete. Hegel may have inspired Marxism but Morgan completed it. Only the theory of primordial communism could explain just why man had a collectivist essence and why he remained estranged during the age of other social forms. Freud, in turn, had to link his distinctive vision of the human condition (and, in his case, its alleviation rather than its final transformation) to a theory concerning what had happened to our ancestors on the way to the super-ego.

The very process which led to a temporary suspension of grand theory itself had deep political roots. In Britain, the Malinowskian revolution – which continues to define the status quo in the discipline – was born of transplanting East European practices to the West and endowing them with a Western rationale. A Western anthropologist had been a man inspired by Darwinism to explore the pre-literate history of mankind; an East European ethnographer was a man inspired by the love of his (often but half-born) nation to explore, codify and thereby protect its culture. A Russian anthropologist was a man filling up his time in Siberian exile. The Easterner 'went to the people' and embraced its culture with passion, as a totality. Bronislaw Malinowski took this populist-nationalist style of ethnic research, transplanted it from the Carpathians to the Trobriands, bestowed on it an ultra-empiricist and quasi-biological rationale which he had learned from Ernst Mach, and called it (at first in jest) *functionalism.* By severing ethnography from speculative history, however, he also separated it from its use as nationalist propaganda . . .

Recently, the hermeneutic turn in anthropology has been linked to the expiation of colonial guilt, which included functionalist anthropology as an accessory to the crime. In consequence, anyone who has doubts about the wilder and irresponsible relativistic claims of interpretive anthropology has been turned into an *ex post facto* imperialist. The yearning to see the social order as the artefact of culture, to see the system of ideas, rather than gross constraints, as the really crucial factor – this hope has manifold roots, over and above the wish to expiate colonialism by total relativism. The idealists, under new names, remain with us and can be heard, loud and unclear. This debate may still be with us for some time.

The collapse of communism and the consequent destabilization of so many East European boundaries has of course greatly increased the intensity of ethnic conflict. The anthropologist's expertise in *culture*, which largely defines ethnicity, has made him a natural oracle in this problem area. Even prior to the dissolution and even the liberalization of the USSR, the late Yulian Bromley, then czar of Soviet ethnography, endeavoured to turn it into the handmaiden of policy towards the nationalities. His struggle to find a sound typology of ethnic groups was in part an attempt to justify the politically determined, inherently contingent hierarchy of units and sub-units of the USSR with an objective or scholarly basis. I have discussed the relations of anthropology to nationalism elsewhere (*Encounters with Nationalism*).

The political loading of anthropology is complex. What is the relative weight of cultural, economic and coercive constraints in social life? Should one endorse the curiously persistent idealist trend (operating under new names such as hermeneutics, interpretivism, deconstruction, post-modernism) which would make social life a reflection of our *meanings*? Does the obligation we have to respect all men also commit us to seeing all ideas as equally valid (an absurd contention, to my mind)? What are the real links of anthropology to politics, to literature?

No doubt the themes linking them are more numerous still. But it is this cluster of issues which is handled systematically in these essays.

Ernest Gellner
Central European University, Prague
November 1994

Acknowledgements

These essays were written mainly while teaching at the Social Anthropology Department at the University of Cambridge, and at the Centre for the Study of Nationalism at the Central European University in Prague. The final preparation of the volume took place in Prague. I am particularly indebted to Sally Hames of the Vice-Provost's office, King's College, Cambridge, and to Sally Reynolds, Margaret Story and Humphey Hinton in the Social Anthropology Department, Cambridge, for much assistance. At the CEU I am grateful for the support of Robin Cassling, Vlasta Hirtova, Anne Lonsdale, Eric Manton, Jitka Maleckova, Jiri Musil, Al Stepan, Sukumar Periwal, George Soros, Claire Wallace and Gaye Woolven. Without Ian Jarvie's generous bibliographical help, it is unlikely that I would have been able to assemble this or indeed any other collection of essays. During this period I also benefited from support from the Nuffield Foundation and Patricia Thomas, and the ESRC and Sir Douglas Hague. Sandra Raphael was an admirable editor and a pleasure to work with. To all these, my warmest thanks.

Sources of the various chapters are as follows:

1 'The Uniqueness of Truth', a sermon before the University of Cambridge, King's College Chapel, Sunday, 31 May 1992.

Also published separately by King's College, Cambridge, and reprinted as 'Squaring the *ménage à trois*' in the *Times Literary Supplement*, no. 4661, 31 July 1992, pp. 13–14.

2 'The Politics of Anthropology', *Government and Opposition*, 23, 1988, pp. 290–303. Modified version of 'The Stakes in Anthropology', *American Scholar*, 57 no. 1, Winter, 1988, pp. 17–30.

3 'Origins of Society', in A.C. Fabian (ed.), *Origins. The Darwin College Lectures*, Cambridge, Cambridge University Press, 1988, pp. 129–40, and given as a special lecture in the *Origins* series at Darwin College, Cambridge.

4 'Culture, Constraint and Community: Semantic and Coercive Compensations of the genetic Under-Determination of *Homo sapiens sapiens*', in Paul Mellars and Chris Stringer (eds), *The Human Revolution*, Edinburgh, Edinburgh University Press, 1989, pp. 514–25.

5 Specially written for a new translation of Freud's *Civilization and Its Discontents*, Everyman's Library (in press).

6 'Malinowski and the Dialectics of Past and Present', *Times Literary Supplement*, no. 4288, 7 June 1985, pp. 645–6.

7 'James Frazer and Cambridge Anthropology', in Richard Mason (ed.), *Cambridge Minds*, Cambridge, Cambridge University Press, 1994, pp. 204–18.

8 'Pluralism and the Neolithic', review of V.A. Shnirelman, *Vozniknovenie proizvodiaschevo khozaistva* (*The Emergence of a Food-producing Economy*), *Man*, 25 no. 4, December 1990, pp. 707–9.

9 'On the Highway to Perpetual Growth' (review of E.A. Wrigley, *People, Cities and Commonwealth*), *Times Literary Supplement*, no. 4406, 11–17 September 1987, pp. 980–2.

10 'An Ideological Might-Have-Been', in Barry Smith (ed.), *Philosophy and Political Change in Eastern Europe*, La Salle, IL, The Hegeler Institute, 1993, pp. 29–46.

11 'An Anthropological View of War and Violence', in Robert A. Hinde (ed.), *The Institution of War*, Basingstoke and London, Comminan, 1991, pp. 62–80.

12 'Tribalism and the State in the Middle East', in Philip S. Khoury and Joseph Kostiner (eds), *Tribes and State Formation*

in the Middle East, London, I.B. Tauris; Berkeley and Los Angeles, University of California Press, 1991, pp. 109–26.

13 'The Maghreb as Mirror for Man', *Morocco, the Journal of the Society for Moroccan Studies*, 1 no. 1, 1991, pp. 1–6.

14 'Lawrence of Moravia: Alois Musil, monotheism and the Habsburg Empire', *Times Literary Supplement*, no. 4768, 19 August 1994, pp. 12–14.

15 'Anthropology and Europe' in *Social Anthropology: the Journal of the European Association of Social Anthropologists*, 1 part 1, 1993, pp. 1–7.

16 'Anything Goes', *Times Literary Supplement*, no. 4811, 16 June 1995, pp. 6–8.

The permission of the editors and publishers concerned to reprint these essays is gratefully acknowledged.

1

The Uniqueness of Truth

Jean-Paul Sartre's *Huis Clos* is an account of a triangular situation, in which three characters are so related to each other that each one of them can both thwart another and yet is also doomed to be thwarted. A kind of three-pronged stalemate is the consequence. Not one of the participants can break out of the situation, but none is allowed even to attain the peace of resignation. They are doomed to torment and be tormented. It is in this kind of context that Sartre comes to make the celebrated observation that hell is other people.

Whether this is indeed the paradigm of the human condition, whether all of us are locked into circles of mutually constraining and festering consciousnesses, and have to allow others to define us against our will, I would not wish to say. But when it comes to the modern attitude to *truth*, it does seem to me that the contemporary situation is triangular, somewhat in this manner.

There are three principal contestants, roughly equidistant from each other. No single one is able to secure a really convincing ascendancy over the others, and liberate himself from the self-image-corroding taunts of at least one other member of the triad. It is all a little like the children's game of scissors, paper, stone: scissors cut paper, paper covers stone, stone blunts scissors.

The three ideological contestants on the current scene, as far as I can judge, are the Relativists, the Fundamentalists and a group which, for lack of a better name, I shall call Enlightenment Puritans. I am embarrassed about naming this position, in as far as it is, of the three alternatives, the one closest to my own, and I wish to avoid a name which already carries a positive or negative charge. A neologism such as I have chosen, even if slightly comic or coy, at least has a chance of entering the scene without prejudice, one way or the other.

Let us begin with the Relativists. They are prominent and numerous in the groves of academe, in many of the humanities and social sciences. They are certainly influential, or in any case very noisy, in the discipline which I am paid to profess. In their repudiation of a single and exclusive verity, they claim to have not merely truth but, also and above all, virtue on their side. They are self-righteous in their vociferous condemnation of Enlightenment Puritans. They see themselves as the harbingers or heirs of a kind of Inverse Revelation, one which revealed not the single truth, but the equal validity of all of them. This new equality of visions had come, they say, with the equalization of men, cultures or nations, and was intimately linked to it. It is its foundation and/or its fruit, and is indispensable to it. It was *because* men had been seen as unequal that a similar treatment had been meted out to their visions of the world. It was *because* the visions had been so invidiously ranked that men themselves had been denied equality . . . And it is by seeing all visions as equal that we shall also confer equality on men and nations. Now that we have come to recognize the equal worth of men, we are also committed to recognizing the equality of visions: or if you like, because we no longer permit ourselves to look down on some visions, that we are no longer in possession of the conceptual tool for putting down men. The equalization of cultures is also linked to the equalization of genders, and anyone disputing the position finds himself in peril of being branded a colonialist patriarch or patriarchal imperialist. The pursuit of unique, culture-transcending truth is damned. The very idea is a cover for domination. Descartes had led to Kipling. Not Kipling, ergo not Descartes.

Relativists do tend to come complete with a halo, and to present their own position not merely as a solution to a problem, but as a mark of moral excellence. They are in practice perfectly capable of combining their formal relativism with adherence to a historic tradition which, for most of its history and for the vast majority of its adherents, was not at all relativistic, but deeply absolutist, claiming to bring a unique and exclusive salvation. The slogan invoked then becomes 'in my Father's house are many mansions.' The insistence on a monopoly of truth was an error outside the faith, and has no place *within* it, as one such distinguished Relativist absolutist explained the position to me. One can only say that if indeed the claim to uniqueness is an outside observer's error, one which can only mistakenly be credited to the genuine inner content of the faith, then the error in question seems to have been widely diffused and very deeply internalized. This obligation to spread the gospel seems to have been an integral part of the gospel itself. If this be a mistake, then missionaries are, all of them, in deep error concerning their own faith. What happens to faiths which incorporate proselytism as an obligation? Are they exempt from the new relativistic toleration?

Our Relativists are open to many charges: affectation, insincerity, self-contradiction, hidden condescension (greater far than the one they castigate in others) among them. Our world is indeed a plural one, but it is based on the uniqueness of truth, on the astonishing technological power of one particular cognitive style, namely science and its application. Science is cumulative, it does not retrace its steps, and, within it, there is an astounding consensus, without coercion. No one quite knows how it is done: the paradox is that whereas science itself is consensual, the philosophy of science, most conspicuously, is not. But though the explanation of the scientific miracle is not available, or at any rate is contentious, the reality of the miracle itself is not. And all those numerous cultures whose independent inner authority our Relativist would endorse, in his eagerness not to be superior, *themselves* accept that, at least in its appropriate sphere, the new science is valid, and eagerly strive to acquire it. The Relativist is guilty of contradiction many times over: not only is his own position articulated in a non-relativistic way and in a non-relative idiom (and allows no place for itself), he also endorses other cultures which in turn deny equality to others – often twice over, once in recognizing the authority of science and once in absolutizing some other part of themselves. If truth can only exist internally to a culture and its norms, in what interstellar or intercultural void does our Relativist articulate his position? There is no place for him to be . . .

For better or for worse, the cognitive asymmetry of the world we live in is one of its most striking features. It is unsymmetrical twice over: one style of cognition is immeasurably more powerful than all its rivals and it is rapidly transforming the world. But this style only operates convincingly in one sphere of human life, without clearly delimiting the bounds of its own applicability.

This inequality of cognitive styles does *not* engender a hierarchy of peoples and cultures. It is not the by-product of the genetic equipment of any particular population pool. The population or culture where this style was born would have been wholly incapable of producing it a few generations earlier than it actually occurred; and since it has happened, other populations have acquired this style with ease, and some of them have conspicuously surpassed the originators of science, when it comes to the business of technological application of the New Science. The new knowledge is not the reward or mark of some general excellence. Nevertheless, the asymmetry of cognitive and productive performance is the most important single fact about our world. To deny it, under the delusion that this furthers the cause of human equality, is at best an absurd self-indulgence. So our Relativists are not quite as entitled to their halo and their complacency as their occasional air of moral superiority would suggest. How do their rivals fare?

Consider the Fundamentalists. They are not always considered as wholly suitable for polite society, but I do not think one should allow such snobbery to stand in the way of our recognition of their importance. They are important not merely because they are numerous and, in some parts of the world, politically dominant. They have a supremely important point: truth does matter. It is not multicoloured and meretricious, at the beck and call of any optional angle of vision.

Fundamentalism is in part a reaction to a kind of facile

relativistic ecumenism, which ensures toleration and mutual compatibility by means of tacitly emptying faith of its content. It affirms that, on the contrary, faith and its content must be taken seriously, that it means what it says (and what the overwhelming majority of its adherents had in the past taken it to mean), instead of merely conveying some anodyne and wholly unspecific exchange of goodwill messages between man and an anonymous, shapeless Nature of Things, a salutation only coded in some kind of more meaty allegory in order to make it intelligible for its educationally less privileged recipients. If Fundamentalism has an accompanying background doctrine, it runs something like this: unless the message is taken literally and seriously, it ceases to have that capacity to guide and orient, which is expected from it. Such bowdlerization of faith is a betrayal. It must be bad to live by a sliding scale of interpretations, falling back on a vacuous minimum whenever convenient, whenever challenged, while sliding up again when favourable circumstances makes possible a suspension of critical faculties. This cannot be good for moral fibre.

The Fundamentalists seem to be well on the way to prevailing in one of the four great literate religious zones into which the Old World was divided at the end of the Middle Ages. This area, the Land of Islam, has disproved the general applicability of the Secularization thesis, according to which the modern world is incompatible with religious domination.

On the contrary, Islam seems to have benefited from modernity: in the past, it was a kind of Eternal Reformation, in which the scripturalist puritans at the scholarly centre struggled, like Sisyphus, cyclically, with a folk crypto-paganism, without ever succeeding in imposing their own vision on the diluted popular version with any permanence. The political and economic centralization imposed by modern conditions, by eroding the local community which had favoured the socially over-incarnate, 'pagan' form of faith, helped the puritan reformers to attain a greater and, it would seem, more lasting and definitive success. They achieved a victory which had never been granted to them in the past. This means that Western, lukewarm, semi-secularized society must negotiate with an important neighbour who does not share its assumptions. The West does of course also have its

Fundamentalists at home – if not in quite such a dominant position – and must learn to understand them in any case. Many of the Fundamentalist visitors have of late made manifest their contempt for the lukewarm, ambiguous, excessively user-friendly belief system of the host society.

The Fundamentalists have a point against the Relativists: you are not serious, you are not consistent, and your position can not really endow anyone with genuine moral conviction. What charge can the Puritans of the Enlightenment bring against the Fundamentalists?

It is in the end also a moral one, which might run something like this: we share your moral earnestness, we share your perception of the inner dishonesty and facility and doublethink involved in relativism, in brief, we share the view that truth is unique and important. But we are just a little more fastidious in identifying that truth which deserves such respect. The symmetrical relationship between a unique principle behind the totality of things and individual observers is a lesson we have learned from you, or from the tradition you defend, perhaps only too well. We share your attachment to the idea of a unique truth, and its importance, and the distaste for its dilution by treating all rival claims as equivalent: but while sharing your aversion for such inflationary devaluation of ideas, we cannot accept any unsymmetrical claims for localized cognitive authority, known as Revelation. Of course, this is how the idea of unique truth first entered the world: an exclusive, jealous, putatively monopolistic revelation replaced the universal *détente* of prescriptural, traditional religions, which had lacked doctrine, content to be danced out rather than thought out. It was jealous Jehovah who taught mankind the Principle of Excluded Middle. But having learned this so well, we turn it upon the Teacher Himself.

The Enlightenment Puritan, as here presented, is not tempted by the facile relativist position – though he may appreciate the tolerance which it seems to commend – and shares instead, with the Fundamentalist, the assumption that truth is unique. But he does not believe he possesses it, or indeed that it is ever available with finality. All that is available are certain loosely defined procedural prescriptions about how the world may be investigated:

all ideas, data, inquirers are equal, cognitive claims have to compete and confront data on terms of equality and they are not allowed to construct circular self-confirming visions. There is some affinity between this so to speak symmetricist cognitive ethic and a morality which insists on treating *people* in an equal manner.

There is alas an important difference between the application of such even-handedness in the two spheres: in cognition, it can claim – over and above any inherent appeal it may have – pragmatic vindication by brilliant success. The scientific tradition which has proceeded in this manner has outdone all its rivals. In the sphere of conduct, it is not clear that any such pragmatic vindication is available. It has indeed been affirmed that those who comported themselves in this manner were the ones who engendered, and were alone capable of engendering, the unique modern world: only a disinterested, religiously inspired commitment to orderly conduct, *for its own sake*, could produce that shift from the rule of predators to the rule of producers which marks the desirable aspects of our society. But it is not quite certain whether this is true, and it is not obvious that everyone would thank them for this achievement. The romantics among us deplore the great change. And, perhaps most important, it is far from clear whether, once the modern world has been brought into being, it *still* favours the style which (on this view) originally brought it into being. So, even if an ethic of equal treatment was pragmatically essential for the attainment of industrial affluence, once it has done its job it may well be dispensable. If so, it cannot claim the authority of being a precondition of the standard of living to which we are all eager to become accustomed. The precondition of the *birth* of scientific-industrial society may not be the same as the preconditions of its successful perpetuation: the two might even be in conflict.

What are the sins of the Enlightenment Puritan? His doctrine is a little too thin, too abstract, too far removed from the earthy and the concrete to be of much appeal to masses or to sustain anyone in a genuine crisis. The idea that an even-handed and atomizing handling of evidence, with an interdict on circularity, in the end leads to a correct understanding of nature (though we don't yet know which one) may be correct (I hold it to be so), but it does not warm the heart, or help a man sustain a tragedy, or behave with dignity when circumstances become too much for him. So our son of the Enlightenment, spurned by the Relativist for his alleged arrogance and presumption, will also be derided – or more probably, just ignored as unworthy of much attention – by the Fundamentalist, locked into a more substantial and comforting, not merely formal faith, which gives him some real guidance as to the natural, social and moral world he finds himself in . . .

The Fundamentalist and the Enlightenment Puritan share a sense of and respect for the uniqueness of truth; the EP and the Relativist share a penchant for tolerance; and the Relativist and the Fundamentalist share a reasonably well furnished, habitable world, as opposed to the arid emptiness of the world of the EP. The Relativist even has access to a whole set of exotic worlds, which are at the same time discreetly connected to all modern conveniences.

Though my own location or identification in this *ménage à trois* can hardly be in doubt, I hope I have described the two positions which are not my own with sympathy and some understanding, without unfairness. Perhaps it does not matter too much: the society and the milieu in which I am speaking has made its own peace with the dilemmas which I have tried to sketch. Its methods of handling these problems have included shrouding them in a kind of decent obscurity, which liberates the individual from any obligation to clarify his own position with any greater sharpness or finality or commitment than he may have a mind to. He is not required to declare himself to others, or indeed to himself. Morally and politically, there may be a good deal to be said for such an ambiguity. George Orwell was wrong to credit *doublethink* to totalitarianism: it has an essential role to play in liberal society, facilitating a blend of conviction and tolerance. Just a touch of fundamentalism may ensure that the mix is not so thin, so disembodied as to lose all moral suggestiveness; the element of Enlightenment prevents the rigidity of dogmatism; and the relativism helps tolerance and the avoidance of unnecessary disputation. The cocktail is generally adjustable to taste . . . It has striking parallels with a well-matured political system, in which absolutist symbols shorn of too much power coexist amicably with pragmatic, effective powers shorn of too much symbolic potency. We know that a political system of this kind works well, and can only wish that less fortunate lands, only recently liberated from a secular absolutism, may also attain a version of it. We watch their efforts to do so, in much more difficult circumstances, with trepidation. But the fact that this can work in politics does not guarantee that it will also work, in the long run, in ethics and serious cognition.

The compromise seems to have worked well locally, and it is unlikely that it will be much affected by my attempt – the attempt of an admiring outsider – to spell out its secret, a procedure which may be a little alien to its own spirit. In any case, this style is not locally in crisis. But perhaps we should spare a thought for parts of Europe less fortunate and, just at present, very much in crisis.

The Enlightenment did not have only one message. It did not restrict itself to the simple and proceduralist doctrine – treat evidence and men even-handedly – which I tried to articulate in its simplest terms. It also had a more meaty and ambitious variant, which argued that if a superstitious and oppressive *ancien régime* was based on falsehood and dogmatism, then a free and tolerant system will be based on *truth*. When the attempt to implement such a reign of reason on earth failed the first time round, those who pondered this failure tried to offer a diagnosis and a remedy. The most famous, influential and well-orchestrated version of the doctrines offering such a remedy in the end became a new world religion, the first one to be formally secular, and it too failed dramatically, almost exactly 200 years after the French Revolution, which had been the first attempt to implement the Enlightenment. If this story has any clear moral, it is that the future lies not with some secular counter-Revelation, but rather in that ambiguous, unstable, uneasy relationship between faith, indifference and seriousness, which I have tried to describe.

On the analogy of the relative success of the local compromise, my own view of that acute and important crisis among our East European neighbours was originally that the watering down of the local faith, by proceduralism and relativism, would be better than its overt repudiation and a possible search for a new absolute revelation. That was my instinct. It turned out that I was wrong; at any rate, that was not what happened. The strategy of managing the transition from a secular revelation to a compromise society, by using the old institutions and the old imagery, but depriving them of the old tyrannical authority – that strategy did not prevail. The way things went, a brutal discontinuity was imposed instead. Given that there is no clear faith to replace the old, how does one engender a compromise ambiguity, if one has to do it at once, without waiting for slow growth? How indeed. Western Europe took centuries to progress from doctrinal absolutism to ambiguous and tolerant compromise, and the process was largely spontaneous. The self-destroyed ideocracy of Eastern Europe is trying to achieve the same overnight and by decree from above. Can it be done?

The triangular predicament with which I began may in fact be a blessing, if only one is allowed to vacillate between the options and they do not press upon one too hard. Perhaps our main thought should be for those who face the same dilemma in circumstances which are so very much less favourable. Blessed are they who only face our problem.

2

The Politics of Anthropology

Anthropology and sociology originally found their more immediate inspiration in an evolutionary or Jacob's Ladder vision of human societies, the idea of Progress. Social forms were seen as located along some great Chain of Being, which eventually leads to this-worldly salvation by this-worldly means. But there the resemblance ends. Sociology was rooted in a primarily historical evolutionism, in the perception, by the generation of Condorcet and Hegel, that human history is a story of cumulative change, and in the hope that the pattern of this change was the key to the meaning of life. History was to reveal the inner potential and destiny of human society. By contrast, the evolutionism which somewhat later, around the middle of the nineteenth century, gave birth to anthropology, was markedly biological and came to be much influenced by Darwin.

Anthropology was born of the desire to explore early or 'primitive' social forms, in the hope of tracing the links between contemporary man and the founding ancestors of humanity. The story becomes complicated by the occurrence, during the third decade of this century, of the great Malinowskian revolution. Bronislaw Malinowski replaced James Frazer as the paradigmatic anthropologist, though their physical deaths in the 1940s occurred in the course of two successive years, only narrowly permitting

Bronislaw to comment on Frazer's death and significance, and thereby obliquely on his own. Malinowski retained the implicit definition of anthropology as the study of simpler societies, but he proscribed, very effectively, the use of the material gathered by this inquiry for the invention of alleged evolutionary lines of development. This was castigated as 'speculative history'. Henceforth, anthropology would be empirical, not speculative.

Frazer had been an evolutionist magpie, gathering a rich harvest of ethnographic titbits from here, there and everywhere. They were torn out of context and used for the painting of a grand canvas of the evolution of the human mind. Malinowski inverted this on both counts: he insisted on the use, and indeed on the securing, of ethnographic data in *context*, and on the use of a form of explanation which related the data to one another, within the unity of a *single* society, or to human needs, rather than to some evolutionary sequence. This is 'Functionalism'. The Malinowskian revolution dominated the British Empire and some other lands of what might be called the Malinowskian sterling zone; he influenced, but did not dominate, the erstwhile North American colonies.

The Malinowskian Empire

The Malinowskian empire survived the political one of which it had been a kind of ethnographic shadow. Lands no longer recognizing the authority of the crown in political matters might well hesitate to defy the Royal Anthropological Institute on anthropological ones. Some rulers of new countries, such as Kenyatta and Busia, possessed much-valued anthropological qualifications. Nkrumah, in the days when he was still trying to make it as an intellectual, without yet possessing the advantage of being a dictator, presented Audrey Richards, one of the leading first-generation Malinowskians, as it were Companions of the Prophet, with a pair of nylon stockings. This happened during the immediate postwar years when nylons were still a sought-after rarity. It must be added, however, that Nkrumah also behaved in a similarly ingratiating manner to British philosophers.

Malinowski was very much a product of the intellectually turbulent last years of the Habsburg Empire. In this he resembled Hayek, Popper and Wittgenstein, who like him had a great influence on Anglophone thought. Roughly speaking, the Habsburg Empire was torn between the cosmopolitan liberalism of the higher bourgeoisie, and the nationalist and socialist leaning of the ethnic groups, including the German speakers. The philosophical expression of the former interest was the ideal of an Open Society, individualist and cosmopolitan, an idea elaborated and made famous by Popper. The latter interest expressed itself largely in the romanticism of *Gemeinschaft*, of a closed community suffused by intimate affective relations, and delimited by an idiosyncratic culture which sustained those relations and endowed them with rich symbolic expression. It found its sacrament in the village green and festival, not in the free market, whether of goods or ideas. Hayek and Popper, of course, voted for *Gesellschaft*, or the Open Society.

Wittgenstein in his so-called mature work switched to a cult of *Gemeinschaft*, in the very curious guise of a theory of language and philosophy. In a coded – but not very elaborately coded – form it contained a theory of society. In his youth Wittgenstein had elaborated the specifications of a kind of universal language, which, being universal, naturally could not be the medium or emblem of any one village green or totem: it could only be the real idiom of a universal *Gesellschaft*, whose members were concerned only with factual assertion and logical form, and simply would have had no means of expressing any cultural idiosyncrasy. In his later or 'mature' philosophy, language became capable of virtually nothing else. Wittgenstein's later view entailed the idea that one could only link each language to an intimate and closed *Gemeinschaft*. Language was, and *could* only be, a set of multi-purpose customs enmeshed in an inevitably idiosyncratic 'form of life' – culture. No humanity without language and no language without *Gemeinschaft*. *Gemeinschaft* thereby became the only possible form of society, and the possibility of anything else was excluded. The closed community carried meanings, and meanings sustained it. Meaning was *only* possible in community, and it alone made community possible. Members of modern society were thus invited to behave as if they lived in a *Gemeinschaft*, and to find their way to their own intimate community by investigating the *ordinary* language of their own society. It would reveal its conceptual norms unto them and be their salvation. Wittgenstein's numerous followers accepted this bizarre invitation with alacrity and enthusiasm. Never in the history of human thought was so much claimed for so little. Cartesian opting out and transcendence of social bounds, by private and independent thought, was declared impossible. The aspiration for something different, for a *Gemeinschaft*-transcending language, Wittgenstein declared to be pathological, and he supposed, contrary to all evidence, that his own philosophical method could and would cure any such strivings. A language tied to a closed community, and eschewing all aspiration to transcendence, thereby became the norm of intellectual health. Those who think otherwise are diseased and he, Wittgenstein, was going to cure them. If you believe that, you'll believe anything.

Wittgenstein was most unusual in that he attributed the drive to universalism, to bloodless cosmopolitanism, as some other Romantics would have said, not to French cultural imperialism or British capitalism or a Jewish conspiracy – these being popular candidates for the role – but to the alleged seductiveness of formal logic and the theory of sets. Thus Wittgenstein bestowed on *Gemeinschaft* a strange new enemy and endowed it with a bizarre new vindication. This gave his position a certain freshness that it would otherwise have lacked, for it would have been but a repeat performance of an old Romanticism, and it gave him his appeal, in the first generation to philosophers and in the second to anthropologists.

Malinowski came from an intellectual background which was in many ways similar to that of the Viennese, with which in any case it overlapped. Wittgenstein's musings about how the language of *Gemeinschaft* works, preposterous though they are when applied to *our* world and language, are in fact rather suggestive anthropologically. Malinowski had a far better appreciation of the respective roles of context-bound and context-free discourse: in their overall positions, Malinowski was the better philosopher and Wittgenstein the better anthropologist. It is when Wittgenstein credits modern thought and language with features that can with plausibility only be attributed to the primitive *and* believes, absurdly, that this provides the 'dissolution' of our problems, that he constitutes the infantile regression of philosophy. The problems of our complex world are to be solved by pretending that our use of language, and hence our society, resembles that of the simplest peoples. The miracle of language can only be explained by the even greater miracle of *Gemeinschaft*. Thus both of them are turned into a kind of terminal, unquestionable, authoritative mystery, which must replace any aspiration to validate our ideas by reference to something external. So members of an open, critical society are invited to comport themselves as if they were members of a closed community, and consult their tribal custom as embodied in ordinary speech. What verbal custom reveals must be final, for we simply cannot have anything else. To seek it was a disease which, after some two and a half millennia, was at long last to be cured. Philosophy must cure any temptation to seek any such alternative. What is astonishing is that this strange message was received with enthusiasm.

Malinowski was even more original than Wittgenstein in the use he made of the elements available in this background. He recombined, in a radically new way, the elements that had figured in the debate between liberals and romantics. The liberals had been cosmopolitan: they liked to see *one* humanity, actually or potentially rational, in all times and places. The romantics valued cultural diversity in both time and space. They gloried not only in the diversity of cultures, but also in the diversity of periods. They cultivated a fine sense of history, of both continuity and change, and above all of slow, meaningful change. For them, the sense of slow organic growth complemented the recognition of the functional interdependence of institutions (not that they used such language), as it had done for Edmund Burke.

Malinowski reshuffled these cards. He retained the romantic stress on cultural diversity in space, but not in time. He repudiated the romanticization of history. Functional interdependence was credited to synchronic institutions, but not to successive ones. Malinowski delighted in the view that history was but a form of myth, serving contemporary ends, like other institutions for that matter. His experience of the rival nationalisms of the Habsburg Empire gave him plenty of support for such a view. In his anthropology, beliefs about the past were to be seen as 'charters' of current practices. This also constituted an ideal methodological principle for the study of simpler societies, devoid as they were of reliable, or any, records. It enabled him to replace the pursuit of past 'survivals' by the search for contemporary *functions*. This made it possible for him to overturn Frazerian anthropology at both its central points: in its pursuit of an overall historic scheme and in its use of context-free evidence. History was irrelevant and context was all-important. It also suited him politically: he could remain a cultural nationalist or particularist, *and* a political internationalist, unsusceptible to the historical rhetoric of nationalism. Notwithstanding relatively minor later influences – structuralism and its obscure later avatars, or a belated, tired, largely Parisian Marxism – social anthropology of the still extensive intellectual sterling zone remains recognizably the same subject as the one set up by Malinowski.

Initially, anthropology had been defined in terms of its concern with the primitive. This concern in Malinowski's time engendered a certain method and style, both of inquiry and explanation: a tendency towards the stress on fieldwork, on context, on the perception of synchronic interconnections. (Its epistemology is Baptist: it believes in knowledge by total immersion.) But once such a style is institutionalized, codified and endowed with a rationale, as it emphatically was in the case of Malinowski, it acquires a life and autonomy of its own, independent of the concern that had initially brought it into being. It is possible to apply the method in fields other than those of the primitive, and it is possible to invoke justifications for it that are in no way specifically tied to the primitive. For instance, it is possible to be sceptical of the historians' or orientalists' fixation on documents, for reasons quite independent of the absence of writing and documents among primitives. Anthropologists are the natural anti-scripturalists of the social sciences.

The best formulation of the general distrust of documents that I know comes from the pen of a man who was not technically an anthropologist or social scientist at all, though his achievements as an investigator are indisputable: the British traitor and Soviet spy Kim Philby. In an autobiography written in Moscow but published in the West – I quote from memory – he notes that it is the naïve and inexperienced spy who thinks he has achieved something if he had succeeded in stealing a confidential document from, say, a foreign embassy. The document in itself is worthless. How does one know it was not written by some junior person eager to ingratiate himself with a senior official and aping his supposed view, while the senior hardly bothered to read it? How does one know it was not a move in an internal intrigue, intended to provoke a reaction and lead to the adoption of views quite contrary to those advocated in the document? What *is* valuable is to be able to speak informally and at length with the members of the embassy in question, and to get a real feel for the way they habitually and naturally think. Once that is understood, it becomes easy to interpret even minor signs that are not confidential. Without that understanding, signs, leaks, documents are, all of them, useless.

It is hard to think of a more convincing, indeed of a more authoritative formulation of the rationale underlying intensive anthropological 'participant observation' than this testimonial from a master spy. A strong sense of the superior power of an approach based on participation, and a sense of the interdependence of institutions and meanings, may lead anthropologists to define their subject in terms of method rather than substance. Anthropology may nowadays be pulled in different directions by its substantive and its methodological definitions. There are still some relatively stable societies, but they are not primitive. There are some primitive ones, but they are not stable. So, ironically, anthropologists are liable to be historians of primitive societies, and synchronic, so to speak, immersionist students of developed ones. Those who investigate primitives can no longer indulge in the fantasy of the 'ethnographic present'.

There are those who seek to define and practise anthropology neither in terms of primitives, nor in terms of field methods, but in terms of the notions of culture and meaning. The original concern of anthropology with culturally very distant, 'primitive' societies naturally impelled anthropologists into a preoccupation with the problem of interpreting very alien ideas and mentalities. Handling this problem, like that of kinship, is one of their professional specialities, so a rather fashionable trend in the subject is inclined to turn the notion of culture, and the interpretation of cultures, into its centre of gravity. The savage has no monopoly of alien meanings: if decoding or conveying such significations, unravelling the systems that engender them, is our particular skill, then there is much left for us to do, even if savages become scarce.

Meaning in America

In this sphere, it is my impression that the situation in America is rather special and liable to take on extreme forms. America was born modern; it did not have to achieve modernity, nor did it have modernity thrust upon it. It has, at most, a rather hazy recollection of any *ancien régime*. As George Santayana and others have noted, America was born of the more extreme elements of what was itself a uniquely individualist and emancipated country. It attained self-consciousness in the Age of Enlightenment, which provided it with a natural and secular idiom for codifying its own vision. These truths we hold to be self-evident . . .

The American Declaration of Independence is one of the most comic and preposterous documents ever penned. Yet Thomas Jefferson was not, in any technical or ordinary sense, a fool. This, however, did not prevent him and his fellows from affirming something totally absurd – namely, that views which, for 99 per cent of mankind, would have been unintelligible or at best blasphemous, heretical and subversive, were actually *self-evident*.

What is the explanation of such egregious folly on the part of otherwise perfectly intelligent, sober, responsible and competent men? The explanation is simple. They took their own rather unusual culture so much for granted that they mistook it for the human condition in general. An individualist world in which men are free to choose their own aims, and select their means by reference to efficiency, seemed to them an obvious world, one in which all men live as of right. What other world could there be?

As it happens, that is not the world in which all men have lived, or within which they live even now. It is on the contrary quite an exceptional world, which emerged at one time on various shores of the Atlantic and adjoining territories, in a manner which is still not fully understood. America has not changed too much, in its tendency to take this world for granted, since the days of the Founding Fathers. For instance, political philosophy, during its recent revival, was and is carried out largely in what might be called the Mayflower style. Society and its rules are made up from scratch: the individual thinker is invited to think away his own special attributes and advantages, to strip away his social role and position, and to use his social nakedness as a kind of premise, indeed as a kind of truth-revealing spiritual exercise, which enables him to excogitate the kind of social order he desires and which he can endorse. The result of this extraordinary experiment is supposed to have some kind of general validity and authority. It is assumed, bizarrely, that the outcomes of this exercise, when performed by various people, would be convergent, perhaps even uniquely determined.

For members of most cultures, the experiment would not be remotely intelligible. But this is not in the least apparent to the upholders of this most recent method in social thought. They are, like the Founding Fathers and the author of the Declaration, culture-blind. These truths they hold to be self-evident . . . America is inclined to culture-blindness because, on the whole, it takes its own luminously individualist culture for granted and sees it as manifestly obvious.

What happens to a culture-blind person when he finally grasps the idea of culture, when he understands the fact that the systems of meaning within which people live differ radically, and that no single one of them is manifestly unique, self-justifying, universal, self-evident? In this sense, *no* truths can be declared to be 'self-evident': self-evidence is a shadow of a culture, and cultures *vary*. Anthropologists are, virtually by definition, recruited among people who have grasped this. But if their own culture or origin combines culture-blindness with very great confidence, the new notion of cultural alternatives, of diverse and incommensurate systems of meaning, is liable to have a very special potency for them, to be widely exciting, intoxicating and utterly vertiginous. It will be addictive and will constitute a revelation.

There is nothing specially illiberal about protecting people from the effect of intoxicating and possibly harmful drugs, or even in imposing such protection in a discriminatory way – imposing it with special stringency on those known to be specially vulnerable. For instance, I well remember driving across the Navajo Reservation, stopping at a supermarket and noting that, though in other ways it was simply just another North American supermarket, it differed from the others in that no booze was available. Encounters with drunk Navajos on the highway made it plain that these restrictions impelled young braves to seek firewater outside the reservation, not without difficulty.

American Indians may be specially susceptible to strong drink; ordinary Americans, culture-blind by background, are specially vulnerable to the ideas of culture and hermeneutics, to the intoxicating notion that systems of meaning differ profoundly, are justified by their own distinct standards, and are separated from each other by profound gulfs, the crossing of which is an arduous and perhaps even perilous performance. The idea that the world is not simply what it is, but that its general nature is an optional artefact, culturally induced, culturally bound, is exciting and disturbing, notably to a person who has had some difficulty in overcoming an initial resistance and incomprehension. It is liable to turn such a person's head.

Now, I do not wish to be misunderstood. I am not, repeat *not*, advocating a Prohibition of hermeneutics. I wish to make this absolutely clear. If anyone accuses me of having recommended such a course of action, I shall consult my lawyers with a view to possible prosecution. I do not recommend any legislative action against hermeneutics. I am a liberal person opposed to all unnecessary state limitation of individual liberties. Hermeneutics between consenting adults should not in my view be the object of any statutory restrictions. I know, only too well, what it would entail. Hermeneutic speakeasies would spring up all over the place, smuggled Thick Descriptions would be brought in by the lorry-load from Canada by the Mafia, blood and thick meaning would clot in the gutter as rival gangs of semiotic bootleggers slugged it out in a series of bloody shoot-outs and ambushes. Addicts would be subject to blackmail. Consumption of deep meanings and its attendant psychic consequences would in no way diminish, but the criminal world would benefit, and the whole fabric of civil society would be put under severe strain. Never!

No. Hermeneutic Prohibition must be avoided at all costs. But voluntary restraint is quite another matter. It would not encourage criminality, and would in any case be more likely to be effective in the long run. What I am willing and indeed eager to propose is the foundation of a Hermeneutics Anonymous, whose members would provide each other with moral and other support in their struggle with temptation and intoxication. Medical supervision would be made available for the limited and controlled use of hermeneutics for legitimate scholarly and research purposes. I have no difficulty in thinking of the name of a most distinguished academic whose acceptance of a life presidency of the association would confer great prestige and authority on it.

It is of course only superficially paradoxical that the American mind should simultaneously be susceptible both to Mayflower philosophizing the idea that one can set up principles of social justice *ex nihilo*, the supposition that it is possible to excogitate a universally binding social order from the mind's own resources, unaided by culture, *and* also to the hermeneutic plague, the reification and fetishism of idiosyncratic and varied systems of meaning.

Hermeneutics, like patriotism, is not enough. It won't do simply to present oneself as a semiotic bridge-builder between various systems of meaning, over-awed by the magnitude of the task, and inviting the reader to be even more staggered by one's findings. Societies are endowed with coercive and economic constraints that are not generally reducible to semantic ones. Changes in a political structure can occur so fast that it is absurd to suppose that the meaning system had changed at the same pace. The relative weight of conceptual and other factors is something to be explored in each case, rather than prejudged. Above all, meanings are a problem and not a solution; culture is a shorthand term rather than a real explanation, and it is never logically terminal.

Hermeneutic intoxication is sometimes accompanied by a certain facile and self-congratulatory relativism. Systems of meaning are credited not merely with a magical potency and efficacy, but also, each in its own zone, with a kind of automatic legitimacy. Whatever anthropologists may say when they talk about their practice out of office hours, when they actually work they are not and cannot be relativists. What in fact they do is give an account of a given society, or some of its practices, against the backcloth of *our* world and not of *its* own world. An anthropologist who would explain witchcraft beliefs and practices of a given society by saying, 'Well, as a matter of fact, in their country, witchcraft works, just as they say,' would simply not pass muster.

Turmoil against Domination

A brilliant, distinguished representative of the American version of the hermeneutic trend is Clifford Geertz. A good deal can be learned about his attitude from a fairly recent and highly entertaining essay of his.[1] A position can perhaps best be understood by seeing what it attacks and, above all, what it attacks with glee.

The object of the attack is the late Sir Edward Evans-Pritchard, a leading member of the Malinowskian school (though one who in the end came to detest Malinowski and was, I believe, detested by him). Geertz does not write of Evans-Pritchard in a spirit of endorsement, but rather in a spirit of severe if admiring criticism. The occasion of the essay is a little-known article by Evans-Pritchard published in 1973, the last year of his life. It is concerned with some of his wartime experiences and is entitled 'Operations on the Akobo and Gila Rivers, 1940–41'.[2] Both the extensive quotations from Evans-Pritchard and Geertz's comments on them are exceedingly entertaining.

Geertz's central point is that Evans-Pritchard's mock-modest,

[1] C. Geertz, 'Evans-Pritchard's African Transparencies', *Raritan*, Fall 1983. Republished in C. Geertz, *Works and Lives: The Anthropologist as Author* (Polity, Oxford, 1988).

[2] *The Army Quarterly*, 1973.

seemingly lighthearted, deadpan account of his own endurance and bravery on the Sudanese–Ethiopian border, acting as a kind of mini T.E. Lawrence, and disrupting numerically far superior enemy forces, at the head of a motley and undisciplined band of Anuak tribesmen, is somehow all of a piece with his formal academic anthropology. Geertz is suggesting that Evans-Pritchard's witty and deceptively low-key boasting about his own war performance and his professional accounts of Nuer, Azande and Bedouin social structure and ideology suffer from the very same defects and are rooted in the same deep traits.

Geertz suggests that Evans-Pritchard's tale should not be swallowed whole. I have no access to evidence about what really happened in 1940–1, but I can only say that anthropologists are often uncharitable if not malicious about each other: had Evans-Pritchard been caught out in exaggeration, one would quite probably have heard of it. I have heard stories of that kind about other anthropologists, but none has reached me about Evans-Pritchard; members of the Africanist network seemed to admire his powers of physical endurance. But Evans-Pritchard's war record is not really to our purpose: the belated conferment of a medal is not on the agenda. What is at issue is his anthropological style and its weaknesses, as corroborated by his reminiscences. What are they?

He wrote clearly. He thought clearly. He was a fully paid-up member of an imperial race and class (close to the end of Empire, but no matter). The clarity of his style and thought, and the imperial attitude, were, Geertz argues, facets of the same coin:

> This easy certitude of perception is a difficult thing to bring off rhetorically, especially when one is dealing . . . with precisely the sort of materials that most gravely challenge it . . .
>
> The so-called British school of social anthropology . . . is held together far more by this way of going about things in prose than . . . by any sort of consensual theory or settled method . . .
>
> There is the suppression of any sign of the struggle with words. Everything that is said is clearly said, without fuss . . .
>
> The main effect, and the main intent, of this . . . ethnography is to demonstrate that the established frames of social perception, those upon which we ourselves instinctively rely, are fully adequate . . .

> This bringing of Africans into a world conceived in deeply English terms, and confirming thereby the dominion of those terms, must . . . not be misunderstood. It is not ethnocentric . . . it is not 'they are just like us' . . . [but] that their differences from us, however dramatic, do not, finally, count for much.

What this final and crucial quotation amounts to is that Evans-Pritchard was, after all, ethnocentric, though only at a very deep level. He represented a conceptual imperialism, the domination of the world by the lucid level-headed tone of educated Englishmen.

But the world is not to be so dominated. All those Africans, Geertz implies, are different in a deeper sense than Evans-Pritchard allows. They cannot really be brought 'into a world conceived in deeply English terms . . . confirming thereby the dominion of those terms'. This kind of intelligibility, and this kind of dominion, have now rightly gone with the wind and are superseded.

By what? A new race, it would seem, of anthropological Hamlets, with a finer sense of the culturally alien, no longer propelled by an imperial arrogance into supposing that in the end all men can be suborned by the categories of the dominators, no longer given to thinking that, in Geertz's words, 'even the strange is more interesting and amusing than it is disturbing or dangerous. It bends our categories, it does not break them.'

These new anthropological Hamlets are so sensitive that evidently their categories are not just bent, but broken, good and proper. You need to have your categories broken to know just how much it hurts. The reward comes in the form of transcendent insights of great depth, but this no longer allows the limpid lucidity of the imperialists. These writers genuinely struggle with their material and spurn to hide the marks of conflict. Not for them 'the suppression of any sign of struggle with words. Not for them the passion for the simple subject-predicate sentences, unmodified and undecorated.'

Geertz does not suggest that Evans-Pritchard was free of inner conflict – he hints at the opposite, quite rightly – but seems to hold it against him that this was not allowed to intrude into his prose. I am a little reminded of Heinrich Heine's comments on German romantic nationalist poets, eager to commemorate the victory of Herman over the Romans in deep forests and swamps: they convey the spirit of place, says Heine, by the use of wooden and soggy verses. It is not obvious to me that, because the world is a diverse, complex and tortured place, which it is, that only cumbersome and ambiguous sentences can do it justice, and that clarity is some kind of intellectual treason. Or, as Geertz would have it:

> The confidence [of] . . . Evans-Pritchard seems less and less available to many anthropologists. They are confronted by societies part modern, part traditional; by an army of wildly contrasting approaches to description and analysis; and by subjects who can (and do) speak for themselves. They are also harassed by grave inner uncertainties, amounting to almost a sort of epistemological hypochondria concerning how one can know that anything one says about other forms of life is as a matter of fact so. This loss of confidence, and the crisis of ethnographic writing that goes with it, is contemporary and due to contemporary development.

It is astonishing that anyone having to cope with all this can bring himself to say anything at all.

What Geertz has done here is interesting. He has added a new twist to the normal hermeneuticist rationale, which previously centred on the existence of self-sustaining idiosyncratic 'forms of life' (Wittgenstein's famous phrase). Change and increasing complexity, epistemological doubts, a more symmetrical and interactive relation between anthropologist and subject: all are recruited as additional confirmations of the new style.

I can accept neither a murky relativism nor a semiotic mysticism. For one thing, I am none too impressed by the 'epistemological hypochondria' (splendid phrase). I have much sympathy for genuine Hamlets and real doubts, but the recent fashions seemed marked less by their apparent scepticism than by their real dogmatism. The argument tends to be: because all knowledge is dubious, being theory-saturated/ethnocentric/paradigm-dominated/interest-linked (please tick your preferred variant and cross out the others, or add your own), etc., therefore the anguish-ridden author, battling with the dragons, can put forward whatever he pleases.

But let me go straight to the heart of the matter. What is really at issue is the denial of relativism, of the doctrine of the logical ultimacy of 'forms of life' or cultures. Cultures are not cognitively equal, and the one within which alone anthropology is possible cannot really be denied a special status. The nature and justification of that pre-eminence is a deep and difficult matter. But it springs from something far more important than the arrogance of an imperial class. It is linked to the very possibility of *reason*. The socio-analysis of Evans-Pritchard's style was highly amusing, but this weapon can only too easily be turned in the opposite direction. What is sauce for the imperialist goose is sauce for the relativist gander. Evans-Pritchard's clarity, whether arrogant or not, enables us to assess his theory of state-less politics, because we know precisely what is being asserted. A 'hermeneutic' account of a political system leaves us wondering whether we have been offered an explanation of social order or merely a description of its atmosphere.

We need an anthropology which does not make a fetish of culture, which recognizes coercive constraints as resolutely as conceptual ones, and we must return to the real world which does not treat conceptual ones as self-explanatory.

3

Origins of Society

I am honoured by and grateful to the Members of Darwin College for inviting me to contribute to the 'Origins' series. I also forgive them the solecism which they have committed in so inviting me – mainly because I think they do not know that they have indeed committed a solecism. The subject which I am paid to teach in this University, social anthropology, has been defined for something like five or six decades by the prohibition, and that is not too strong a word, of speculation about origins. This is not just a precept built into the mores of the community which teaches the subject, but has in effect become part of its definition. I remember how, when I was becoming qualified in the subject by doing a Ph.D. on a North African topic, I once mentioned Ibn Khaldun, the very great fourteenth-century sociologist of that part of the world, to my supervisor. His reaction was to say: 'If you are going to talk about that, well, you can take yourself off and go into another subject.' So I did not stress Ibn Khaldun again until I actually had my Ph.D.

Now members of Darwin College would not attempt to bribe a policeman to let them park a car in some restricted street, because they know that they ought not to corrupt people. Nevertheless, they have done this to me, in a sense, when I was offered an inducement to talk about origins. And the reason I am indeed talking about them is not because of the bribe, but because I think that prohibition of speculation about origins does call for serious discussion and revision. So I do have some serious scholarly reasons for doing that which, according to the prevailing mores of my discipline, I am not meant to be doing at all.

When I was asked to give the lecture on which this chapter is based, I was asked to talk about the origin of *society*. When the programme actually appeared, I saw it was in the plural and referred to *societies*. And this shift is entirely apposite: the relationship of the plural to the singular, of *societies* to *society*, provides one of the main and crucial clues for discussing the origins of society, the origins of human sociability as such, the origins of the kind of social order that we call a society. Of course, all this involves speculation. But such speculation ought not to be without interest, and it is precisely the relationship of the plural to the singular which enables one to make some advance in reformulating the question, and makes it much more manageable. If you don't know the answer to a question, tinker with its formulation. That's a principle I learnt when I was a professor of philosophy.

The really crucial feature of what we call human society is its astonishing diversity. This diversity is not only very interesting in itself: it also provides the clue to the origin of what we call *society*.

The range of things which are called a human society is very extensive, and diverse societies do astonishingly different things. This is well known to be a problem, or to give rise to one, namely that of relativism. Given that there is diversity, and that sometimes diverse societies encounter each other or even live on the same territory, how do we know which is better, which embodies principles that should prevail? That is indeed a serious question, but it is not the one that concerns me here. The question is not: how do we cope with the consequences and implications of this diversity? – but rather: how is diversity possible at all? This is a Kantian question.

People do not normally regard this as a problem. Diversification has obvious advantages. It gives one variety. The more options are tried, the greater the chance of success. The fact that people are capable of constructing such very diverse social orders, and such very diverse cultures, has one immediate implication: a species capable of this diversity over space is also capable of diversity over time, and hence of sustained growth, whatever the desired direction might be. The specification of that proper direction is what bothers people who are troubled by the problem of relativism.

But the sheer *possibility* of diversity also constitutes a problem, and a very fundamental one, for the following obvious reason. Evidently human beings are not genetically programmed to be members of this or that social order. You can take an infant human being and place it into any kind of culture, any kind of social order, and it will function acceptably. No doubt there are genetic constraints on what men can do. But these constraints are far wider than the constraints imposed by any one society. Each society narrows them down for itself, so to speak.

In other words, the diversity which is exemplified *between* cultures is simply not tolerable *within* any one of them. How is the unrestrained diversification of thought and conduct, of a cancerous growth in all the directions permitted genetically, inhibited in any particular society? This is the first question one has to ask about the origin of distinctively human societies.

How is this particular human kind of herd possible? Gregariousness as such is nothing distinctive; humanity has no monopoly on it, and gregariousness consequently doesn't present a specific problem. What does make human society so distinctive is not perhaps the existence of cultural diversification (there is some small measure of it in other kinds of species), but the truly fabulous range of it. The problem is: what *prevents* humans from developing too fast and too wildly, given that the genetic constraints are far too wide to explain the stability and homogeneity of specific human *societies*?

There is another human trait which I will discuss in an attempt to reformulate the question. In order to approach it, I will mention what is probably the most famous, but least tenable, theory of the origins of human society, namely that of a social contract. This theory maintains that human society originates in a number of individuals who get together and, for their mutual advantage, draw up an arrangement by which they abide thereafter, and that this is how society comes into being. I shall not discuss the theory at length, because it is well known to be absurd. The point I wish to make is that its absurdity contains lessons which have not been sufficiently exploited.

The objection to the social contract theory is of course that it is patently, brazenly, obviously circular. It presupposes the very thing which it is meant to explain, namely the existence of a being capable of a contract, a being, that is to say, with the ability to conceptualize a situation distant in time and abstractly specified, and effectively to bind himself to behave in a certain kind of way if and when that situation arises. But the people who decry and ridicule the contract theory of society do not go on to exploit the illumination which this gives us as to what is distinctive about human societies. It is precisely the capacity to fulfil abstract obligations and to conceptualize situations drawn from any one of a very wide and perhaps infinite range of situations. The number of situations which you can bind yourself to carry out is very wide, and presumably has that famous infinity attributed to language, which constitutes the key premise for the Chomskian approach to language and the rejection of behaviourism in linguistics.

How is a society established, and a series of societies diversified, while each of them is restrained from chaotically exploiting that wide diversity of possible human behaviour? A theory is available concerning how this may be done and it is one of the basic theories of social anthropology. The way in which you restrain people from doing a wide variety of things, not compatible with the social order of which they are members, is that you subject them to ritual. The process is simple: you make them dance round a totem pole until they are wild with excitement and become jellies in the hysteria of collective frenzy; you enhance their emotional state by any device, by all the locally available audio-visual aids, drugs, dance, music and so on; and once they are really high, you stamp upon their minds the type of concept or notion to which they subsequently become enslaved. Next morning, the savage wakes up with a bad hangover and a deeply internalized concept. The idea is that the central feature of religion is ritual, and the central role of ritual is the endowment of individuals with compulsive concepts which simultaneously define their social and natural world and restrain and control their perceptions and comportment, in mutually reinforcing ways. These deeply internalized notions henceforth oblige them to act within the range of prescribed limits. Each concept has a normative, binding content, as well as a kind of organizational descriptive content. The conceptual system maps out social order and required conduct, and inhibits inclinations to thought or conduct which would transgress its limits.

This is one of the central theories of anthropology and, until a better one is found, I shall remain inclined to believe that it must be valid. I can see no other explanation concerning how social and conceptual order and homogeneity are maintained *within* societies which, at the same time, are so astonishingly diverse when compared with each other. One species has somehow escaped the authority of nature, and is no longer genetically programmed to remain within a relatively narrow range of conduct, so it needs new constraints. The fantastic range of genetically possible conduct is constrained in any one particular herd, and obliged to respect socially marked bounds. This can only be achieved by means of conceptual constraint, and that in turn must somehow be instilled. Somehow, semantic, culturally transmitted limits are imposed on men.

The sheer diversity possible in a species of this kind also makes social change possible, change based not on any genetic transformation, but rather on cumulative development in a certain direction, consisting of a modification of the semantic rather than genetic system of constraints.

But this possibility of progress, which in our culture we think of as somehow glorious, presents a problem. Initially, the main difficulty facing societies was to *restrain* this excessive flexibility. The preservation of order is far more important for societies than the achievement of beneficial change, a possibility which only arrives later, when conservation can be taken for granted and when openings for genuinely beneficial change are available. Progress is possible because *change* is possible, because the internal constraints on men allow such a wide range of conduct. But most change is not at all beneficial; most of it would disrupt a social order without any corresponding advantage. Before we can explain how beneficial change is possible, we must first show how too much change, with all kinds of chaotic effects, is avoided. This is not a Conservative Party political broadcast, but the point needs to be made. Conservation is the initial problem for a labile population, and it appears to be solved through deeply internalized concepts.

The question of course arises, which came first: this extraordinary ability and variety of possible conduct, or language? Obviously I do not know, but the point that has to be made is that the two are clearly correlative. Once you have the possibility of an astonishingly wide range of behaviour, it has to be restricted somehow, and there has to be some kind of system of signs indicating the limits. This I assume is central to the origins of language. Language makes possible that astonishing kind of variety by allowing it to be contained. It consists of a set of markers delineating the bounds of conduct, bounds whose *genetic* limits have become far too broad for any one social order. Only a species endowed with something like language can have a wide range of genetically possible behaviour; and a genetically broad range of conduct necessitating some mechanism – i.e. language – which restrains that which nature has failed to restrict.

Part of my point is that a number of things not normally connected must clearly have come together: the possibility of a wide range of conduct, the means of signalling the optional items within that range which come to be adopted by any one herd (in other words, language), and the presence of ritual which socializes individuals into that system. Once you have this collection of traits, although you do not yet have the actuality of growth, you do have the potentiality of growth. So sociability proper, semantic rather than genetic transmission, language, diversity, ritual enforcement and the potential for growth, make up a set of features which must all have arrived more or less jointly.

Our problem is: how do you generate an entire community which differs from an animal herd, not merely in the range of its potential cultural flexibility, but also in the capacity of its members to respect contracts? Ritual on its own does not yet give us the full answer: the kind of obligation instilled by ritual is not yet a contract. It is too rigid. It is not negotiable, and it is not optional from the viewpoint of the individual who is subjected to it. It confers status on the individual subject to it, but it does not yet enable him to subject himself to contract. A status is, if you like, a kind of frozen contract; and a contract is optional, open to choice, a variable status. But a frozen status, like single-party elections, is a fraud, a travesty, not really a contract at all.

So one also needs to ask: by what conceivable steps can one proceed from a system of individuals grouped in social order, reasonably stable, no longer genetically constrained, to the kind of society that *we* consider normal, which we consider a real society, and which the authors of social contract theories consider normal – a society in which men can commit themselves abstractly, at a distance, to a *kind* of behaviour, no longer frozen either genetically or ritually? Those who hit upon contract as a foundation of society gave a bad explanation, but in effect offered a good definition of our kind of society, of what it is that we are endeavouring to explain.

The ritually constrained system does not yet give us the kind of society that we can regard as normal and acceptable. A number of things had to happen after the emergence of a ritually, conceptually constrained system, before an order emerged in which people could optionally, rather than rigidly, conceptualize and choose alternative patterns, and effectively bind themselves to abide by them. In other words, something further had to happen before the contract could become a model of social conduct. And once again, I think we should speculate concerning what those features were.

First of all there was the Neolithic revolution, the development of a system for the production and storage of food. Human society was already highly diversified, even before this occurred. The adoption of food production and storage was clearly within the potential of a concept-using and ritually restrained society, but it enormously expanded its possible size and complexity.

But it was also a tremendous trap. The main consequence of the adoption of food production and storage was the pervasiveness of political domination. A saying is attributed to the prophet Muhammad which affirms that subjection enters the house with the plough. This is profoundly true. The moment there is a surplus and storage, coercion becomes socially inevitable, having previously been optional. A surplus has to be defended. It also has to be divided. No principle of division is either self-justifying or self-enforcing: it has to be enforced by some means and by someone.

This consideration, jointly with the simple principle of pre-emptive violence, which asserts that you should be the first to do unto them that which they will do unto you if they get the chance, inescapably turns people into rivals. Though violence and coercion were not absent from pre-agrarian society, they were contingent. They were not, so to speak, necessarily built into it. But they *are* necessarily built into agrarian society, if by this one means a society possessed of a stored surplus, but not yet of the general principle of additional and sustained discoveries. The need for production and defence also impels agrarian society to value offspring, which means that, for familiar Malthusian reasons, their populations frequently come close to the danger point.

The trouble with the popular image of Malthus is that it is a bit ethnocentric and assumes a kind of stable institutional background, within which, if famine strikes, people die off at the margin: they wait patiently in a queue, and the people at the end of the line perish. But it does not work like that. The members of agrarian societies know the conditions they are in, and they do not wait for disaster to strike. They organize in such a way as to protect themselves, if possible, from being at the end of the queue. So, by and large, agrarian society is authoritarian and strongly prone to domination. It is made up of a system of protected, defended storehouses, with differential and protected access. Discipline is imposed, not so much by constant direct violence, but by enforced differential access to the storehouses. Coercion does not only underwrite the place in the queue: the threat of demotion, the hope of promotion in the queue also underwrite discipline. Hence coercion can generally be indirect. The naked sword is only used against those who defy the queue-masters altogether.

There are various kinds of situations where centralized domination does not occur, where some kind of balance of power engenders participatory and egalitarian polities. Nomads, some sedentary peasants in inaccessible terrain, and sometimes also trading cities, all exemplify this. But the overwhelming majority of agrarian societies are really systems of violently enforced surplus storage and surplus protection. These systems can vary in all sorts of ways, from collective tribal storehouses to governmentally controlled silos.

Political centralization generally, though not universally, follows surplus production and storage. It helps take us out of the first kind of social order, the system of ritually sanctioned roles, which might generically be called Durkheimian. Food production increases the size of societies: within large societies, the logic of rivalry and pre-emptive action generally leads to a concentration of power. A formalized machinery of enforcement supplements or partly replaces ritual. Food production and political centralization, and also one further very crucial step, jointly constitute a necessary rather than a sufficient condition of the next transformation, which leads towards the kind of society we are trying to explain. That additional third factor is the storage, not of a material surplus, but of meanings, of propositions and of doctrine. This doctrinal and conceptual storage is made possible by *literacy*. This is that extra step. The feasibility of the storage and codification of ideas is as profound in its implications as the storage and socially enforced distribution of a surplus.

There is an asymmetry between the two storage discoveries. Material surplus generally, though not universally, makes for political centralization. And although political power and centralization in agrarian society is fragile, often unstable, it is nevertheless extremely pervasive. By contrast, the codification of concepts in writing does not lead quite as frequently to doctrinal centralization. Moreover, ideological doctrinal centralization has two aspects: organizational and ideological. The carriers of the codified origin may or may not themselves be centrally organized, and that organization may or may not have a single logical apex, a single guiding principle. The clerisy may or may not be united in a single organization with central leadership, and the ideas may or may not have an apex, and so the two centralizations, ideal and organizational, do not necessarily go together.

The theory about what may then happen, and what seems to have happened at least once, runs roughly as follows. If the doctrine is centralized and endowed with a single apex, for instance, a single, exclusive, jealous deity, this may have very striking effects. The point about the ritually instilled concepts of preliterate, ideologically uncentralized, Durkheimian societies is that there is no need for them to be logically coherent. There is no earthly reason why the ritual accompanying the opening of the pasture should be in some way logically consistent with the ritual which accompanies weddings.

The point about the Durkheimian social order is that these concept clusters, these clusters of expectations and obligations, not only come in packages, but are also profoundly holistic in another way: they are not broken up into their elements. The various clusters do indeed tend to be articulated in the same style, thereby providing simple societies with that social coherence for which they are often envied. But they are not logically coherent, and indeed they are not expected to be.

I suspect there is a law which affirms that social and logical coherence are inversely related. From the kind of society endowed with a very high level of social coherence and logical *in*coherence, how does one reach the opposite condition, which appears to be ours, where a fairly high degree of logical coherence is accompanied by a minimal degree of social coherence? If the favoured explanation of the origins of logically diversified but socially harmonious conceptualization is ritual, then the favoured explanation of the emergence of this other conceptual style is the impact of a rationalistic, centralizing, monotheistic and exclusive religion. It is important that it was hostile to manipulative magic and insisted on salvation through compliance with rules, rather than loyalty to a spiritual patronage network and payment of dues. It is this that leads to the exclusion of that facile cohabitation of diverse conceptual schemes, of a logical tolerance which is so characteristic of simple societies, and also of what may be called non-Abrahamic traditions.

It is a plausible theory, and again, until we have a better one, I think it is the one with which we must continue to work. Of course, the jealous deity did not achieve all of this unaided. One may suspect the mysterious exclusivity if one High Spirit had to have other support. It probably did have to be a high *spirit*. The person who noticed and took at face value the government of mankind by concepts, and built a theory around it, was Plato. Ironically, he did it at the very moment when locally and socially specific, ritual-born concepts were being replaced by script-born, potentially universal, trans-ethnic ideas. His Theory of Ideas confirmed the control of conduct through authoritarian concept-norms, by the attribution of transcendent origin and authority to those norms. The Platonic theory of ideas is, all at once, a transcendence, yet also a kind of coming unto self-awareness of the Durkheimian world: it recognizes that a society is a community of minds framed by *concepts*, which are, all at once, ways of clustering objects *and* ways of imposing obligations on men.

At the same time, he also sketched out what is really the generic social structure of agro-literate societies, namely government by warriors and clerics, by coercers and by scribes. In his version, the two ruling strata happen to be conflated, and top clerics were meritocratically selected from the authorized thug class. In historical practice, the details of this kind of government vary a great deal. Plato is relevant because he offered a marvellous blueprint of how this kind of society works and how it justifies itself.

His crucial mistake, however, was very much an intellectual one. He saw clearly enough that, in this kind of world, the binding concepts are unequal, forming a kind of hierarchy, with a top concept ruling all the others. The Concept of the Good, as it were, generically incorporates and warrants the authority of all the others, which guide conduct at more specific levels. That theory may satisfy intellectuals, who are flattered to hear that their professional tools of trade, namely concepts, should be so sacred, and that the Top Concept should rule them all and all of us. But most of mankind simply will not quake before a High Concept: they will, however, quake before a High God. This personalization was essential for the effective imposition of a centralized vision. To concentrate the mind of humanity, the apex of the system had to be *personal*, and the carrier of anger and wrath. But, at the same time, to achieve the effect which concerns us, it had to be a *Hidden* Deity which would set the rules and norms, but be too proud or too distant to interfere in day-to-day management of the world. It had to scorn making exceptions, it had to be distant and orderly, it could not be a kind of head of a bribable and interfering patronage network, which is what High Gods are in many other systems.

Once this notion of an orderly, distant, commanding, single apex prevails, certain other things became possible. The shift from ritual to doctrine, as the central tool for sanctioning the restraint which keeps society together, takes place, and this shift is supremely important. What goes with it is that the compulsion should no longer be attached to individual concepts, but rather to certain second-order features of conceptual living altogether. Concepts must be orderly and be applied in an orderly manner and be part of orderly systems. The orderly behaviour of concepts and of men is really attained by one and the same revolution.

Conceptually bound conduct, as stated, involves compulsion which is no longer genetically prescribed, but is instead culturally variable and ritually fixated. Concepts have a kind of grammar; at the place where one concept operates, another one could also be slotted in. Concepts are seldom *wholly* idiosyncratic; each is a kind of alternate within a system. But their grammar is initially rather rudimentary in a Durkheimian world, because they don't break up into units, and shifting or replacing them is fairly restricted. It occurs only within limited sub-systems: there is no universal grammar, no incorporation of all ideas into one single system with one set of rules. But once a sense of compulsion no longer attaches to individual concepts, but only to the whole orderly system, to orderly thinking as such, and to the orderly break-up of concepts into constituent elements, something else becomes possible: a society which is a system of contracts rather than a system of statuses, and a nature built up from evidence, on the expectation of symmetrical order, and a society where both concepts and men are equal. Revelation, the unsymmetrical attribution of authority to some ideas and some men or some institutions, becomes morally repellent.

In one sense, *any* concept is a ritual: it is a named cluster of expectations and obligations, triggered off by socially prescribed conditions and contexts. What we have called a Durkheimian society lives in accordance with its pantheon of concepts, with their own hierarchy, and some are much more important than others, and are sustained by specially weighty rituals. The system as a whole is relatively fixed and non-negotiable. Now contrast this with a monotheistic, iconoclastic, puritanical, nomocratic world: a distant, hidden, rule-bound and rule-imposing, awe-inspiring God has proscribed magic, ritual, ecstasy, sacred objects, and enjoins a rule-bound morality on his creatures, and similarly, imposes law-abiding regularity on all nature. He concentrates all sacredness in Himself; piety is henceforth to be manifested in sober orderly conduct, in an undiscriminating observance of rules.

The sacred is now symmetrically diffused in the world. No men are priests, special mediators, or rather, all men partake in priesthood equally. All men, *and* all concepts, are equal under God. Society is still concept-bound, but the concepts under which it lives and by which it is bound are equal, symmetrical and orderly. Reverence attaches to all of them equally; or rather, it attaches to their formal properties, to the fact that they form part of a unified and orderly system, and not to their specific and distinctive traits. None of them are specially underwritten by specially weighty rituals: the most potent ritual of the Protestants is absence of ritual, their graven image is the absence of graven images. All occasions in life now acquire equal weight, all affirmations are equally binding: no need for special oath-confirming rituals.

To put it pedantically, the authority of concepts has shifted to their formal, second-order characteristics. Now *Nature* in the modern sense becomes possible: it constitutes a unified law-bound system, within which no object, no event, no theory is sacred. There are no pre-empted, entrenched doctrines – which is the essence of theological religion. Equally, rational production (which is a precondition of capitalism, though not co-extensive with it) also becomes possible: it means the free, unrestricted choice of means in the pursuit of clearly specified and isolated aims.

A society makes the first shift from a religion centred on ritual and magic, and committed primarily to confirming and perpetuating stable status groups, when it acquires a class of literate scribes whose speciality is the codification of *doctrine*. In their competition with freelance shamans and possibly with other rival social groups, the scribes will stress the authority and primacy of doctrine, over which their literacy gives them a kind of monopoly. 'Reformations' are liable to be endemic in this kind of society: the scribes will seek to promote the exclusive authority of the doctrine as against rival forms of the sacred. Reformations, however, generally fail; but on one special occasion a Reformation succeeded, at least in part, and a new kind of world emerged.

I am not putting forward an idealist theory of the emergence of modern society in terms of its ideology just because I have been stressing these aspects. I do not in fact hold any such theory. The elements which I have been stressing and trying to sketch out are necessary but not sufficient; obviously a number of other things had to happen before a modern society could emerge. The separation of the clerical guild from the warrior stratum in the government of agrarian society, and a rivalry between them, and the occasional victory of the unified clerical organization was important; so was the neutralization of various groups of hereditary or professional coercers, effective political centralization, and the emergence of free production-oriented strata. All this made possible a simultaneous cognitive and productive explosion. One thing which held the earlier status system rigidly together, apart from the old conceptual style, was also a system of rigid kinship; men had been caught between kings and cousins, and only escaped one of these to fall into the power of the other. At least two important theories have recently been put forward concerning the erosion of this constraint, those of Jack Goody and Alan Macfarlane. I do not know whether these theories are true, but they provide a model of how we could well have reached the point at which we find ourselves.

Once, however, social and economic conditions were favourable, this new thought style could emerge: it allows concepts to be freely dissociated and recombined, without sacralizing any of them. Constraint and compulsion are only imposed at a second level: men are obliged to think and produce in an orderly way. They are no longer tied to given specific concepts, to ways of looking at things, to given roles, to given production techniques.

One of the great codifiers of the new vision was David Hume. His famous theory of causation says in effect that there are no inherent or given or obligatory clusters of things. Anything can go with anything, and the clusters can only be established by observation. First, all separables are to be separated, and then their real associations established in the light of evidence, and of evidence alone. This is a recipe and a model for cognition, but it could equally of course be a recipe for market behaviour, the rules of which were plotted at the very same time by Hume's good friend, Adam Smith. The combination and recombination of productive elements, unconstrained by conceptual clusters, by social roles in effect, is the essence of the liberal entrepreneurship hallowed by Adam Smith. Its principles are the same as those which also underlie an unconstrained cognitive exploration of the world, codified by Hume and by Kant.

The story offered here ends up with the kind of society which the contract theorists naïvely took for granted when they invoked the contract as an explanation of that order which makes contract possible. The wide range of conceptualization, the free attachment of obligation at a temporal distance to any freely chosen content, is what we mean by contract. A society which has these features is also egalitarian, in the sense that it does not allow frozen systems of statuses; and it is also protestant in a generic sense, in so far as it does not allow a segregated species of privileged cognitive specialists. Individuals and concepts are equal and form part of a system where the *form* may be hallowed, but the content is variable. This society is also *nationalist* in the sense that, for the first time in history, something happens which was inconceivable in the earlier period: the high culture, transmitted by writing and formal education, comes to constitute the pervasive culture of the entire society, defines it, and becomes the object of loyalty.

What I have done in effect, as anyone familiar with this topic will have realized, is to give a very potted version of Durkheim and Weber, fused so as to form one continuous story. Durkheim's problem was, why are all men rational? By this he meant – why do men think in concepts and why are they constrained by them? He understood the problem of conceptual thinking much better than empiricist philosophers, or empiricist anthropologists for that matter, such as Frazer. He understood that, if concepts were formed simply by the process of learning from nature, by 'association', a semantic cancer would rapidly develop. There would be no limits on either behaviour or concept formation. If association engendered concepts, there would be no limit on the content of concepts, and the astonishingly disciplined behaviour of concepts and of men would be inexplicable. The fact that concepts mean the same thing to all members of a given community would become a mystery. So would the fact that they also impose discipline on men. This problem could not be solved in conventional ways, and Durkheim indicated the direction in which the solution lies.

Weber's question, of course, was not why all men are rational, but why some are more rational than others, where rationality is envisaged in marked contrast with Durkheimian rationality. It is the new and special rationality which concerned him, one that no longer quakes before ritually instilled concepts, but only respects certain formal rules concerning the deployment of all of them. Weber put forward a theory, which I have represented in a simplified and exaggerated version, concerning how that new world came about, thereby making possible the cognitive and productive explosion.

He also made plain the cost of such a world. The price of the separation and levelling of all elements, the full utilization of the potential involved in uniting all concepts in a single orderly logical space, and obliging them to disassociate and re-associate at our convenience, is considerable. The price, of course, is the separation of fact and value, and the ending of that comfortable endorsement of social arrangements to which mankind had become habituated.

One hears many complaints about the absence of a good legitimation of our social order. The suggestion is that this really is a scandal, and that philosophy had better do something about it. If my account is correct, philosophy cannot possibly do anything about it. Admittedly, a large number of substitute re-legitimations or re-enchantments is on the market. They are not worth much.

What I have put forward is of course a theory; it is speculative.

I have brazenly sinned against that famous injunction proscribing speculation about origins. The speculation, however, would seem to be more or less compatible with available facts; or at any rate, it is not blatantly in conflict with them. It explains them better than any available alternative, and it suggests further ethnographic, historical and other enquiries. As a good Popperian, I ask no more of theories. The irony of anthropology is that it was born of a passionate preoccupation with the question of origins. Somewhere between the forties and the eighties of the last century, eventually encouraged by Darwinism, this preoccupation engendered a distinctive discipline, which endeavoured to use contemporary simpler peoples as a surrogate time machine. That was what virtually defined the subject.

Then, in the 1920s, in the conceptual sterling zone, all this was overturned. It was overturned in an extremely fertile way, by Bronislaw Malinowski. It is said that the greatest pleasures are overcome revulsions, and perhaps the most powerful taboos are attractions suppressed. The new taboo on speculation concerning origins was indeed very powerfully internalized. Perhaps it is time to change once again. The point about pre-Malinowskian anthropology was that its data were not very good, but its questions were extremely interesting. Malinowskian anthropology is by now perhaps a bit the other way around. The data are admirable, the questions may be a bit stale. Perhaps the time has come to combine a high quality of data with a revitalization of questions. They may indeed be questions about origins.

References

Burtt, E.A. *The Metaphysical Foundations of Modern Physical Science.* International Library of Psychology, Philosophy and Scientific Method; Kegan Paul, London, 1925.

Childe, V.G. *Man Makes Himself.* Library of Science and Culture, 5; Watts, London, 1936.

Durkheim, E. *The Elementary Forms of the Religious Life,* trans. J.W. Swain. George Allen and Unwin, London, 1915; reprinted 1976.

Durkheim, E. *The Division of Labour in Society,* trans. G. Simpson. Free Press, Glencoe, IL, 1933; reprinted 1960.

Ellen, R. (ed.) *Between Two Worlds. The Polish Roots of B. Malinowksi.* Cambridge University Press, 1988.

Firth, R. (ed.) *Man and Culture: An Evaluation of the Work of B. Malinowski.* Routledge and Kegan Paul, London, 1957.

Frazer, J.G. *The Golden Bough.* 3rd edn, Macmillan, London, 1907–15.

Goody, J. (ed.) *Literacy in Traditional Societies.* Cambridge University Press, 1968.

Goody, J. *The Development of the Family and Marriage in Europe.* Cambridge University Press, 1983.

Goody, J. *The Logic of Writing and the Organization of Society.* Cambridge University Press, 1986.

Macfarlane, A. *The Origins of English Individualism: The Family, Property and Social Transition.* Basil Blackwell, Oxford, 1978.

Sahlins, M. *Stone Age Economics.* Tavistock, Chicago, 1972.

Weber, M. *General Economic History,* trans. F.N. Knight. Adelphi Economics Series; George Allen and Unwin, London, 1927; reprinted by Transaction Books, New Brunswick, NJ, 1981.

Weber, M. *The Protestant Ethic and the Spirit of Capitalism.* London, 1930; reprinted by George Allen and Unwin, London, 1965.

4

Culture, Constraint and Community

The existence of culture among species other than man is debatable. There are writers who have gone as far as to affirm the absence of culture among other species.[1] The claim that culture is incomparably more important among men than among members of any other species is far less contentious. This much less disputable premise is all we really require for the present argument.

What is meant by *culture?* Basically, a non-genetic mode of transmission, located in an on-going community. A community is a population which shares a culture. One might say that *culture* refers to whatever is transmitted non-genetically. The two notions, culture and community, are intimately linked.

Culture and community are defined in terms of each other: culture is what a population shares and what turns it into a community. A community is a sub-population of a species, which shares its genetically transmitted traits with the species, but which is distinguished from that wider population by some additional characteristics: these in some way or other depend on what the

1 See Robert A. Hinde, *Individuals, Relationships and Culture: Links between Ethology and the Social Sciences* (Cambridge University Press, Cambridge, 1987), p. 3: 'we can thus speak of the possession of "culture" as being a uniquely human attribute.'

members of that community or sub-population *do*, rather than on their genetic equipment. It shares a series of traits which are transmitted semantically: what is reproduced is *behaviour*, but the limits imposed on that behaviour depend on markers carried by the society and not by the genes of its members. Cultural behaviour is not dictated genetically and cannot be reproduced, either by some genetic inner *Diktat* or even by a mere conjunction of genetic programming with external non-social stimuli. Hence its boundaries or limits must be defined by something or other in possession of the community within which this reproduction of behaviour takes place. Such non-genetic delimitation of boundaries of conduct or of perception, in the keeping of a community, is about as good a definition of *meaning* as we possess. Meaning, culture, community – these notions interlock with each other. The circularity of their definitions, their interdependence, does not matter.

What the human species does share genetically is an unbelievable degree of behavioural plasticity or volatility. The diversity in actual conduct found among members of this single species is quite incredible: they do very different things, they speak remarkably different languages, observe different codes, and so forth. It is reasonably obvious that these differences are not transmitted genetically: infants drawn from one population pool can be socially and linguistically incorporated and successfully reared in totally different communities. If the new community possesses a self-image incompatible with some traits which are genetically transmitted, some trouble does ensue. If, for instance, a community which thinks of itself as belonging to one pigmentational category socializes an infant adopted from another such category, the child in question may later have some difficulty in securing full moral incorporation. This, however, is not in conflict with the claim that the child in question normally experiences no difficulty in successfully assimilating all the socially or semantically transmitted traits.

Racialists are defined by the conviction that some socially important traits are specially common, or even exclusively present, in certain *genetically* defined populations: that some genetically defined populations possess strong concentrations of either desirable or undesirable characteristics. It is doubtful whether this is true to any significant extent: the traits considered morally significant seem to depend far more on socially than on genetically transmitted elements. Morally exciting or repellent features have often been transformed historically with a speed which makes it most implausible, or impossible, to attribute the metamorphosis in question to genetic change.

What *does* seem genetically based in humankind is the plasticity, the volatility itself. All members of the species are endowed with it and no other species possesses it. But possibly the most important single sociological fact about mankind is that this plasticity is very seldom much in evidence *within* single on-going communities. On the contrary: members of the same community in the main resemble each other to a marked degree. Generally they speak the same language, both in a literal and in a broader sense; they use similar linguistic tokens; and the general way in which they use them, their *culture*, is also fairly similar.

This point may need some modification with respect to complex civilizations, which contain a wide diversification of roles within their social structure, and where the occupants of diverse roles often do markedly different things, wear different clothes, are obliged to speak in a different manner, are dominated by distinct values, and so on. Though such diversity indisputably prevails among the members of complex societies, this does not really militate against our main point: men are, all things considered, astonishingly well-disciplined and restrained in their conduct and their thought. Members of simpler societies may, as Durkheim stressed, all do and think and feel the same things, whereas members of more complex societies may complement each other by their diversity; but neither the former nor the latter normally stray very much from what is culturally expected of them. Where diversity of roles is expected or imposed by culture, behaviour is none the less constrained within rather narrow bounds. Genuinely chaotic and unpredictable conduct, crossing the bounds of culturally recognized alternatives, is astonishingly rare.

To sum up the argument so far: if we look at mankind interculturally we find an amazing diversity. If we look at mankind within any one community/culture, we find an equally amazing discipline and restraint. Question: how can a species, genetically granted by Nature such remarkable freedom and licence, nevertheless observe such restraint, such narrowly defined limits, in its actual conduct? Man is born genetically free but is everywhere in cultural chains. How is this possible?

What are the necessary conditions of this cultural enslavement? What are its sufficient conditions? And what are its functions, or, to give functionality its old Aristotelian name, what is its Final Cause? In a world in which natural – and social – selection can be assumed to operate in some measure, Final Causes or Functions are of great interest: they provide significant clues to efficient causes. That which serves a purpose, which in turn is a precondition of survival, legitimately constitutes an element in the explanation of that survival.

To begin with the function: it is reasonable to suppose that without *local* homogenization, standardization, discipline, human communities would be unviable. Highly unpredictable and wildly diversified members of a local group or herd simply would not be capable of cooperating. They would cease to exist as any kind of group and, presumably, as individuals. A plausible theory is available which claims that *Homo sapiens sapiens* acquired his intelligence in the course of working out devices for predicting and managing the waywardness, deviousness and cunning of his fellows: we were propelled into intelligence, so to speak, by being obliged to keep up with each other's smartness.[2]

There may be a great deal in this account of the Gadarene or competitive rush into cleverness, but it could only have worked if the waywardness and unpredictability stayed within certain well defined limits. I can stretch my intelligence to its limits in my attempts to outsmart a clever chess player or poker player or intriguer. But if he is so volatile that that he is in effect playing a series of quite unconnected games (as happens in Tom Stoppard's play *The Real Inspector Hound*) then no effective strategy is possible. In fact, he ceases to be any kind of a player, and there is no game.

[2] See N. Humphrey, *Inner Eye* (Faber, London, 1986).

What is the necessary condition of this essential, indispensable, intra-cultural or intra-communal discipline? A species which is genetically capable of such diversity, but at the same time requires great homogeneity and discipline within arbitrarily selected sub-populations, simply *must* be capable of operating and recognizing an extremely rich system of markers, which set bounds to what is and what is not done in any one community. Given the astonishing internal complexity and external diversity of cultures, and also their well demonstrated capacity for rapid transformation, it seems to me obvious that this system of markers must also possess the features which, as a result of the central ideas and insights of Chomsky, have now come to be associated with *language*: the system of markers must be able to achieve infinite results by finite means.

A language is, so to speak, a modular system of markers, within which the same elements can be combined and recombined in a wide variety of ways, engendering the delineation of quite distinct and alternative boundaries of conduct. For instance, a language containing the notions of seven days of the week, and the opposition 'work' and 'non-work', can command the members of a given culture not to work on Sundays; and within the same system of ideas, the notion of prohibition of work on any other day is also easily intelligible, as is the idea of the obligation to work on this or that day.

The semantic/cultural constraints on conduct are exceedingly rich twice over: in any one language, prohibitions other than those actually imposed are conceivable and understood. In other words, members of the culture live in a *world* such that the actual state of affairs is but one possibility among others. Its possibilities greatly exceed its actuality, but they are understood and, in a sense, present. A world is a system of intelligible possibilities, only a small fraction of which is actually realized. Without a language and its modular combination of diverse elements, it is not clear whether it makes much sense to talk of a sentient being living in a world. A world only comes into being for conceptualizers who can specify the options, the unrealized possibilities. A set of stimuli do not add up to a world. A modular system of markers, generating alternative possibilities, all of them conceptualizable, but only one actually realized – *that* is a 'world'. Without language, there is no *world.* Animals without language, living only within realized possibilities plus perhaps a small range of fears and anticipations, in a way do not inhabit a *world* at all.

The second and more abstract sense in which mankind is rich in possibilities is that, over and above the alternative possibilities present in any one language, we are evidently capable of acquiring and internalizing more than one set of elements ready for combination. Languages and cultures differ radically in the ways in which they construct a world. Men evidently have the capacity to internalize and submit to quite distinct visions. Languages are rich, but mankind is also rich in alternative possible kinds of language.

A culture is a system of constraints, limiting an endlessly labile set of possibilities, within bounds which are themselves also very complex, and which apply to a very wide range of situations. It seems to me quite inconceivable that the principles making such a complex system possible should be invented and erected *ad hoc* in the case of each culture; still less that each prohibition, each proscription within it should all be invented and instilled separately. Chomsky has popularized the argument that the data available to a language-learning child simply are not rich enough to enable it to catch on to the structure of the language it is learning to acquire. It could not learn to speak, were it not for the fact that the child is already highly and, so to speak, generically language-prone. I am arguing that, similarly, we should not be able to live in a culture were we not already very prohibition-prone. We are culture-prone as well as language-prone, and these two intimately linked susceptibilities must be rooted in some well-structured general predispositions, without which our volatility would be our undoing.

The *specific* prohibitions to which we are subject are culturally idiosyncratic: but our strong tendency towards observing some reasonably coherent set of prohibitions, and our sheer capacity to perceive them with precision and to comply with their requirements, is an attribute shared by the entire species. Moreover, the linguistic and the cultural discipline predispositions in great measure overlap. Language is, initially and basically, a system of prohibitions. *Am Anfang war das Verbot.* In the beginning was the prohibition. Language consists of markers indicating what thou shalt not do. The rules governing the combination of the elements are deployed to form markers, and are themselves obeyed by a linguistically and culturally most biddable humanity.

The referential aspect of language has of course been greatly exaggerated by empiricist theoreticians, who project our own empirical fastidiousness onto other users of language. Referentiality is not wholly absent among earlier users, in so far as the markers need to be triggered off by *something*: but that something is in the main social and only in a much smaller measure natural. Social stimuli dominate and trump natural ones. Sophisticated scientific languages, whose terms are *operationalized*, as we now say, in terms of natural conditions, and at the same time become fairly independent of social ones, constitute an exception, a late and unusual development. A referential system, sensitive to nature and blind to society, is a rare achievement, a part of what we mean by 'science'.

Diversity is the clue to the history of mankind and, one may add, to the success mankind has had in dominating the planet. This diversity has two aspects, intra-social and inter-social. The fact that societies differ so markedly allows diverse societies to explore diverse options or strategies: many cultures have adopted ways which were not markedly successful. What brought mankind to its present condition is that so very many options could be tried out. It must be assumed that the successful ones were always in a minority, perhaps a tiny minority. It did not matter from an evolutionary viewpoint, in so far as so many alternatives were tried, and the successful ones could be emulated by the others or eliminate them.

Intra-social diversity (compatible with finely tuned conformity and discipline) is just as important, though for another reason. It and it alone permits the great complexity of social organization, which in turn allows the exploration of cultural alternatives of great power. Options could be tried which simply would not be available to societies whose members resembled each other closely. This was one of Emile Durkheim's central insights. It was he who proposed the distinction between Mechanical and

Organic Solidarity, where the former engenders social cohesion based on the similarity of the cohering elements, be they individuals or groups, while the latter achieved cohesion based on complementarity and on mutual interdependence. Whether or not Durkheim was right about the mechanisms of social cohesion, there can hardly be any doubt concerning the point that great diversity of roles permits an incomparably wider range of possible social organizations, much broader than that which would have been possible on the basis of a mere accumulation of elements which fundamentally resemble each other.

This point had already been made by Adam Smith, *nur mit ein bisschen anderen Worten*. It was he who most eloquently and persuasively proposed the idea that the key to progress was the Division of Labour. The system of differentiated and minutely proscribed activities which make up a given society is not predetermined, but can be elaborated and developed to a point of refinement where it greatly enhances our well-being and prosperity. That was Smith's point.

Durkheim later suggested that what really mattered were the socio-political rather than the economic consequences of the division of labour: its impact on human sociability was more important than its impact on the production of pins. But Adam Smith was not unaware of the political importance of the phenomenon either. What was wrong with Smith's theory was that, perhaps because he lived so long before Darwin, his basic anthropology was so naïve: it took far too much for granted. It simply assumed, as *given*, certain basic features of human nature, which in reality are most mysterious and must not be taken as self-evident: our capacity to conceptualize very specific aims, very specific procedures, often stretching over long periods of time – in other words, our capacity to enact and persist in highly distinct and specific roles. This presupposes a conceptually organized world within which alternatives are easily grasped. This capacity may seem obvious to people addicted to a kind of panhuman ethnocentrism, to seeing our shared human condition as natural, obvious, a given and unquestioned birthright. But in reality, it is nothing of the kind. Other species lack it. After Darwin, we need to explain our distinctive endowments.

The division of labour requires and presupposes this ability to conceptualize. Not all specializations, role specificities, are economic, and not all of them are beneficial: but before we can specialize economically, and specialize in a manner which enhances our efficiency and productivity, we must first of all be capable of conceptualization which is both precise and persistent and independent of immediate stimuli. We must master and respect a conceptual, modular system of behaviour-limiting markers. This is a gift which is not shared, or shared only in incomparably smaller measure, by our primate cousins.

So we return, via Adam Smith, to our initial point. Man is defined by his plasticity, which enables mankind to display its amazing diversity, both within individual societies and between them. But this potential for diversity would be useless were it not also restrained by some compensatory mechanism. This compensating mechanism restores behaviour to relatively narrow limits in any one cultural milieu, but not to the *same* limits in all milieux. Assume that man is indeed as volatile as manifestly he is, but also that learning and knowledge operate in the manner in which simple-minded empiricist philosophers supposed they did work: by the interaction of individual minds with 'experience'. On this model, each individual would build up his own system of associations, in the light of an inevitably diversified and idiosyncratic experience. Divergence between individual minds would be enormous, and ever increasing at a tremendous rate. Our minds would suffer from semantic cancer, because meanings would expand through idiosyncratic associations. Would such volatile minds ever be capable of either communicating or co-operating? It is unthinkable. Without plasticity, no diversity; and without diversity, none of that rapid exploration of alternative strategies which has made mankind what it is. But without cultural restraint, the plasticity would become malignant and excessive, moving much too fast. It would also be unable, through its very volatility, to *retain* any advantages gained. It would simply, as it were, skate over them and move on much too quickly. Any gain would rapidly be lost. So the plasticity needs to be counterbalanced by restraint and constraint. Language constitutes the major part of the system of markers which indicate the tolerated boundaries imposed in any one culture at any one time.

Note that two famous definitions of man – man is a rational

animal, and man is a social animal – are not really basic or elementary, but derivative. They are, both of them, corollaries of our more fundamental point – mankind is the plastic or volatile species. This being given, rationality and sociability become necessary consequences: the volatile animal cannot survive unless he is both rational and sociable. Or rather, he must be rational, and in order to be rational, he must also be social. The idea of rationality used here is that of Emile Durkheim: it simply means being susceptible to and restrained by shared, socially imposed concepts. A volatile being devoid of this capacity would be *far too* volatile.

But man must also be social: it is difficult to see how a very small community could either perpetuate a really rich system of markers or inhibit an over-rapid development of such systems. Every new deviation from the norm could and would, much too easily, become a new norm. It takes a population of a certain size – not a very large size, but at least a band – to impose a sensitivity to the distinction between what is accepted usage and what constitutes a deviation. Rationality and sociability are corollaries of volatility; without them, the plastic animal would be too unconstrained to be viable.

So speech and plasticity came together: neither is possible without the other, twice over. Each presupposes the other; each renders the other necessary. It is hard to conceive full language existing prior to volatility of conduct: what use would this highly adjustable, rich system of markers be? A rich, alternative-engendering system of markers, accompanying a rigid, invariant, genetically dictated form of behaviour, would be a totally useless or noxious luxury. A chained being has no use for the capacity to conceptualize alternative paths to freedom. But it is equally impossible to imagine the absence of language *after* the arrival of volatility. So it is reasonable to suppose that the marks of volatility of conduct are indices of the origins of language.

But if speech is the necessary condition of restraining *excessive* plasticity, is it also sufficient? The doctrine that it is indeed is one form of sociological idealism. This is the view that it is our systems of meaning which constrain us, and *suffice* to make a society or to define it. Another way of putting this would be to say – give me the system of meanings, in other words the culture, and I will tell you what kind of society you are dealing with. No system of constraints over and above culture need be considered: the specification of the culture will suffice. I have very grave doubts about the adequacy of this widely held view.

Now it does indeed seem to me true that, culturally and linguistically, we are astonishingly biddable, docile and well-behaved; and it may also be true that, for pre-agrarian mankind, such a culturally oriented anthropology may indeed be appropriate and perhaps very nearly sufficient. I am not sure that this is so, but it is at least conceivable, and it may constitute an approximation of the truth. Pre-agrarian humanity does not have very much to fight about, and the mere description of a shared culture may constitute something approaching a near-complete account of the maintenance of social order in the society in question. Perhaps it lacks elaborate coercive systems. There are also some grounds for doubting this, but at least it is a *prima facie* possibility and deserves investigation.

It does, however, lose all plausibility when we come to food-producing, resource-storing societies. As no principle of resource distribution is either self-evident or self-enforcing, but many are *conceivable*, and every single one is unfair to *some* participants, these societies are inherently conflict-prone and have to be endowed with coercive systems, which in turn go beyond the cultural system. One and the same cultural system of shared meanings and markers is compatible not merely with diverse occupancies of key positions in the society, but also with quite diverse authority structures and methods of enforcement. Structure and culture are often independent of each other to a marked degree. One and the same culture or marker-generating semantic system may be compatible with quite diverse organizational, coercive systems.

My point about the difference between foraging and agrarian humanity could be put as follows: mankind is susceptible to two kinds of constraint, cultural/linguistic and coercive. All in all, men obey the grammatical and cultural rules of their community without needing much in the way of sanctions, though it could be said that the ridicule which follows phonetic or sartorial solecisms is a sanction of a kind, and a very powerful one at that.

But when it comes to the occupancy of positions in the economic and political hierarchy, sanctions rather more potent that the mere 'grammar of the culture' are generally required.

My claim is that the balance between these two kinds of constraint changed profoundly with the discovery of agriculture and the presence of a stored surplus. Among foragers, semantic systems were no doubt reinforced by some violence, which was presumably also important in the allocation of roles to individuals; but among agrarian societies, elaborate coercive structures reinforce and maintain the society and its organization to a far greater extent. Perhaps this is a mere matter of stress: physical violence was no doubt also present among foragers, and placid submission to mere custom, without threat of force, is not unknown among agriculturalists. But even if it is a matter of stress rather than of a radical discontinuity, a very significant shift in the balance between these two elements must have taken place.

Our general point was that man is basically plastic, but that in any one society his comportment is restrained within remarkably narrow limits. The genetically under-determined species is constrained by new, semantically transmitted bonds. What mankind *is* given genetically is, precisely, that leeway, *and* the capacity to construct an open-ended system of markers, which will compensate for genetic flexibility or under-determination. Man is also endowed with a remarkable docility in the face of these systems of markers, and a capacity to recognize the limits which they impose and to comply with them. In terms of this overall scheme, our point concerning the Neolithic Revolution, and the implications of food-production and storage for the size and complexity of societies, is this: very complex systems of roles arise with food production and storage, and these can no longer be sustained by culture alone, but also need systematic duress. To put all this in an old-fashioned way: production and storage bring about the state, or institutional coercion. We can speak of the state proper when the agents of this institutional coercion are concentrated in one part of society.

Culture, or the constraint of conduct by conceptual means, is of course not absent or unimportant in the agrarian age. Agrarian societies generally aspire towards stability, and their complex organization tends to be underwritten and supported by a correspondingly elaborate cultural machinery. Where simpler societies had the dance and the story, these societies possess doctrines as well as myths, in the keeping of a corps of ideological specialists. The basic formula for these doctrines is that what is *must be*, and rightly so. The proofs offered in support of this sacralization of social reality cannot possibly be genuine and independently valid. Hence the agrarian age must appear, to those no longer enslaved to it, as an age of superstition and coercion. This is precisely how the Enlightenment saw it.

A general formula which may be applicable to agrarian societies is that they need *both* cultural/semantic and elaborate coercive systems of social control. Their complexity and demands and, one might add, their inequity are all so extreme that, without coercion and fear, social order would crumble. But coercion alone would never have been able to sustain these elaborate societies either: what they need is, so to speak, coercion at *a distance*. A herd of concept-less animals cannot be constrained to do something highly specific and to do it *now*, by the threat of dire punishments at a later date. Animals will only obey rather crude instructions, enforced by crude and currently perceptible sanctions. They can admittedly be drilled into performances or abstentions, but the range and refinement of such internalized instructions is rather small. They could never engender the intricate and sensitive patterns of conduct presupposed by the complex social order which we take for granted. Complex human civilizations require men to do very minutely circumscribed things, and to do them in the light of sanctions that are not immediately present and operative. Complex civilizations would not be possible unless men were capable both of *fear* and of abstract, alternative-conceptualizing *thought*. They need coercive action at a distance, fear at a distance, which is finely tuned, precise, discriminating. We need to be both clever and frightened.

Or one might put it all as follows: semantic or cultural systems alone do not suffice as compensations for our genetic under-determination. They need to be supplemented by coercive systems. This need becomes conspicuous and overwhelming at the point at which the institutionalization of food production and storage opens up the possibility of populous, complex and diversified societies. Coercion without meaning is blind, meaning without coercion is feeble. Meaning on its own enforces cultural but not political conformity. Only jointly can force and signification construct those masterpieces of social organization which emerge in the agrarian age. De Maistre observed that the executioner is the foundation of social order. But he is not sufficient. Civilized humanity needs to be under the sway of both executioners *and* generative grammar.

The simultaneous presence of semantic and coercive techniques for imposing order on behaviour is reflected in the prominence, and in the insulation, of the specialists of legitimation and the specialists of violence. These two supremely important and dominant social categories generally preside, in some kind of often uneasy cooperation, over complex societies. Their pre-eminence constitutes eloquent testimony to the fact that the maintenance of social discipline is highly problematic, and that it is seldom attainable without them. Society could not manage without their help and, once endowed with them, cannot easily resist their demands. So they generally secure great privileges for themselves. The markers delimiting the boundaries of sub-groups and of required behaviour need to be serviced and maintained, and this confers power on the priests. The tools of coercion likewise need to be deployed and kept in readiness, and that bestows power on their frequently monopolistic possessors. Why are these two categories so frequently distinct and separate? Presumably the nature of the two sets of skills is such that their deployment, and/or the training which leads to the acquisition of virtuoso status, are not easily combined. The correct question seems to me not why institutions such as divine kingship or priestly rule are occasionally encountered, but rather why they are ever absent. The separation of, and rivalry between, these two categories of dominators may well constitute one of the important clues to the question of how we managed to escape from the agrarian order. Priests helped us to restrain thugs, and then abolished themselves in an excess of zeal, by universalizing priesthood. First Canossa, then the Reformation.

We now know that it is indeed possible to escape from the

agrarian age of Fear and Faith. We know it because we have indeed escaped from it, though the romantics among us would prefer to say that we were expelled from it. We know it happened, though we do not fully understand how this escape or expulsion came about. What we do know is that the rules of the game have changed radically once again. Both coercion and culture are still with us, but in a wholly new form. Coercion has diminished in degree, at least in liberal societies. Agrarian society was inescapably Malthusian, with population constantly pressing on resources; the distribution of those resources could not but be invidious, and hence required a good deal of coercive enforcement, often very brutal. Post-agrarian society is affluent and can afford, or at any rate has frequently allowed itself, the luxury of a marked relaxation of coercion. Coercion is by no means absent, but it is greatly softened, at any rate in some societies.

When we come to the new role of culture, we find not just a change in degree but in kind. In its cognitive life, this new kind of society respects *science*. This is made up of a curious system of markers largely disconnected from any social triggers, and related in a systematic manner to something extra-social ('nature', 'experience'). As a set of imperatives, it only commands hypothetically, and relates to the choice of means, not of ends. It is not expected to be stable.

In its productive life, this society is similarly unusual: stability is not expected here either, and there is an unconstrained free choice of methods and personnel. In other words, both cognition and production are liberated from the restrictive constraints on role and method innovation which had dominated them, in the interests of social stability, throughout the agrarian age. It is as if that genetic volatility, which had characterized man for 200,000 years or so, had at long last, and for the first time, been allowed to manifest itself to the full, not merely in the form of variety *between* cultures or societies, but *within* one of them. A kind of society has arisen which could tolerate a relative liberation of human plasticity, even within the bounds of a single social order. The explosion of cognitive and productive innovation is of course linked to a rather special new and inwardly imposed restraint, which can for convenience be referred to as distinctively modern rationality. This mysteriously allows men to be orderly and social, even while they freely recombine elements of production and cognition. An inwardly sanctioned constraint leads producers and researchers to observe and respect formal rules, even in the course of substantive innovation. Discipline has moved on to a higher plane, permitting an astonishing amount of innovation at ground level, while social order is preserved.

So constraints are not absent in this society either, but they take a new form. The compulsive sacralization of important concepts, which had so preoccupied Durkheim, is replaced by the second-order sacralization of procedural propriety, of the rule of treating like cases alike, of conceptual tidiness, of the unification of referential concepts in an ideally unified system, and of their separation, to a remarkable extent, from the markers delimiting social conduct. The crucial imperatives are formal, not substantive. No individual concepts are heavily underwritten and rendered immovable by awesome ritual. Our literal rituals are playful and semi-serious. A unified and orderly and open system of referential concepts now lives in relative isolation from the markers guiding social conduct.

The requirement of orderly symmetry is at the heart of both the social and the cognitive ethic of modern society. Absence of ritual has become the most potent ritual, absence of graven images the most pervasive fetish. Both inculcate orderly and experimental treatment of nature and help engender the technology which is the new basis of society. Bribery by economic growth in some measure replaces fear as the cornerstone of the social edifice.

The importance of the sociology of Max Weber lies in the fact that it offers a theory of how this new kind of restraint has come into being. As so often, the merit of the theory resides more in its highlighting of a previously unperceived and important problem than in the solution it offers for that problem. Weber has made us sensitive to the difference between a world in which formal order is sacred but all specific objects are equal, and the older world in which some substantive objects were much more sacred than others – the world analysed by Durkheim.

This new kind of society, and also its associated vision, quite transforms the relationship between High Culture and Low

Culture,[3] which had been in mutual tension throughout the later part of the agrarian age. High Culture had been perpetuated by script and formal education, Low Culture by informal socialization within the local community. The new nature of work, which consists of the context-free manipulation of meanings and people, not of things, requires the overwhelming majority of the population to be in possession of a High, literate culture. Its acquisition is the most valued qualification for most individuals, and a precondition of effective membership: men passionately identify with it, and this is known as 'nationalism'. Social control now operates in part through such nationalism, or the ardent identification with either an existing or a desired nation-state. It is also enforced by a centralized and pervasive state, and made palatable by a shared stake in affluence and the promise of its continuous enhancement.[4]

My argument has been that genetic under-programming must have been linked to the presence of a compensating system of cultural/linguistic restriction. These cultural systems and systems of coercion have complemented each other in diverse ways at different stages. The volatility must obviously have had its own genetic preconditions, so that our volatility, and our endowment with compensating talents and propensities, must have arrived jointly. The consequence has been the emergence of a species in whose life both social or semantic transmission and institutionalized coercion have become far more important than genetic mutation, making it possible for change to be astonishingly rapid.

[3] See S.N. Eisenstadt, *The Origins and Diversity of Axial Age Civilizations* (State University of New York Press, Albany, 1986).

[4] See E. Gellner, *Nations and Nationalism* (Blackwell, Oxford, 1983).

5

Freud's Social Contract

Civilization and its Discontents is a foundation myth, an account of the origin of the present social order and indeed of the emergence of humanity, an anthropogenetic theory. It is also a version of the social contract, a theory concerning what validates the moral order – admittedly, a somewhat half-hearted and less than enthusiastic account, a less than glowing endorsement. It contains a suggestion for a modification of the contract, for a diminution of its severity, but this is accompanied by an undisguised fear of the possible social consequences of such a softening of the terms. The lukewarm ambivalence of Freud's social contract is one of its most marked features. The tone is: this is the best we could do . . . Perhaps we can do just a little better, by being less severe on ourselves: but I am terrified at my own audacity in making such a proposal. There are some among us who may take advantage of it. It might lead to a catastrophe. (Ambivalent thought on the side: *would* it be a catastrophe?)

Social contract theories are indeed a *kind* of foundation myth. They constitute a very special subspecies, which distinguishes itself in important ways. Standard foundation myths generally invoke supernatural, or at any rate quite exceptional and supernormal powers and beings. These powers make possible the exceptional initiating events, which then constitute the very beginning of the world and/or of the social order, and thereby legitimize the order so engendered. The fact that the events and powers are so exceptional, and the fact that they occur at the beginning of time, jointly validate the society they bring about. Such myths are the natural charters for religiously oriented societies, with their deeply internalized, absolutized status differences. Those differences are made authoritative just because they are so suffused by the transcendent. The awe which status inspires in such a society is mirrored in the exceptional nature of the events which brought about the prevailing system of ranks.

By contrast, the whole appeal of social contract theories is that they set up the social order on the basis of something mundane, human, ordinary, namely the voluntary contract between two or more men. Nothing tremendous and extra-terrestrial is required for the setting up of society – only goodwill or good sense. Setting up a social order is a good *deal*, and its preconditions are those of good deals: it is beneficial to both or all parties concerned. The switch from foundation mythology to social contract theories is also the transition from societies of transcendent status to societies of immanent, voluntary consent. The superficial, temporary nature of status in such societies, linked as it is to a merely transient occupancy of a position in an instrumental, rather than sacramental bureaucracy, or to a similarly contingent bank balance, and the absence of any deep internalization, are reflected in the mundane nature of the deed which sets up social order itself. Hierarchical societies with ascriptive status have myths; egalitarian mobile societies have contract, roughly. The transition from status to contract is mirrored in the move from myth to contract.

Freud's version is unusual in a number of respects: for one thing, precisely, it combines a foundation story or myth with a contract and, in consequence, it faces all at once the problems confronted by each of these kinds of intellectual production. Each of them faces a kind of regression: myths naïvely assume a background world within which the world is created, contracts assume a background moral obligation which underwrites the primal contract itself. The contract element in this Freudian version differs from other contracts in that it is not rational, but emotional. It postulates a pattern of feeling, not of thought or calculation.

The story of course takes place within nature, within the world. Freud's thought is naturalistic and empiricist, not to say materialist – all that goes without saying. Freud's critics are liable to say that the Unconscious he discovered or postulated has all the attributes of the old Transcendent: it is powerful, menacing, and only selectively accessible, as specified by the theory which postulates its existence, which at the same time confers privileged access and authority on the propounder of the theory itself and his acolytes. So outsiders are deprived of access and cannot really criticize the entire structure. All this may be true and, from the viewpoint of the internal logic of the belief system in question, the Unconscious may indeed be the functional equivalent and replacement of the old higher religious realms. Nevertheless, from the viewpoint of understanding Freud's theory of the origin of morality and society, it is also exceedingly important that this new version of the transcendent is formally located within nature and history. The founding myth and the terms of the basic social contract are terrestrial, not celestial.

The naturalism of both the foundation story and the contract story is important. It means that the foundation story must lay claim to historical truth, as indeed must the contract episode. In Freud's case, as indicated, the contract itself is emotional rather than rational: this follows in any case from its location in the Unconscious, and anything else would hardly be in the spirit of Freud's thought. Earlier versions of social contract theory presupposed, somewhat comically, a set of previously asocial but mysteriously rational individuals, coming together and setting up law and order in the interest of all, though possibly against the interest of some. Bertrand Russell once commented on the oddity of a contractual theory of the origin of language, based on the supposition that a group of hitherto speechless elders would solemnly agree henceforth to call a cow a 'cow'. Freud's vision of man does not lead him to any such implausible vision of instant rationality: the social order is set up by an event which brings about a certain emotional constellation, which then sustains society, rather than on the acceptance and implementation of a rational argument.

Quite apart from the fact that a rationalist version would hardly be consonant with the Freudian vision of man, it would also not work for another reason: Freud is far from sure that the setting up of social order really is rational in the sense of being in the true interest of those who do so. He keeps wondering whether the price of it all is not too high, and this is indeed the main theme of the book. So if, *per impossibile*, an attempt to set up society rationally had indeed taken place, it might well have failed: one of the miracuously rational elders taking part in the primal constituent assembly, a beneficiary of his mysteriously self-generated rationality, might have stood up and denounced this palaeolithic Maastricht, and made a speech containing precisely the central argument of *Civilization and its Discontents*, warning his colleagues of the grave danger of the path on which they were about to embark – *Beware of the road to emotional serfdom! Do you realize what you are letting yourselves in for? Once you set up this here super-ego, you will no longer be your own masters!* – and, assuming that his listeners too were endowed with this precocious or preternatural rationality, they would have perceived the wisdom of his words and heeded his warning, and society would not have come into being. Freud himself clearly wonders whether this might not have been better, but alas there is nothing much we can do about it now. It is too late to reverse that fateful decision. The primal bond is both tragic and irreversible, though it can, it appears, be softened.

So the Freudian social contract must be a pattern of feeling rather than ideas. The older contract theories became fashionable during the period when men switched from religion to reason in the pursuit of social foundations. Freud's version of the contract replaces the earlier ones at the point in the history of thought when the cult of reason gives way to a celebration of feeling or instinct, when romanticism prevails over rationalism, when its earlier victory in literature and (partially) in philosophy seems at last to be confirmed and completed by its triumph in science, medicine and psychiatry – a victory it owes more to Freud than to any other single man.

Both foundation mythologies and philosophical social contract theories in general suffer from certain weaknesses. Mythologies tend to indulge in a kind of childishness and narrowness. They tell us how the world began and, in the course of telling the story, assume the existence of a world within which the world is being born . . . Thus, for instance, the Judaeo-Christian story tells of the origin of mankind with the primal couple, but then assumes that their offspring interact with *other* people! This led some Africans, who had been told the story by missionaries, to infer, as they told the anthropologist Isaac Schapira, that some unmentioned incest must have occurred which explained the existence of those *others*, and that this was the real clue to the whole story. The narrative circularity of mythologies, which assume a world within which the world comes into being, is matched by the logical circularity of philosophers' theories: they have great difficulty in explaining how, in a world where only the primary contract makes other contracts binding, the initial contract, itself devoid of any prior underwriting, could itself also be binding. The regress of validations applies to contracts as it does to anything else.

It will be interesting to see whether or how Freud himself, attempting to offer both a myth and a contract, can escape the difficulties which haunt both genres. But first it is best to see what actually his argument, or multiple (not necessarily harmonious) arguments actually are.

Freud starts with a certain hedonism, the 'Pleasure Principle', even though this subsequently becomes greatly modified. Freud's hedonism is naïve, unsophisticated, quasi-Benthamite in its formulation (pleasure and absence of pain), in brief, it is very *pre-Freudian*. The picture we owe to Freud, which once stated is clearly superior to its predecessor, is of man subject to strong irrational drives, whose specific objects are identified by an intricate privately coded system of interpretations, in the main hidden from the agent himself. Neither the general character of the drives nor the manner of selection of their objects is at the service of human contentment.

It was Freud who had overcome the empiricist model of human nature twice over, once by showing that our desires were dark, turbulent, animal-like, unrealistic and indifferent to reality, and furthermore not at all transparent, nor engendered as echoes or aftertastes of sensations, but mediated by a devious, complex, internal Enigma machine, whose operation is unintelligible to its possessor. This is how we behave, and though romantic literature had told us so for some time, what really put a seal on the recognition of the fact was that *Dr* Sigmund Freud, clinician and therapist (not some mere scribbler or philosopher) had said so. But, although he had taught us to see mankind in this manner, he himself remained attached – not so much in his conclusions, but in the baseline of his argument – to the old hedonist-empiricist way of looking at human conduct, a view worked out by the British empiricists, and one for which Freud's half-acknowledged mentor Nietzsche had such a profound contempt.

What is worse, he not only uses this as a baseline, he does so without any philosophical sophistication. He affirms that the answer to the question concerning what men demand of life 'can hardly be in doubt'. The answer is, he tells us: 'They strive after happiness; they want to become happy and to remain so.' What he really taught us was that, more often, they are determined to make themselves miserable.

Is the Pleasure Principle, as he calls it, really beyond the reach of doubt? Any beginner reading Sigmund Freud knows full well not merely that it is in doubt, but that it is false: only Freud himself seems on occasion immune to his own teaching, preserving a kind of archaic logical stratum of an earlier doctrine. We know from Freud – and from literature, and from life – that men often passionately seek their own misery. The doctrine that they primarily seek their own happiness can only be made true by a suitable definition, by equating 'happiness' with 'whatever it is that a man seeks'. Then, of course, the doctrine that a man seeks his own happiness and nothing else becomes necessarily, tautologically true: a man seeks what he seeks. But, although the bland (and initial, provisional) endorsement by Freud of the hedonic principle does owe its plausibility to the tautological element in it, yet he does not stick consistently to this sense either, in so far as it leads him to say that all this leads man 'in the main, or even exclusively' to seek happiness. But if it is at all possible to seek something else, even if not 'in the main', then the tautology lapses; and in any non-tautological sense, the initial proposition is untrue anyway . . .

This is not the only muddle which Freud fails to clear up, and which weakens his argument. Human conduct can be characterized in a third-person terminology, as the obedience to drives, or it can be seen (as the empiricists generally saw it) in first-person terms, as the response to inner sensations of pleasure and pain. Drives can certainly exist without sensations, and more contentiously, sensations may exist without striving. (Arguably, if a sensation is described as pleasurable or painful, this already includes the notion that the sensation in question will be pursued or avoided, as the case may be.) It is not obvious which of these terminologies is preferable for an effective characterization of conduct, and the general insights of Freudianism would, I think, lead one to favour a language of drives rather than sensations. In fact, Freud uses both and combines them, in a manner which arouses one's fear that tautological versions of the same formula are used to establish the formula in another, more contentious sense.

Man can indeed only act from drives that he actually possesses: that much is tautologically true. But translated into sensationalist language, on the assumption that every drive is experienced inwardly, it leads to the Pleasure Principle, the enslavement to inner satisfactions. But the claim that inner sensation accompanies any and every drive is questionable, and the drive tautology, when translated into sensation language, is no longer true. Freud used the language of drives both for long-term trends, patterns of behaviour, and for their inward echo, or the mechanisms responsible for trends or behaviour (though he often mistakes a metaphor for a real specification of mechanism). Eros and its sinister counter-force both appear on three levels, in the individual, in a total civilization and in all organic life . . . (The whole drama is astonishingly like the play within the play in Chekhov's *The Seagull*, which is after all of roughly the same period and is meant to reflect *fin de siècle* modernism and its inner *trouble* . . . Chekhov made his tragic young writer say it all rather more briefly.) To invoke a spirit standing behind all organic life, behind the emergence of our entire civilization, which at the same time accounts for the private miseries of individuals, really looks rather like a piece of wildly indulgent *Naturphilosophie* . . . Clearly, Freud was a metaphysical poet.

Freud was endowed with a low level of philosophical sophistication or fastidiousness, and had little if any sense of the kind of problem which Ernst Mach had so powerfully injected into Austrian philosophy, namely the relationship between data and explanatory notions. Mach and others had endowed Viennese thought with a powerful *logical* super-ego, but this does not seem to have been internalized by Freud at all. He makes some perceptive observations about the philosopher Vaihinger, who would let religion in by the back door as a pragmatic fiction, an attitude Freud disliked, noting elsewhere that the only religion worthy of the name (presumably, psychologically effective) is that of the common man. Also, at the end of *The Future of an Illusion*, he pursues, without determination or depth, the theme that our knowledge is determined or limited by our intellectual structure . . . Given the use he makes of the idea that it is also determined by our *unconscious* psychic structure, and that both views raise the problem of how we can then claim validity for our theorizing, he might really have taken the problem a little more seriously. His lack of patience with a sophisticated approach to explanation comes out, for instance, in his irritation at the suggestion that the Unconscious might simply be an explanatory device, and not the name of a real thing. How could something which has such powerful consequences, he asks irritably, be merely a construct of our explanatory strategies? There is this coarse-grained quality in his thought and we must accept it, though I for one find it embarrassing. Freud uses physicalist language both in a descriptive sense and in an explanatory sense, and subjectivist language once again both as description and as explanation. He requires only a low level of concreteness, precision and testability in all of them, and the matter is not helped by his facile switches between them.

What does he do with his hedonic principle, having established it in a manner which leaves it full of ambiguity? All in all, he interprets it as the subjection to inner drives. He then leaves this topic for a descriptive discussion of civilization and the affirmation of his main thesis, namely 'that what we call our civilization is largely responsible for our misery, and that we should be much happier if we gave it up and returned to primitive conditions.' This general contention replaces or sums up the previous survey of frustrations or part-satisfactions. What he means by civilization appears to be in part the establishment of social order, of rules imposed on individuals, and in part a kind of higher civilization haunted by elevated, abstract, demanding ideals. All civilizations have their discontents but some have more discontents than others, you might say. After a digression in which he invokes his earlier findings in *Totem and Taboo*, he proceeds to the use of *love* as social cement, as the formation of civilization in the sense of large social units.

Here he comes to offer his first contribution to answering the questions – how is society possible at all? – how is order either maintained or legitimated? The answer is, in effect, through the modification of sexual love. His first experience must have suggested to man, says Freud, 'that he should make genital erotism the central point of his life'. But now something interesting happens: by way of insurance, it seems, men generalize their love. To love a single object puts you at its mercy, but to generalize your love – well, it distributes the risk. Love of mankind would seem to have begun, if Freud were right, as an insurance against risk. One woman may let you down, in fact she probably will, but if you love humanity there will always be someone left who hasn't yet deceived you. I find this neither a persuasive explanation nor exactly a rousing sermon in favour of the religion of humanity or universal love, but let it pass. Anyway, the thinning out or distribution of love is complemented by its regulation, its delimitation by rules. Love diluted by diffusion and restricted by rules enables men to form large units, which for Freud constitutes part of the essence of that civilization he is trying to explain and evaluate. Big is beautiful. No specification yet of the mechanisms which *obliged* love to submit either to dilution or to regulation. But at this point Freud indulges in a harsh characterization of (his) 'present-day civilization': he observes that it

> makes it plain that it will only permit sexual relations on the basis of a solitary, indissoluble bond between one man and one woman, and that it does not like sexuality as a source of pleasure in its own right and is only prepared to tolerate it because there is so far no substitute for it as a means of propagating the race.

Freud admits that this is an extreme picture which has proved impossible to put into execution. All the same: it is this, it would seem, which our civilization *wants*. He goes on to make a curious remark that not only civilization, but also something else within us thwarts us. The ultimate foe is within us. The enemies of our satisfaction are multiple. But there would seem to be no doubt but that civilization, i.e. social order, is one of them, and crucial and important among them. This order in turns owes something to the enemies within us, aggression or its thwarting, or its role in the thwarting of love . . .

The actual argument of *Civilization and its Discontents* is odd, and not very tidy or fully coherent. The baldest summary – civilization thwarts our instinctual needs and makes us unhappy and neurotic – is of course very simple, seemingly lucid and barely contentious. But in fact, the moment one looks at the proferred argument in any detail, curious lacunae and incoherences appear. Originally, says Freud (chapter IV), it is *love* which engenders social units. Sexual love, says Freud, engenders a family unit when it ceases to be intermittent, becoming permanent. *Continuity of lust* appears to be the very first social cement. Leaving aside for a moment the transition from authoritarian patriarchy to the brotherhood of guilt (a transition crucial for Freud, but at this point he himself deals with it rather cursorily), we are led to consider how this primordial cement can be put to more general use: initially, it only binds together those linked by genital love, plus at most the offspring of that love.

To engender larger units, more is required. Freud seems to consider the attainment of social size an important element of civilization, noting that 'one of the main endeavours of civilization is to bring people together into large units.' Small may be beautiful, but large is civilized. So sexual love must be doubly transformed: its aim must be inhibited and deprived of its narrow, literally sexual aim, and at the same time it must be extended to a far larger class of people. Briefly put, instead of desiring a few people sexually, you must love many people platonically (though Freud insists that the latter love remains rooted in the former). It all ends in that thwarting civilization which is the source of our discontents, which restricts sex to the minimum compatible with survival (one and one only heterosexual partner at most), and a reprobation of sexuality as a source of pleasure.

One gets the general picture and, for all its exaggerated character (which Freud recognizes), it is not a bad account of the state of mind of many people in the second half of the nineteenth century. The account of Freud the Liberator has on occasion been challenged by the claim that the Vienna of Strauss and Schnitzler was so permissive that it needed no liberation. In fact, the permissiveness was selective and restricted. You could get anything you wanted from the flower-girls, no trouble at all. The demographic situation which allowed the *K. und K.* ('Imperial and Royal') army to turn all its educated recruits into officers and still leave them a mass of peasants to command, also meant that there was an enormous reserve army of peasant daughters available for domestic service – or prostitution. For them, 'liberation' could be a disaster, not an alleviation of the human condition. As late as 1944 I heard a Silesian recruit, when a fellow soldier dared refer to his sister, expostulate angrily that he would have him know that his sister was respectably married, in a tone which betrayed that this was a precarious and important achievement, and one not to be taken for granted. The very mention of the sister triggered off fear and anger. In brief, Freud's text is a better guide than *Fledermaus* to the social and psychic realities facing the citizens of the Dual Monarchy.

But to return to Freud's argument. Restricted and generalized love leads to those larger units which, in his view, are of the essence of civilization. But what force ensures this restriction and generalization? Here the argument does not actually tell us, though of course we can turn to Freud's other books for help. Does libido turn in upon itself or is it aggressiveness which provides the inhibiting force? Is love a friend or an enemy to civilization – it seems to provide the initial impulse to the formation of bonds, yet it needs to be thwarted, at least in part, if those bonds are to be extended beyond the minimum.

This unclarity concerning the role of love in the attainment of sociability is made worse by the introduction of the next important character in the drama, namely aggression. Aggression is important (who would deny it?), but it is precisely its apparently unambiguous badness which, by contrast, gives the strong impression that love, the other partner in the plot, must be wholly good. This cannot be quite right, in so far as both partners require some measure of thwarting and regulation at least, and the question remains – what force is responsible for that restraint? Freud's tendency here to condemn aggressiveness so totally is in interesting contrast to its role in Plato's scheme in *The Republic*, where what Plato calls the spirited element has an important part to play in both maintaining internal order and external defence, and as a kind of mediator between what Freud would call the super-ego and the id. In *Civilization and its Discontents* Freud seems persistently to come close to a kind of Manichean dualism – love good, aggression bad – which is compatible neither with what he says elsewhere nor with the requirements of his argument, nor with the facts of the case. Would Love alone, freed of the presence of the enemy Aggression, lead to universal harmony? In Freud's own terms, the answer is obviously no. Does libido thwart itself, or is it aggression which thwarts it, or does aggression thwart itself? Is the super-ego made strong by internalized fear, or thwarted love, or thwarted aggression? The text wobbles on these problems, or even claims that there is no problem.

Freud's impulsion towards a starkly dualistic, Manichean account of our psychic life, indeed of all life, emerges vividly and without cover in chapter VI. Here the ultimate polarity of Eros and Thanatos makes its appearance, where all libido is united into a single force, credited both with the preservation of living substance and with the building up of larger units, but at the same time it is assigned its negative counter-force or *Doppelgänger*, making for dissolution and destruction, the death instinct. Here usefulness is granted to the destructive drive, in so far as it can help an organism survive by aiding in the destruction of its enemies. But at the same time, its failure to find such deployment makes it turn inwards, reinforcing that self-destructiveness which is at work in any case . . .

The trouble with this excessively Manichean version is that it doesn't even make much sense in Freud's own terms. Is love all good, engendering only fusion and those sought-after, civilized larger unities? No, evidently not, for in its natural forms the units it promotes are too small, and the units which it is *forced* to seek are unsatisfying to it, not to mention the fact that it is not allowed to enjoy its objects properly, in the original and instinctually satisfactory sexual sense . . . So aggression, especially when turned inwards, is partly good after all, at any rate, helpful in the achievement of the positive object of creating larger units . . .

In chapter VII Freud does indeed focus on the usefulness of aggression in generating that inner self-discipline so necessary for civilization, and which makes civilization so painful. He is a little bothered by a contradiction which he declares to be only superficial, between the origin of conscience in the internalization of an external authority, and its origin in the inner strength of that very aggression which is being thwarted. Freud believes this contradiction is apparent. After this, he reaches one of the most intriguing parts of his theory.

All contract theories as stated face the problem of the regress: if the contract alone set up moral obligation, what (prior!) obligation can underwrite and establish the authority of that contract itself? Freud's theory is a version of a contract theory, meant to explain the emergence of the social order, even though it is one necessarily written in the idiom of feeling not of thought, located in the Unconscious. Society is set up by conscience (plausible enough), by a sense of guilt. Society is a brotherhood of sin. The sense of guilt arose through the joint act of the brothers in the primal horde, when they killed the authoritarian father. But here too there is a regress! How could the primal killing explain the emergence of conscience if, before it, they had no conscience? They could *do* it, but how could you make them feel *sorry* about it? *Murder most foul* was required for the establishment of society: providing the murder was not so difficult; the problem lies with the sense of foulness. How can you feel it to be foul if you do not *already* have a conscience? If your problem is the origin and establishment of conscience, then the murder on its own, pre-foul so to speak, won't give you what you want without blatant circularity. If you need conscience to know that you are sinning at all, then the first sin can't give you conscience! A terrible question, which puts the whole of the Freudian theory in doubt. Is there a way out?

Freud sees the problem, and he thinks he has an answer. The participants in the primal killing of the father did not yet have a conscience: after all, they were about to take part in the act which would engender both conscience and hence true society, and if they already had a conscience anyway, they might have spared themselves the trouble. (But if they did *not* have a conscience, the act would do nothing for them – they would take it in their stride. What is one murder more or less to conscience-less proto-man? There's the rub!) Either way, it's no good. Ah, but though they had no conscience, they *did* have ambivalence. 'His sons hated him, but they loved him too. Very much.' And *how* they both loved and hated him! They hated him so much that they killed him, but they also loved him so much that, having killed him, conscience was born of their regret. 'After their hatred had been satisfied by their act of aggression, their love came to the fore in the form of remorse for the deed. It set up the super-ego.' Kant had to postulate a self-wrought feeling, living precariously between Nature and the Noumenal, which would mediate between sinless Reason and amoral sensibility, so as to make obligation and morality possible. Freud uses ambivalence for the same end.

So the act of killing is the starter motor, extraneous to the main psychic engine, which breaks through the deadlock and sets the process going. Freud is clear that, in *subsequent* generations, it no longer matters whether the deed is actually committed: the ambivalence of feeling on its own, even without an act, has become sufficient, now that it faces the now properly established super-ego, which after all (as he stresses) does not bother to distinguish between wish and deed, and punishes either of them with equal vigour. By then you can sin, you are equipped with the required organ for sin detection, and better still, you can (and do) sin without actually doing anything. The wicked thought suffices. An inherent and inescapable ambivalence performs the same role in Freud's system as original sin in theology: it ensures the ubiquity of sin. This is required, for otherwise society would not be able to function. But for all this to work, one must indeed thereafter possess a super-ego which punishes even ambivalence as harshly as it punishes an actual deed. There is no further need for the act. *Am Anfang war die That, aber spaeter ist die That ueberfluessig. Gefuehl ist alles.* (In the beginning was the deed, but later the deed becomes redundant. Feeling is everything.)

Once the engine is running, it feeds itself, it has no need for the starter motor. But to transform mere ambivalence (or fear of outer authority) into a conscience, a super-ego, an *act* is absolutely required, or so Freud maintains. The historic reality of the primal murder is an essential part of his theory. Goethe's emendation of Scripture – *Am Anfang war die That*, in the beginning was the *deed* – acquires a very definite and precise meaning in Freud's hand. No guilt-inspiring deed – no humanity, no society. The historic reality of the primal and bloody contract is an indispensable part and parcel of his theory.

The final conclusion of the volume is something we shall return to: Freud the prophet of the reduced demands of the super-ego, whether in the individual neurotic or civilized humanity at large. The very final passage once again indulges in the binary Manicheanism, as if love were wholly beneficial and its 'equally important adversary' constituted *the* danger – whereas in fact the argument (if valid) shows them both to be essential for life, for civilization, for the emergence of greater aggregates. But before proceeding to an evaluation of the overall position, something more needs be said about the details of the position itself, partly in the light of Freud's other relevant and closely related works.

Freud is not merely a critic of over-severe morality (though this is perhaps the most important aspect of his work and influence), he is also a terrible morality snob. He is not merely the man to point out the discontents of civilization, he is also exceedingly proud of them. It is clear that he feels that *we* (the better class of person, if you know what I mean) have the privilege of enjoying a better and more vivid kind of discontent, and we would not be seen dead without our discontents. They constitute a badge of cultural rank. Without our discontents, we should be *déclassé* . . .

This is closely related to a curious feature of his particular version of the social contract, namely, that it is virtually unrelated to the problem of the *state*. The state is hardly mentioned, and only occurs in a tangential context. The point is, Freud is not terribly interested in social order imposed by fear of something external, and he really has a barely disguised contempt for people who only behave themselves because of such an external, politically inspired fear. The institutions of external coercion do not interest him too much, not merely because he is a clinical doctor, not a political scientist, but also because he prefers the better company of those who know *innere Führung*, and is loth to slum it with those who need the carrot and the stick. (He is scared of them, but that is another matter.) This order sustained by external fear occurs in the primal patriarchal tyranny which preceded the first tyrannicide-patricide, and the fact that such a political system is also repeated in the form of authoritarian government throughout history, and is required for the lower cultural orders, is not his main concern. He knows it, of course, deplores it, is frightened by its implications (the fear is quite specially intense in *The Future of an Illusion*), but it is not really at the very centre of his attention. What does interest him, *and what he respects*, is the kind of social order which, relatively speaking, dispenses with external sanctions and works through internal ones. He is concerned with the civil society of inner-directed conscientious men, something like Kant's Kingdom of Ends, an association of rational agents deeply respectful of each other's rationality – except that, in Freud's version, the bond is not shared reason but shared guilt. His version of the self-wrought feeling of obligation, as Kant describes it, is Oedipal not noumenal. And, although he considers it pathogenic and inimical to contentment, and aims to reduce its demands (an endeavour in which he has, I think, succeeded on a massive scale), he is nevertheless proud to have such problems and, I think, would, had the choice ever been offered him, have contemptuously rejected any opportunity to return to a condition of a weak super-ego and strong external fears.

Here we come to an internal problem of his theory. All men have super-egos but some men have more than others. Moreover, the distribution of the two types is not random but very systematic. Excessive conscientiousness at least seems to be related to a demanding, solitary and jealous deity, and, on the other hand, to the emergence of societies in which the role of external authority is diminished and that of internal authority enhanced, and which, presumably in consequence, are less oriented to coercion and more to production. (Or is the connection the other way round? That is the issue between Marx and Weber. Freud presumably favours the psychogenic explanation, but the mechanism he proposes is quite different from Weber's.) In brief, not only social order as such, but its higher varieties also need to be explained. Freud both does and does not observe this distinction.

In other words, the problem of the establishment of social order occurs not once but at least twice: Emile Durkheim, for instance, developed a theory of the original emergence of inner compulsion in *The Elementary Forms of Religious Life*, while dealing with the second transition in *The Social Division of Labour*. Max Weber did not deal with the first contract at all, but dealt with the second one in his most celebrated work on *The Protestant Ethic and the Rise of Capitalism*, in which he offered an explanation resembling Freud in at least two respects, namely, invoking unconscious processes and being indebted to Nietzsche. But, like Freud, Weber in the end could not resist telling the story twice, once as it occurred during the Reformation and once during a dress rehearsal in the Old Testament. Freud, though not much concerned with the economic aspects of the second contract, did have an acute sense of its general importance, and certainly believed it to be related to the emergence of a morally demanding, magic-spurning monotheism. Hence his *Moses and Monotheism*, which ends up as a repeat performance of *Totem and Taboo*.

The trouble is, while Freud did have a sense that there were indeed two problems, he only had one solution, and so he had to repeat it and make it do double duty. *Moses and Monotheism* is one of the outstanding pieces of crime fiction of the century, far more gripping than Agatha Christie or Dorothy Sayers. A murder has been committed *and* concealed for centuries. But the murderers – they were a whole collectivity – did not bargain with the acumen of Sleuth Sigmund. He noticed the crucial clue, the existence of a highly conscientious community, and, once on the scent, was not dilatory in unmasking both the concealed deed and its perpetrators. No community (a fortiori, no excessively concientious, moralistic community, spurning external sanctions) without conscience, no conscience without shared guilt, and so a shared murder. The sheer existence of society is *the* clue to the commission of a murder, for where there is society there must have been murder: the existence of a *conscientious*, magic-avoiding, moralistic rather than manipulative spirit clinches the matter. These murderers may have thought they were clever when they concealed their deed, but they had no idea how they were giving themselves away, at any rate to a perceptive investigator with psychoanalytical insights, primarily by the fact that they had a severe conscience *at all* (rather than by what they specifically thought they had on their conscience, which hardly matters; all consciences are the same, Oedipus rules OK).

No direct evidence for the murder? But of course, what would you expect: the crime could hardly have a deep psychic impact unless it was repressed! The absence of surface evidence is itself the clearest evidence, in the best analytical tradition. The Jews had invented, or adapted and popularized, a moralistic, severe, monotheistic religion (actually initiated by the Egyptians under the impact of their own imperial expansion, but soon repudiated by them). In this religion morality, not magic, was central. Could there be any doubt about how they could attain such a condition? No doubt at all, at any rate for Sigmund. They must have committed a collective murder, and moreover, the victim must have been the very personage who brought them this pure faith – Moses. It is all so blindingly obvious, once he spells it out. Of course they suppressed records of the crime, but the truth will out – it is precisely their moralism that gives them away. Once on the track of the truth, some historical claims – fragmentary, ambiguous and inconclusive though they would be on their own – confirm the matter. Jewish moralism, so marked throughout history, is based on a kind of doubly distilled super-ego. All nations are descended, at least culturally, from the participants in the primal murder, but the Jews did the Father in twice over, the second time round murdering not literally a father but something much like one, namely a demanding spiritual leader and innovator . . . With such a history, who can wonder at the pervasiveness of conscientiousness, self-hatred and neurosis in such a group?

A number of curious things follow from all this. Freud is widely credited with the theory that anti-Semitism is unconsciously inspired by resentment against the historic originators of an excessively demanding faith. (I have always found this hard to swallow: was the Ukrainian peasant, setting off on a pogrom, really motivated, albeit unconsciously, by resentment against a religion, but for which he would still be worshipping Perun, and drinking and beating his wife even more than he was doing anyway? This never rang true.) In fact, Freud's theory here is rather more subtle. The Christians at least owned up to the fact of deicide, even though they blamed it specifically on the Jews; the Jews deny the very occurrence of the event. So the guilt of the Jews is not so much the killing of Christ, but the historic suppression of the murder of Moses . . . Their sin was not deicide but the suppression of a surrogate deicide . . . They deny the crucial killing without which conscience and society are not possible. Freud does not make it clear whether the actual inclusion of a Dying God theme in a religion strengthens or weakens the sense of primal guilt. Is public celebration of divine martyrdom (Christianity, Shi'ism) more or less effective than repression of the recollection (Judaism and, presumably, mainline Islam)? As so often in psychoanalysis, the evidence can be deployed either way.

The trouble with Freud's theory of morality and religion is that it fits some cases and not others. It does indeed fit divine (or near-divine) martyrdom religions such as Christianity or Shi'ism, but it does not fit faiths in which this element is absent, such as Judaism or Sunni Islam. In the case of Judaism, of course, it is precisely the suppression of the crucial fact which, according to him, explains everything – but can this be extended, for instance, to Sunnism, or indeed to other world religions? Was there also a historically suppressed killing of the Buddha and of Confucius, or did these higher moralities succeed in imposing themselves without the benefit of murder of the Teacher?

Something must be said here about Freud's method. It is sometimes claimed that Freud must have been an implicit Lamarckian, that the transmission of the primal guilt and the awareness of it presupposes the transmission of acquired characteristics. This does not seem to me to be necessarily so. The mechanics of transmission could be cultural: the shift from mere ambivalence, conflated love and hate, to permanent guilt, under the impact of a particularly horrific deed and the perpetuation of awareness of it, could be explained in terms of a cultural mechanism operating on an unchanged genetic base. Freud was aware of the problems, and his (as usual, schematic and semi-metaphorical) solution, invoking the notion of a collective mind and recognizing the difficulties involved, could certainly be reformulated in some such terms, though he does not himself do so. What he does say is at any rate compatible with such an interpretation, even if this interpretation is not dictated by his actual words.

Though not guilty of Lamarckism, of the doctrine of the genetic transmission of acquired characteristics, Freud is open to the charge that he makes himself an easy present of social transmission. The perpetuation and diffusion of the recollection and socio-moral effects of the primal crime presuppose cultural (though not necessarily genetic) transmission of information. But how is that possible? Freud does see the problem, but does not give much of an answer to it, other than suggesting the existence of a collective mind, no doubt as the locus of perpetuation of the recollection of the shared guilt. Language and the possession of the conceptual equipment (conscious or other), which would as it were fix the nature and implications of that guilt, are taken too easily for granted. The machinery for the possession and transmission of shared, yet circumscribed and definite, collective representations, is simply assumed, but no theory is offered concerning how so remarkable an achievement was possible. Here as elsewhere, Freud is open to the charge of naïve mentalism, of taking our intellectual competences too much as given and unproblematic.

At this point, it is useful to compare him with that other author of a modern version of the social contract, Emile Durkheim, who, like Freud, does not credit early man with a rationality which would have appeared *ex nihilo*. What Freud takes for granted, Durkheim turns into the central problem of *The Elementary Forms of Religious Life*: how can we possess shared, disciplined, compulsive concepts, which can then guide our social comportment? Whether or not he answers the question correctly (invoking ritual as such, of any kind, rather than, like Freud, a murder turned ritual), he does formulate the question extremely well, and I suspect that any return to serious theorizing about the origins of society will have to return to his articulation of the problem. Durkheim's formulation focuses on the problem of how we can ever single out the obligatory and constrained conduct, and how members of the same community can do it in unison, whereas Freud is preoccupied with identifying the enforcing drive, while ignoring the first and really more difficult question. How can the id-thwarting force locate the object to which it is meant to lead us?

It is the simultaneous emergence of a species genetically under-determined in its behaviour *and* equipped with a mechanism for restraining this wide potential of conduct, in any one group, which makes culture and cultural transmission possible. It makes possible that transmission of a social compact which Freud presupposes but cannot explain, but also makes possible a wide diversity of cultures and basic social compacts, which indeed is the case, and which Freud by implication excludes. The real original, pan-human social contract was the emergence of the sheer possibility of cultural compulsion and transmission, which is a kind of blank sheet making possible a whole variety of more specific contracts, social orders each with its own blend of coercion and conviction. The very first and great transition, which in effect engendered man and society, offers a kind of generic questionnaire to each society, making cultural diversity and non-genetic transmission possible, but leaving the filling-out to individual cultures. Freud, unlike Durkheim, asked the wrong question.

What follows from all this is that Freud's question is misconceived and wrongly formulated, in so far as it seeks, like the theorists of old, for one *single* social contract for all societies (thereby landing itself with the awkward question concerning the diffusion of the primal guilt-information, which leads to comic answers whichever way you play it), and which also of course helps account for the main empirical difficulty facing Freud, namely that, while some societies fit his model, others do not. There is no single model. Freud's own historic importance ironically lies in the fact that he helped along a transition from one kind of contract to another, from an authoritarian hierarchical order to an affluent, permissive, egalitarian one. The main historic effect of his account of the basis of social order in general was that it diminished the authority of the one prevalent at the time, by crediting it with human, all too human roots, and with pathogenic fruits. The fate of his own work illustrates the diversity of contracts – which is incompatible with the main thrust of his argument.

There are indeed grave problems with his theory of the genesis of conscience and society (the two being virtually equivalent in his presentation of the problem) as found in both *Moses and Monotheism* and *Totem and Taboo*. As we saw, the real historic occurrence of the primal slaying is something he holds to be essential for the theory. At the same time, of course, it need not (and hardly could) occur in every society and every generation. We know full well it does not. So some civilized and conscientious people benefit from a primal crime not merely not committed by them, but not even committed by their own direct ancestors: cultural diffusion spreads out the benefit of society formation to others, who had not, strictly speaking, earned it by their own endeavours and guilt, people who had made no contribution to the formation of conscience and society by doing in a father. These innocent yet cheating free-loading beneficiaries of the primal murder committed by others are, in a sense, moral parasites. They live off the hard work, or rather, the hard murder of others without contributing to it, free riders who secure their social order and remorse on the cheap, members of the social guilt club who have failed to pay their dues, men who enjoy their Oedipus as some people watch TV programmes without paying their licence fees. No society formation without father immolation!

But it would seem that, strictly speaking, it does not absolutely have to be your own dad or grandad who was done in. But just how many times did it have to occur? One solitary parricide would hardly do for all mankind, would it? Did it have to occur prior to the dispersal of *Homo sapiens sapiens* or did it have to be repeated in each isolated sub-segment of mankind? How big a load can we place on cultural diffusion of guilt, freeing some of mankind at least from the need to take part, literally, in the grisly deed?

And there is one rather acute problem: the murderous brothers, having done in father, set up conscience and society proper by abjuring access to their own sisters and instituting exogamy. But supposing the neighbouring gangs do not oblige by doing the same? Supposing, as is only too likely, the primal murder is not synchronized between various primal bands? The group which has performed it has also, on Freud's theory, generously initiated a free (indeed, obligatory) woman exchange, which is a kind of corollary of the murder of the previous monopolizer of women, simultaneously a disavowal of his methods and greedy possessiveness, yet also an atonement for his murder: but no sexual GATT obliges their neighbours to reciprocate. On the contrary, they are most liable to perpetuate protectionism in this touchy matter of females, and constitute not so much a *Geschlossener Handelstaat* as a *Geschlossener Heirats-Stamm*. So our premature pioneers of social morality and free trade in women, Friedmanites of sex, having regretfully exported their newly tabooed sisters, heroically exercising their recently acquired conscience, receive nothing in return for their sacrifice from their pre-primal-murder, pre-conscience and hence still endogamous neighbours, and so are condemned to extinction . . .

As a matter of fact there is one modern state at least, post-independence Algeria, which did behave in something of this style, placing great difficulties in the way of its own female citizens who might wish to marry out. In brief, Algeria behaved as if the entire country were still a patrilineal tribe which gives internal claimants priority over women, allowing bride-export only when, after proper notice, no internal groom has presented himself. The fact that Muslim tribes generally tend to have this custom, unlike most other patrilineal societies, is a bit of a puzzle for anthropologists. For Freud, there is no problem at all: given the absence of patricide in Islamic theology, it all follows. This is just what you would expect – no killing of the father, so no exogamy. But by the same token, Muslims on his theory should have weak super-egos . . . unless of course, like the Jews, they did really kill their own Law-giver, but suppressed the fact? What all this amounts to, once again, is that Freud's theory simply does not allow for the great actual variety of human cultures and patterns of prohibition.

These are specific problems, but there are also general ones. What is Freud's standing as a theoretician of the origin of man or of human society? One cannot confront his views with anthropological orthodoxy, for at present there is no such thing. What happened in social anthropology, at the very time that Freud was making use of anthropological material and blending it with psychoanalytical theory, was that anthropology itself was turning its back on questions of origins, rejecting them as speculations which were inherently too unsound to be settled or pursued. Some anthropologists have since defied this taboo and returned to the topic, but they have remained relatively isolated figures, and one cannot yet speak of any general consensus in this area.

It is a curious fact that, in his method of proceeding, Freud commits in an exaggerated and provocative form the very methodological sins which anthropologists learned to abjure during the same period. Moreover, the first chapter of *Civilization and its Discontents* is actually devoted in the main to an exposition and defence of such just a methodology. He invokes the method of recovery of survivals, comparing the mind to a city in which archaeological remains enable us to reconstruct and even perceive much of its past. He does not really face the objections which persuaded the anthropologists to abandon such procedures – the fact that the 'survival', even if genuine, is torn from its original context, or the fact that survivals are invented or interpreted in a circular way so as to turn them into explanations of the present. It is a curious fact that the first and as it were the founding generation of social anthropologists who did adopt this anti-past-reconstruction stance, at the same time often admired Freud. Did they grant him methodological licence which they denied to themselves, or did they simply refrain from taking his genetic stories literally?

Apart from sins against anthropological method as codified in his own time (and perhaps due to be modified again), there are those general logical failings which have in effect made Freud the very paradigm of *non*-science. Very, very stratospheric abstractions, like Eros and Thanatos, are reified. They are given both a kind of physicalist interpretation (broad behavioural tendencies) and yet also a sensationalist one, as experienced drives, and are credited with an explanatory power over and above any descriptive one, where the explanation is in fast more a metaphor than a genuine specification of the manner of emergence of the thing to be explained. Even the metaphors fall over their own feet: at times, we are presented with a dramatic binary world in which creative love confronts destructive aggression in an eternal duel, yet at the same time love is not wholly or even largely good, but needs to be tamed by inward-turned aggression, while by the same token aggression is indispensable for the erection of larger loving totalities . . . As descriptions, the links of these stories to the concrete details of the real world are so utterly loose that they can be and are applied to any material at will. Freud invokes these abstract though, to him, terribly earthy and potent forces, yet does not ever attempt to operationalize them, so that their presence and effects could be independently checked. It is left to his intuition. More than this: his notion of the Unconscious achieves a kind of additional de-operationalization, by allowing these forces to have *any* manifestation. In his work, when these forces are bounced off the super-ego, they reappear as agents and fortifiers of their own repression. It is as if all apprehended criminals were readily able to be recruited and socialized into the police force, without even any training. Can our instincts really be so readily turned around?

One further notorious trait of the Freudian method, the fact that the theory itself permits reinterpretation of all data on a privileged basis (unconscious meanings trump manifest ones and are preferentially accessible to the analyst) is not particularly conspicuous in this work: Freud doesn't actually dispense with historical data when dealing with, say, biblical history (a disregard he actually commends when dealing with individual patients). He is cavalier with the evidence, but does not deny its relevance in principle. The illusion of the *Allmacht des psychoanalytischen Denken*, to which he is so easily liable to succumb in clinical practice, does not quite take over in his historical speculations. There is a residual respect for the autonomy of historical evidence.

So what remains? Freud captures, better perhaps than anyone else, the manner in which the educated middle classes of the developed world in the early twentieth century perceived themselves and their relationship to society. In liberal societies, men lived by conscience, not by fear. They were proud of this (and Freud himself was very proud of it and of the sublimation of instinct into creativity, which was a mark of his social and cultural class), yet with a naturalistic background vision of man, they had become uncomfortable about the excessive prohibitions imposed on nature by conscience. Their naturalism made them distrust the absolutist, external-authority pretensions of conscience. The theoretical justifications of the authority of conscience were at the time under critical scrutiny, and it did not look as if they would emerge from this too well. Some men still accepted its dictates, virtually in the very terms in which Freud summarized them: take, for instance, the case of T.G. Masaryk, Freud's senior by a mere six years and, like Freud, a southern Moravian, and one who also naturally gravitated towards Vienna. Masaryk, a liberal in many ways, still believed, as he told Karel Čapek, that sex should ideally be restricted to a unique one-to-one relationship of one man to one woman. (He disliked sexual mysticism and blamed it on Catholicism and its excessive demands, so in a way resembling Freud.) But such men were becoming rare.

Kant, Marx, even John Stuart Mill, looked forward to a fusion of *is* and *ought*, a condition in which man's inclination and his conscience would become as one. Kant did not believe this could be the case in this world (where a painful dualism was our inescapable lot, a view he shared with Freud); Marx did not believe it could happen under the current socio-economic dispensation, whereas it would in effect define the highest social form due to appear in the future (Freud's critique of Marxism is the most convincing passage in the entire book); and Mill thought it would take quite a time, though it might come in the end. Freud did not believe that such a reconciliation would ever be on the cards, and reported, accurately, common experience on this point. It was just because (unlike Kant) he saw both libido and conscience as springing from the self-same mundane roots, that he did not believe they could ever be fully at peace. Conscience is the satisfaction of libido by other means, but that does not mean the two will come to terms. On the contrary, their underground affinity endows them with great opportunities and inclinations for mutual torture. They were destined to continue to torment each other, though the torment could be diminished a bit, with Freud's help.

The discontents were here to stay, make no mistake about that, but palliatives are available, and Sigmund knows about them. At the same time, near the very end of the essay, he falls back into that facile reductionism of the views of *others* which his own general position allows him: 'One thing only do I know for certain and that is that man's judgements of value follow *directly* his wishes for happiness . . . they are an attempt to support his illusions with arguments.' (Emphasis added.) *Directly*? Had he not shown that the moral theories sustaining the severe super-ego have the opposite effect? Has he forgotten the deviousness with which the super-ego finds its rationalizations, the cunning with which it indulges in torture? He returns here to the naïve and reductive hedonism which otherwise he has helped us overcome. More important: if this is so, if our reason is such a slave to our passions (in a sense rather different from that with which David Hume had endowed this famous formula), what is the point of reasoning about this matter at all? How does he come to make an exception on his own behalf and advise us, rationally enough, to tame or domesticate the super-ego? Advice he was indeed obliged to give: unlike his predecessors Schopenhauer and Nietzsche, who also saw conscience naturalistically as the satisfaction of lusts by other means, but who as mere scribblers were then able to take refuge either in a pessimistic aestheticism or in a quite unspecific 'transvaluation of values', Freud was a doctor and had to guide patients. He retained this attitude, albeit with quite becoming hesitation and ambivalence and reservations, when he switched from individual patients to treating mankind as a whole. So he did recommend a solution, or at least an attitude. Freud is probably the most influential moralist of the century, but, heaven knows, this is not due to the rigour of his reasoning . . .

So the discontents *could* be diminished at least. This is what he recommended or, at any rate, he supplied the charter for a new attitude, for a change in moral climate which, presumably for deep social reasons, was taking place anyway. Freud grew up in a society which had still remained, all in all, similar to that faced by the Enlightenment intellectuals, who thought they themselves might live by the light of Reason, but who were frightened of the prospect of the masses also being freed from anything else to restrain them. Freud was close in spirit to the attitude of Voltaire, who locked the doors when atheism was discussed in case the servants overheard and, freed of the fear of God, then murdered him. Freud had the same fears, and already expressed them with special intensity in *The Future of an Illusion*. Freud differed from his Enlightenment predecessors only in stressing that Reason was and had to be rather painful, even, or especially, for the Enlightened: for it was extra inner pain, not just Reason, which made them so enlightened, and capable of being both social and creative without the help of the fear of the Lord. They might live by Reason alone, but it was tough going. As for the others, never mind whether it was painful, the trouble was that it was insufficient! We'd have to be careful with *them*! Very careful indeed.

However, in the end he turned out to be wrong about this: a new society was emerging in the twentieth century, based on advanced industrialism and diffused affluence. Its principal method of social control shifted from coercion by fear and the proximity of starvation, to generalized bribery by economic growth, and increased participation and diminution of social distance, due to a new and mobile occupational structure. This society turned out to be less demanding, severe and punitive than its predecessor. It bribed rather than terrified, and it was altogether more permissive. All in all it works, at any rate so far and in socially favourable circumstances. Under the old order, strict control over rather scarce resources, enforced by brutal coercion, was the main method of social management. It included the rationing of sexual resources. Roughly speaking, only the socially acceptable and conforming ones (and, of course, those who were powerful) had access to the brides. Now, the astonishing but repeatedly confirmed promise of ever increasing and ever easier access to resources replaces fear as the method of maintaining order. Regimes collapse not when they no longer inspire fear, as of old, but when they fail to deliver economic growth. The relaxation of control which is inherent in this new order is extended to the sexual sphere. It would be both difficult and pointless to try and exempt it. Freud's ideas about the feasibility of a mild diminution of the severity of conscience, whether valid or not, did not *cause* this change: they had, as indicated, profound social roots. He did, however, provide the rationale for it.

In 1945 liberal consumerism eliminated, by war, one ideological rival, who aimed to combine industrialism with a restoration of hierarchy and a measure of severity, and a cult of violence. This alternative ideology, with its recognition of instinctual needs and its disavowal of the humanist universalist ideal, might well have acclaimed Freud's ideas (and surreptitiously I suspect benefited from them), but it was prevented by its racism from doing so. It did implement a possibility Freud mentions, namely the reversal of the trend towards the universalization of love, in the name of a return to natural selection. In 1989 the conclusive end of an economic confrontation eliminated a further rival, one who had aimed at the political imposition of righteousness on earth. This alternative did control resources severely, partly as a means of imposing discipline and partly because it was not very efficient at producing them, and it extended this severity to the sexual sphere. So, for the time being, permissive liberal consumerism has no rivals, at any rate in the West, and Freud had drafted its social contract, in the form of an anatomy of its discontents, plus some recommendations concerning how they are to be handled. Social life is a compromise with instinctual needs which, in itself, is unavoidable and has unavoidable costs, but with good sense guided by the illumination he brought, the cost can be markedly diminished. In truth, it was the new basis of social order and not the Freudian vision of man which made the new permissiveness possible, but for all that, it was good to have a well-drafted charter for the new morality. The diversity of possible social contracts (Freud himself made a contribution to a radical change, though he was most fearful of its possibility and inherent dangers) illustrates the misguided nature of Freud's very question, which assumes *one* contract, quite apart from any doubts one may have about his answer.

Freud may well have been wrong about both the original social contract or its biblical second reading, but he took the lead in drawing up a new social contract for the emancipated educated classes of the twentieth century, *and* for the entire, far more permissive society which emerged with general affluence later in the century and which, all in all, accepted the moral lead provided by the educated classes. There are many not one social contract, and Freud helped to draw up a new one suitable to new circumstances. He was the leader among the gang of brothers who didn't exactly kill conscience, but cut it down to size. They were ambivalent about their own ambivalence, and he advised them to live with this condition. He was, when all was said and done, exceedingly proud of that super-ego which made sure of his own discontents.

The old conscience issued categorical imperatives, the new one negotiates a private settlement with the help of an enormous new corps of counsellors (probably Freud's most important progeny, more so than the elite analysts proper), who have taken over pastoral duties in a naturalized and secularized world, a brotherhood of acknowledged ambivalence rather than outright sin and a shared murder, and who do so in a diluted Freudian idiom, with other elements added to the mix according to taste. The modern liberal state avoids not merely a statutory wage policy, but also, as much as it can, a statutory morality – and for much the same reasons, namely both the difficulty *and* the redundancy of enforcement, and the absence of premisses for determining first what it is which is to be enforced.

When one lacks conviction concerning rules or aims, one also lacks the will to enforce them, whether it be a matter of wages or the limits of legitimate sex. Better have a free market in both spheres. Contrary to Freud's fearful anticipation concerning what would happen when the mob was told that religion was an illusion and that there were no rules any longer, in fact the *mass*, largely embourgeoised by a new occupational structure and new types of work, seduced by affluence and a wider social participation, is quite willing on the whole to behave itself in return for the promise and reality of ever-increasing wealth. Though freed of fear of severe punishment and informed of the demise of the deity, the mass has not gone off on a rampage of murder and rape, and all in all has gone on paying taxes and driving on the right side of the road. As *the* social bond, the anticipation of ever-increasing affluence has replaced the recollection of a shared murder.

But the new permissiveness needed an explanation: the disavowal of the authority of guilt inspired by a vicarious, ancient, and in the end also rather hypothetical and speculative parricide will do as well as any. Of course we retain our Oedipus but he is now restrained, we have distanced ourselves from his claims, toned them down in view of their excessiveness and in the light of the requirements of mental hygiene, and by seeing them in context, psychologically, as one natural fact among others. Where superego was there shall ego be. The Surgeon General has determined that conscience can be dangerous to health. Thanks to Freud, this warning notice is now widely distributed in our society.

Freud may have been wrong about the primal social contract, and indeed was wrong in his assumption that there was only a single one, applicable to all mankind and all types of society. But he helped prepare the phrasing of one particular basic constitutional law, that of modern, liberal, permissive, consumerist society. Where the preamble of the Declaration of Independence of a puritan, individualist Republic proclaimed the rights to life, liberty and the pursuit of happiness to be self-evident, there Freud's preamble to the as yet unwritten basic law of our society says as much about shared Oedipal guilt and instinctual renunciation, but significantly adds that these are to be limited as far as feasible. The limits are to be freely negotiated in the light of individual circumstances, but these are the new self-evident aspects of man's social coexistence. Pursuit of happiness is vindicated again, but there is a warning that not too much of it is to be expected, given that we are what we are.

Liberal consumerist society may in due course face grave problems, it may or may not prove stable but, for the time being, it works. It may founder when consumerism is satiated or becomes self-thwarting, it may court ecological disaster, or it may founder on the conflict between its need for cultural homogeneity (manifested as nationalism) and ethnic diversity either inherited from the past or engendered by new migrations. In the meantime, however, where favoured with economic success, it is working well enough. Freud's particular fears for its viability proved unfounded, and he actually helped it a lot by providing it with its moral theory, its self-justification.

So morality is now left to individual negotiation, and this is carried out in Freudian idiom. As against men such as Masaryk, who tried to go on playing by the old rules, which in Masaryk's characteristic case were virtually word by word such as Freud had credited to the old order, Freud provided the tools for articulating or privately renegotiating a more flexible new set of, no longer commandments, but, how shall we put it, indicative guidelines. Flexible self-knowledge (in fact: guided and negotiated self-choice) replaces the Tables of the Law. All this probably makes *Civilization and its Discontents*, and its supporting fables, the most important single text for understanding the moral climate of the twentieth century.

6

Past and Present

It is customary to trace the idea of Progress back to the quarrel of the Ancients and the Moderns: it was at the point at which Western Europeans presumed to think that they had surpassed antiquity, and that the Renaissance was well and truly over, and the religion of Progress was born. I beg to dissent from this view. The real essence of the idea of Progress is not that we in particular are better than the ancients, in literature or anything else, but that *generally* speaking, later means better, that later forms of humanity tend to surpass earlier ones, that there is a global, cosmic mechanism or principle, given which things improve, by and large, passing not through two stages but through an endless series or gradations of improvement. Claims to have detected the operation of this principle emerged among thinkers in the later part of the eighteenth century. In the nineteenth, biologists argued for something similar, and the truth about history appeared to be a truth about all life, perhaps about all being.

This is a powerful, indeed an intoxicating idea. Like other key philosophical ideas, it not merely explains, it also justifies. It justifies the ways of God to man; indeed, the most influential and fully orchestrated philosophy of progress – Hegel's – was profoundly and systematically ambiguous on this point. It was left deliberately unclear whether Progress was God's gift to mankind, or whether, more simply, God *was* Progress.

Romanticism and anthropology have this in common: they are, both of them, spin-offs, corollaries and, in part, reactions to this progressive vision. Romanticism repudiates the uncritical and total endorsement of the Moderns. It finds merit in untutored, backward, traditional folk practices, or in medieval institutions or styles, real or imagined. In extreme forms, it may repudiate the modern altogether, as an aberration; in more moderate and characteristic forms, it merely seeks and finds continuity, it perceives the seeds of the present in the past, the fulfilment of the past in the present. Romantics have a sense of history. They talk as if they had invented and patented it, and perhaps they have.

Anthropology as a distinctive inquiry likewise originated in the progressive or evolutionary vision. Its fascination with the savage was rooted in seeing him as an ancestor, socially or institutionally or intellectually speaking, even if he was biologically speaking a cousin rather than an ancestor. It was, for all practical purposes, the study of retarded cousins, whose retardation could be assumed to make them closer to our shared grandfathers, notably those far enough back to have left no written records, and who consequently could not be studied by the normal historical methods.

Romantics delved into the villages and folk cultures of their own society. Anthropologists, by contrast, were interested in very distant cultures. The work of the Romantics had political implications: in an age of irredentist nationalisms, the limits of a culture were soon to become the limits of the territorial claims of the state which found its *raison d'être* in protecting that culture. But the age of nationalism was also the age of colonialism, and the work of anthropologists therefore also inevitably had political repercussions, though not in the same style: there is no record of a colonial power claiming a given territory because, for instance, the natives were matrilineal or practised animism.

Thus anthropologists and Romantics went their separate but parallel ways, respectful of the past, using the present as evidence for the past: a nearby present as evidence of a recent past in one case, and a distant present as evidence for a distant past in the other. In the altogether new form of the debate between Ancients and Moderns, in the debate between Westernizers and Populists, between partisans of an open, individualist, rationalistic *Gesellschaft* and those of an integrated, communal, spiritually fulfilling *Gemeinschaft*, Romantics and anthropologists were often on the same side of the fence.

In the emerging social sciences, this conflict was mirrored in styles or methods of inquiry. One party saw the correct method as the working out of the interaction of individual men's aims, views and environment, rather in the way in which prices are determined by supply and demand, leaving little room for any mystical sense of culture and continuity. On the other side, there were those who favoured the historical, institutional or cultural method; and they too thought that their method had universal applicability. In fact, both sides rather vacillated between holding their own recipe to be universally valid, and using it in a prescriptive, normative way, as a touchstone of pathology. Of course, they were diametrically opposed to each other in their identification of the pathological: who was the poor patient, modern man or the savage?

This great European debate constitutes the background of modern anthropology. But anyone familiar with this confrontation who took a good look at the fertile and brilliant tradition of social anthropology as practised in Britain and its intellectual dependencies since the 1920s would promptly feel puzzled and disoriented. Something simply does not fit. Some strange dissonance disrupts the habitual natural affinities and oppositions. The tradition in question displays some, but some only, of the expected traits. A sense of the interdependence of institutions, and of the way in which human actions owe their meaning to a pervasive culture at least as much as to individual aims – yes, certainly. But it is the near-cynical, irreverent attitude to the past of the Malinowskian tradition in anthropology – still, all in all, the dominant style in the intellectual sterling zone – which constitutes the main deviation from the normal, expected intellectual alignments. Its most characteristic doctrine is that the past is and ought to be the slave of the present. Not only mythology, but 'history' itself, is seen basically as a set of alleged past events which men and communities select – or invent – in order to justify and explain their present practices and predilections. Mythology and history are assimilated to each other, and both are seen as 'charters' – Malinowski's preferred term in this context – of contemporary institutions. Real history is not factually accurate history; real history is that which acts on the present in the present, by fulfilling a present social and emotional need.

This great reversal of priorities is virtually the defining feature of Malinowskian anthropology. The past is seen as significant not because it possesses an existence and agency of its own, but through its function in the present. This is of course entirely in line with the whole Malinowskian style, which sought to explain the beliefs and practices of savages in terms of their social role or functions in the societies in which they occurred. This view was known as functionalism.

Just how and why did Malinowski manage to effect this diplomatic revolution in the alignment of ideas, in the customary elective affinities, fusing a romantic sense of the interdependence of institutions and the pervasiveness of culture with a rather unromantic devaluation of the past? Bronislaw Malinowski, the uncrowned Anthropologist Laureate of the British Empire, died in 1942, and was born in 1884. The centenary of his birth in 1984 led to a minor flood of research into his youth and the influences which formed him in pre-First World War Austrian Galicia, in Cracow and Zakopane, by young scholars such as Andrzej Paluch, Andrzej Flis, Grazyna Kubica and Jan Jershina in Poland, and Edwin Ardener in England. This has enabled us to understand how this reshuffling of European cultural cards came to re-orient and redirect anthropology.

The Polish and Continental roots of Malinowski had previously been neglected. The Malinowskian revolution was once hailed as virtually self-explanatory and self-justifying: the manifest merits of its ideas sufficed to explain its famous victory, its conquest of the anthropological world of the British Empire, as it was in its tranquil autumnal glory. Speculative second-hand, fragmentary, discontinuous data, and an implicitly or even explicitly contemptuous devaluation of the primitive, were replaced by thorough, painstaking fieldwork. Wrongly, I think, accused of serving colonialism, the Malinowskian recipe for fieldwork style and interpretation was certainly by far the best way of making good scholarly use of the vast array of accessible, peacefully governed, but more or less well-preserved exotic cultures assembled under the imperial political roof.

So much for the usefulness of those ideas; but what of their roots? Malinowski was a Cracow Pole, well pleased with Habsburg rule – his doctorate in 1908 was awarded him *sub auspiciis Imperatoris*, a great and rare honour – who combined cultural nationalism with political internationalism. He knew that redrawing political boundaries would not terminate the oppression of one culture by another in eastern Europe – it would merely redistribute the roles of oppressor and oppressed.

Like other educated Poles, he was exposed to the two great intellectual currents of the nineteenth century: Hegelianism and positivism. The former taught in effect that world history was world judgement, that national fulfilment lay in a national state – for nations, life begins, not at forty, but with state formation – and that consequently Poles, having then no state to call their own, were either second-class members of the world-historical process, or were called upon to redress the temporary mistake of history and set up their own political unit. Alternatively, they turned to a kind of inverse Messianic Hegelianism: it was the suffering of state-deprived Poland and its eventual redemption which conferred meaning on history. Malinowski neither cared to consider himself second-class nor was attracted either to irredentist nationalist activism or to collective Messianism. Hence there was little to draw him to a philosophy, fashionable though it may have been, which could only lead him to such an unpleasant dilemma.

But happily there was no need for him to be any kind of Hegelian. He was on the other side of the great divide. His thesis, which was so greatly honoured by Kaiser Franz Josef himself, was a sympathetic study of the new wave of positivism, notably Ernst Mach's. The Machismo which Malinowski found so appealing, included both a rejection of transcendent entities – alleged unobservables were to be turned into constructs out of observables – and a biological-functionalist attitude to thought: both the nature and the justification of ideas lay in their service to the organism. Ideas were functional.

What was original in Malinowski was that he directed these two ideas quite particularly at the past, at history. The past was no longer to dominate the present, to determine it, and to set its tasks: on the contrary, the past was to be seen as having been shaped by present needs. There were plentiful examples of this process of construction in central and eastern Europe: hardly a nationalism existed which did not fiddle the past for its own ends. However, Malinowski took the extreme position of seeing all visions of the past as primarily functional in the present. This itself in turn was his own 'charter', and it allowed him to do two things at once: revolutionize anthropology under his own leadership, and get himself off the hook as a Pole, one who otherwise would have been obliged to settle his account with History.

Everyone knows the story about the competition prize offered for a book about elephants, and how the Pole submitted a study of 'Elephants and the Polish Question'. Superficially, Malinowski seems to contradict the moral of this story. He never wrote a book called 'Argonauts of the Western Pacific and the Polish Question', or even 'The Sexual Life of Savages and the Polish Question'. But we should not be deceived. He did *really*. The very same positivist-functionalist set of ideas by means of which he overturned the reign of Frazer also provided a splendid and original escape from the dilemmas which Hegelian-type philosophies impose on stateless nationalities. So the Polish Question was, after all, hidden inside the anthropology.

The paradigmatic anthropologist of the age, who had indeed deeply stirred and stimulated him, was Frazer. Frazerian anthropology had consisted of a speculative reconstruction of the development of pre-literate human mentality, on the basis of a vast array of very fragmentary data, carefully assembled but torn out of context. Malinowski's functionalism insisted that all such evidence be restored to its context, and his fieldwork method consisted of an exhaustive exploration of social contexts. The idea that the past be treated as a slave of the present, and not vice versa, was a very neat corollary of the positivist onslaught on unobservables. In pre-literate societies, the past is a kind of transcendent, being well out of cognitive reach. Malinowski was quite clear that Frazer was the last king of classical anthropology, and he himself the first king of a new, functionalist anthropology. Frazer was the old priest of the anthropological Sacred Grove and he, Bronislaw Malinowski, slew and succeeded him, perpetuating and reincarnating him because he had also destroyed him.

Malinowski's victory within the British Empire was virtually complete. For a long time, most anthropological chairs were occupied by his intellectual progeny, though in America his impact was less total.

Even today I do not think that any of the loudly trumpeted assaults on the Malinowskian régime have really overturned it. But there have been modifications. Athough, ever since Malinowski slew Frazer, no new aspirant has slain him in turn, the old priest, or his cult, has changed considerably.

The first change came early. The shift from 'functionalism' to 'structural functionalism', associated with the name of Radcliffe-Brown, meant in effect the dropping of the biological stress, of attempts to match – and thereby explain – social institutions with basic biological needs. This programme may have been implicit in the pragmatist-style positivism which Malinowski took over from Mach, but it doesn't work very well. Human societies do of course have a biological base, and recently sociobiology has revived the interest in it with a new sophistication. But the variety of social forms, often erected on frequently identical or similar biological bases, is so great that it is probably best, at least for the majority of social scientists, to concentrate on the social factors which explain the differences, rather than the biological ones which explain the shared substrate.

The most important change, however, is probably the serious return to history: the tendency to ask anthropological questions of historical material, and historical questions of anthropological material. What was valuable in the Malinowskian myth of the 'ethnographic present' was the insistence on a sense of the interdependence of institutions, and the requirement that the way in which they mutually constrain each other should be thoroughly explored and documented, and that facile explanations, in terms of the location of isolated institutions in terribly abstract evolutionary schemata, which are then supported by 'data' that are but shadows of the schema itself, should be avoided.

This idea can be and has been retained and is compatible with a concern for history; in fact, it can give historical investigations a new sensitivity and richness. It does not require a ritual abolition of the anthropological regime, merely its more effective deployment. British anthropologists such as Jack Goody or Alan Macfarlane have in effect done this; American ones such as Eric Wolf or Marshall Sahlins or Clifford Geertz had never stopped doing it.

We need neither pretend that we have no history, nor revere it as a cosmic judge and taskmaster. The political and methodological dilemma faced by Malinowski early in the century no longer needs such an extreme solution – though the exaggeration he practised, probably knowing full well what he was doing, has cleared the air for us. The dominant style of inquiry into nations without history was devised by a member of a nation with a history too painful to be seen as providential.

7

James Frazer and Cambridge Anthropology

James Frazer is probably the most famous anthropologist – certainly the most famous British anthropologist, and quite probably the most famous anthropologist altogether.

His dates were 1854 to 1941. It was a very long life, a life that began deep in the Victorian age, but lasted right into the Second World War. The dates are significant. To the outside world, he is still perhaps *the* anthropologist. Within the anthropological profession, his position is somewhat different. He is King Harold – the last king of the old regime – slain by the Conqueror. The Conqueror, in the case of the British social anthropological tradition, is a Pole: Bronislaw Malinowski. There is indeed a marked similarity between the Harold to William relationship and that of James Frazer to Bronislaw Malinowski.

Before that particular great leap, we find quite a different kind of history of the subject. Real history, with a kind of *continuous* regime, where you can say what happened and who influenced whom, with a sustained interaction – a kind of continuous moral climate – and a continuous set of institutions – all that only visibly begins with Malinowski. Before him, it was all like a kind of Chinese painting, where the background is missing and you get only isolated images. There are indeed various figures which most people might have heard of: Tylor and Morgan, McLennan and Marrett, Maine and Robertson Smith. But precisely what the relationship between them is is not all that clear. It is only known to specialists. It is not part of a *lived* history. It is all rather like English history before Harold, with funny names like Ethelred and half-mythical figures like Arthur and Alfred, with blanks between them and with no *continuous* history, no stable context.

The history of anthropology is rather like that. Frazer himself does have a clear image, because he was indeed the last of the old lot – and before him, not exactly darkness, but no cumulative story: at least no familiar, immediately recognized, clear and familiar story. After him the continuous story does begin: and this is not an accident, because the changeover from the ideas of Frazer to the ideas of Malinowski is itself of the essence. Malinowski engendered a shared style, practised by an entire professional community, and thus made continuity and comparability possible. It acquires a kind of dense quality: those within the anthropological community *know* the history, as part of their living environment.

Naturally, the Battle of Hastings in this case was very slow and, of course, not physical. The relationship between Harold and William – or rather in this case between James Frazer and Bronislaw Malinowski – was complicated, intimate and ambivalent. In a physical sense, this Harold lived on for a very long time. James Frazer only died in 1941. Bronislaw Malinowski, his successor as Number One Anthropologist, died a year later. So he only just had time to make a posthumous appreciation of his predecessor, in which he said Frazer was the greatest of the old school, leaving it quite clear – without having to say – whom he considered to be the greatest of the new school. So he commented on the great revolution in which he succeeded Frazer and, implicitly, on the irony of the relationship, which many people have noticed. As the paradigmatic anthropologist, Frazer was killed and replaced by Malinowski during the inter-war period.

The central starting-point of Frazer's famous, great book, *The Golden Bough* – great in both a physical and an evaluative sense – is the sacred grove at Nemi, the place where there was a curious rule of succession: the priest at Nemi was succeeded by whoever slew him. So it was not exactly a job which gave its possessor the best possible life expectancy. Frazer presents *The Golden Bough* as an attempt to explain this strange – strange even by classical standards – and brutal and exceptional rule; and by the end of *The Golden Bough* you are supposed to understand why it had to be so. That at any rate was the pretext; the real underlying theme is more complicated. However, this *is* the nominal topic: it takes umpteen volumes to explain why that strange custom prevailed in that grove some twenty or so miles south-east of Rome. The relationship between Frazer and Bronislaw Malinowski was similar. Malinowski 'slew' Frazer, intellectually speaking, and so became king of the Sacred Grove of Anthropology. This is the central and obvious irony of their relationship.

A few more general observations about Frazer: he is the last of the great anthropologists – at any rate, in Britain – in the sense of offering an overall picture of the human mind and of human history. After him – and this was part of the Malinowski revolution – anthropologists were meant to look at individual societies. Theorizing about man and society at large, while not excluded, was no longer at the centre of the subject. For instance, you cannot get a Ph.D. for it and enter the profession: a field monograph is required for that. On the whole it became the kind of thing people do in their retirement, or when asked to give the Reith Lectures.

The one anthropologist since Frazer who has had a similar impact, who has become a world figure with an enormous impact on literature and who offers a comprehensive picture, is Claude Lévi-Strauss. There is a certain similarity between the two men. In each case you can sum them up in the following formula: a powerful, unifying, philosophical insight, plus a vast amount of ethnography, a vast amount of detail concerning diverse, usually exotic and strange customs or myths. The insight gives unity to the mass of material, the mass of material, presented in a lively and vigorous way, gives substance to the insight. Naturally the insight is not the same in the two cases.

In the case of Frazer, the insight is associationist psychology or – to put it another way – the image of the human mind which you find, above all, in David Hume, and which continues to be the kind of picture of mind and man offered by British Empiricists from their beginnings in the seventeenth century to Russell. The model sees the mind as a kind of snowball of sensations: a kind of accumulation of data provided by the senses. The *association of ideas* is the key notion used to explain how the human mind works and also – in the case of Frazer, by extension – of how human society works. Frazer is an intellectualist twice over: not only does he think that man is primarily a theoretician, but he also supposes that society is a reflection of human ideas. One way of summarizing Frazer is to suppose that Hume's theory of mind is correct, and suppose that you tried to make sense of all the ethnographic reports that have come in from the diversity of human culture. If you try to make sense of that mass of data in the light of the Humeian model of the mind, the result will be *The Golden Bough*.

In the case of Lévi-Strauss the basic insight is something different, a notion that in a way is the inverse of Hume's picture. It is not that the mind and its content are built up from the data, but the data themselves are made possible by a pre-existing structure or system of polarities or of extremes. The best way to illustrate the difference in the two insights – the Hume insight which underlies Frazer and the structuralist insight which underlies Lévi-Strauss – is to do it in terms of something Hume himself raised, namely, *the missing patch of blue*. Hume's central doctrine is that all our ideas are but a kind of aftertaste of our experiences; you have an experience of a given patch of blue, the aftertaste stays with you, and that *is* your idea of blue. It is a general theory of ideas – the opposite of Plato's theory, which would make things and impressions into faint echoes of abstract Ideas. For Hume, ideas cannot arrive in any other way.

But then Hume, who was a very honest man, thought of one counter-example to his own principle. His own principle was that there are no ideas without previous perceptions – you cannot have an *after*taste without the *initial* taste. Any aftertaste presupposes a previous experience. That, in Hume, is the general law according to which the human mind is constructed. No ideas without impressions. But then, being an honest man, he notices an interesting counter-example: imagine a kind of scale of shades of blue as you might have, say, in a shop which sells wallpapers. You can choose your preferred shades of blue, and on a kind of scale you are offered all the shades of blue from very very dark blue to very very light blue. But, for some reason, one particular shade is missing. Well, says Hume, if you had the whole scale you would notice the gap, for suddenly at this point the jump from one shade to the next is a bit greater than usual. So you can *imagine* that particular missing shade of blue, even though you had never previously experienced it. You *can* fill the gap. Hume noticed this contradiction of his general principle that all ideas are but aftertastes of previous experiences. He notes it, but then just goes on to live in a sort of peaceful coexistence with the counter-example to his own theory, and does not worry about it any further.

The way you could sum up the difference between the implicit picture which underlies Frazer and the structural picture which underlies Lévi-Strauss is that what Hume considers an *exception*, for a structuralist like Lévi-Strauss is, on the contrary, the *norm*. You would not be able to perceive and conceptualize different shades of the blue unless your mind were already endowed with the polarity between extremes, into which various shades could *then* be placed. In other words, the spectrum of polarities *precedes* the contents of the mind. I am never quite clear whether Lévi-Strauss wants one universal mind for all mankind, or one mind per culture. But the polarities of sensibility or conceptualization are there already to receive the various shades. Anyway, Frazer's anthropology is based on Hume's model, and Lévi-Strauss's on the generalization of the *exception* which Hume acknowledged.

One further point about Frazer's position in history: I have described his position in the history of anthropology, but in the wider history of thought he can usefully be compared to Bertrand Russell. Once again, one can offer a kind of formula for the main position of Russell. He changed his mind a great deal, but the main kind of position with which he is associated is: *David Hume plus modern logic*. He restated the basic philosophy of Hume at a time which possessed a new and more complicated logical machinery, which he used in an attempt to answer the question of how mathematics works. This is the simplest formula for the general position of Bertrand Russell. Similarly, Frazer is Hume's philosophy, Hume's theory of mind, plus a preoccupation with the diversity of human cultures. So, in both cases, you get a kind of Augustan eighteenth-century attitude, adapted to the latter part of the nineteenth century and the first half of the twentieth. Both exemplify a kind of updated Cambridge reformulation of an Enlightenment view of mind. In both cases we find somewhat similar values.

Frazer was an Augustan in at least two senses. This emerges when one turns to the layers of theory which are to be found in *The Golden Bough* and in the work of Frazer generally.

The top layer – the official doctrine, which is in effect the main theme of *The Golden Bough*, behind the pretence that it is all aimed at explaining the murders at Nemi – is a combination of Hume's associationism – the snowball theory of mind – with evolutionism in the sociological sense, i.e. the notion that the main fact about human society in history is a progression from lower to higher forms. In brief, associationism plus evolutionism. The basic idea is the adaptation of associationism to the problem of diversity in human culture. And the answer is – there is indeed an enormous variety, but do not be deceived – there is also an underlying unity, and the underlying pattern is progress from the lower forms of thought to the higher ones. This is Frazer's main and official theory.

The further crucial feature of his particular version of evolutionism – of seeing an overall pattern of development and improvement – is a three-stage theory. The famous three stages offered by Frazer of the development of the human mind are: *magic, religion, science*. That is the overall *official* theory of *The Golden Bough*. The human mind begins with magic, proceeds to religion and ends with science. He does not believe that any of these elements is ever present *alone*. It is rather that magic predominates at the beginning, and science predominates at the end and religion predominated in between. But the other elements are also ever-present; it is a matter of relative dominance.

Robert Fraser's *The Making of the Golden Bough* demonstrates in great detail something which has always been obvious to me, namely that Frazer's theory of magic is a direct adaptation of associationist principles developed by Hume. His terms, like 'sympathetic magic', have passed into common speech. That sort of magic is based upon the idea that the connection between *things* resembles the connections by which we associate *ideas* – we associate A with B either through resemblance or because they happen to have appeared together. One thing reminds us of the other. And similarly magic – or magical connections – are based on the application of this principle. The underlying notion of magic is that nature can be manipulated by employing connections which we can identify by this natural operation of the human mind, by finding links between things through associated connections, similarity or contiguity.

Magic doesn't work, and Frazer's theory is that, because it failed to work, mankind proceeded to religion. This conception of religion is basically animistic: it is based on the existence of spirits behind things. While the magician manipulates nature, the priest appeases the spirits behind nature, who are assumed to be responsible for what happens. That does not work either, and then mankind proceeds to science, the essence of which is looking very carefully at what *really* causes what, instead of being misled by accidental associations.

We sort out the real connections by the experimental method. This, for Frazer, is the basic pattern of human history. There were various things wrong with this. Magic fits the model of the human mind as specified by David Hume very well, religion not nearly so well. Animism is not based on some kind of association. It is the postulation of a new explanatory principle of an event. You can perhaps fit it in if you try hard enough; you can say that the individual mind experiences, in its own individual psyche, the connection between consciousness and will and experience, and some similar association can then also be projected on to nature. But it does not fit nearly so well as magic. It is really the invention of a radically different hypothesis. Secondly, it is all a bit absurd. The idea of mankind progressing from magic to religion because magic failed to work, would seem to presuppose that at some point, say, in the first millennium BC, when the shift occurred from the simpler religions to the more theoretical world religions – the so-called Axial Age – there was some sort of world congress of shamans, at which they read papers to each other, and said 'Well, we've been keeping records of this here magic lark, and the failure rate is appallingly high. It really does not work. We must now think of something else. How about animism?' This is not very plausible. People do not keep such records, and most societies are simply not bothered by the failure rate of their magical practices. There are always ways around this and, moreover, they do not compare notes. It never happened like that.

You might think that the intellectualist account of the next transition is a bit more compatible with Frazer's vision. Something like this did happen in the seventeenth and eighteenth centuries. In the seventeenth century scientific theories were developed which seemed to fit facts rather better. With the coming of Copernicus and Galileo, there came the success of theories based on theorizing and observation, as opposed to revelation. This was then echoed in the eighteenth century by philosophers who thought about this success and developed a theory of scientific method. They advertised the success and their explanation of it, and converted much of mankind to it. So Frazer's model might possibly fit that particular transition. Perhaps you could fit the scientific revolution, and its philosophical echoes, into his model. But the first transition doesn't fit at all, and it is absurd to try and make it fit.

But to return to the layers in Frazer's thought. The top layer is evolutionist/associationist theory – using the associationist's theory of mind to produce an evolutionary pattern of different kinds of thought, engendering the variety of human cultures. The second layer is rather different. This is the second layer in which, once again, Frazer was very Augustan, very much a kind of throwback to Hume, and this incidentally is relevant to the tangled topic of Frazer's relationship to religion. But this layer manifests a different aspect of his Augustan attitude, and one questionably compatible with his evolutionism/associationism. If you look at his passages about the influence of Oriental religion in Europe, you find a kind of throwback to the attitudes of the Augustans, Edward Gibbon, for example. You can find this approach in the famous chapter on the expansion of Christianity in Gibbon's *Decline and Fall*, or in another work of David Hume, *The Natural History of Religion*. There is, in this view, a crucial contrast between the religion of classical antiquity and the scripturalist monotheism which replaced it. As in the cases of Hume and Gibbon, Frazer's sympathies are clearly with classical antiquity and not with Christianity or the world religions. The contrast is the following: ancient religion was basically a civic cult; it inculcated civic virtues of living or dying for your city, a kind of ethic of social cohesion and obligation. By contrast, what replaces it is other-worldly and egotistical – it teaches men to be concerned with the salvation of their own individual souls, and not to be concerned with the world, except incidentally, at most as a kind of moral gymnasium, where they prove their worthiness for another life. It is a transition from civic this-worldliness to egotistic other-worldliness. Well, this is a perfectly possible attitude. Note, however, that it doesn't fit with the top layer of Frazer's thought, which assumes that what people do when they practise magic or take part in religious rituals, or subscribe to religion, is the same as that which people later do when they practise science. They are, in that view, basically intellectuals, *theorizing* about the world. Magic had one theory about the world; when it doesn't work it is replaced by the second one, and when that doesn't work either, it is replaced by the third one. It is assumed that man down the ages was a kind of scholar, a don sitting in his study, shifting from one theory to another, as his thought progressed. Well, of course, this is nonsense: theorizing about the world, and about nature, is one activity among others and, for most people and at most times, *not* the dominant one. When people take part in ritual they are not theorizing; they are expressing their participation in a social order. The intellectualism of the main theory is one of its weaknesses, but the paradox is that, in the second layer of Frazer's thought – when he concretely compares the religions of the classical Mediterranean with the world monotheisms which replaced it, warmly favouring the former – he is not talking as an intellectualist at all, but as a kind of comparative sociologist, interested in social structures and social cultures, religion as *ethos* or social cement, not religion as bad scientific theory. Frazer's second layer sees religion as the expression of a social order, and is not compatible with the first layer. So there is a tension between the two layers – though both are very Augustan, they still contradict each other.

Finally, there is the third layer, what you might call the *Waste Land* layer. Of course, Frazer – because of the richness of the material, its cohesion, and the vividness of his prose – had a very great impact on literature. His presence is very vivid in T.S. Eliot's *The Waste Land.* But Eliot's use of Frazer is totally contrary to the spirit of Frazer himself. When Frazer was presented with *The Waste Land*, he found it unintelligible. One may suspect that had he understood it, he would have found it distasteful. T.S. Eliot was *not* Augustan. Frazer was also used by Freud and, when the use was explained to him by Malinowski, he laughed his head off.

Now the point is this: the literary – which is, I think, the most common use of Frazer – is what you might call a *Jungian* use. Frazer assembles all his rich material about bizarre beliefs and practices from all over the world, he groups it together and he finds a great deal of similarity of pattern. There is a great deal which is common. The solution to his main formal problem about the rule of succession to Nemi in the end is that it is not so bizarre after all – something like it is found all over the world. There are *many* other examples of succession by murder or the killing of the priest or the king. And the theme of *The Waste Land* is just that: the land is waste because of the lack of vigour of the monarch. So Eliot does borrow the main theme from Frazer.

But, if there is a similarity in the myths and the rituals of mankind, what *is* the explanation? Frazer did have an answer – the laws of mental association, as laid bare by Hume and the British Empiricists. But there is another explanation, put forward in its simplest form by the psychologist Jung: namely, that all these patterns are dredged up from a kind of store, a shared collective unconscious. There is a common reservoir of symbols or archetypes (or whatever you wish to call them) and these then reappear all over the world. Claude Lévi-Strauss had quite a different answer later – the similar underlying *structure* of the human mind, not a shared content, would engender the same patterns of mythology all over the place. The Jungian explanation proved more persuasive to the literary mind than associationism. So the way in which Frazer has assembled his material lends itself to this Jungian interpretation. It is in this form that Frazer has made possibly his most influential contribution. I don't think this was his most meritorious contribution, but this is the form in which he has made his greatest impact. People evidently like dredging *The Golden Bough* and the assembled material for an account of the rich shared imagery and symbolism of the human mind. This was hardly Frazer's intention, but the way he arranged the material lends itself to it.

What more is wrong with Frazer? Some of it has already been stressed: the intellectualism, the assumption that early man was primarily a theorist rather than a practitioner, and all that goes with it: the lack of social context – the lack of the notion of culture as a unity. It is here that the new regime set up by Malinowski reacted against Frazer. Its main principle was insistence on *context*, and the seeing of the whole set of cultural features and institutions rather than tearing individual bits and fitting them into a collage. This avoided the magpie method which was so very characteristic of Frazer.

But over and above the intellectualism, the contextlessness, there is another further crucial weakness in Frazer: he did put enormous weight on the association of ideas. The presupposed theory really is very bizarre. Let's take him at face value and present the doctrine the way he put it in *The Golden Bough*. It begins with this bloody, macabre ritual – a rule of succession, rather – with the priest prowling in the sacred grove near the lake at Nemi – knowing that sooner or later he will be killed by someone who wants to be his successor. Why? Why does he put up with it? Why did he get himself into such an unenviable situation? And why on earth does his successor risk his life only to secure a post which is not exactly a sinecure, a job where you're going to be done in by the next successor, and so on? Why do they do it? Answer: that's how the human mind works, you see – by the association of ideas and, in this particular case, the association of ideas of prosperity of the land and the vigour of the king/priest. This mistake in association makes for the acceptance of an invidious rule. In reality, the potency of the ruler/

priest and the productivity of the land are not connected, as scientific agronomy will tell you; but the plausibility of magical association makes it seem so. So people become victims of the association of ideas. A strange theory. It really credits association with a hold over human behaviour which is truly astonishing. I for one am not going to get myself killed for the association of ideas. I can associate anything with anything, but I draw a line when it gets me into danger.

If you fail to be convinced by this criticism, it can be strengthened. The trouble about association is that almost anything *can* be associated with anything. The expression *free association* is really a pleonasm. Hume himself began by distinguishing various kinds of association. Similarity is one of them, but then so is contrariety. You associate A with B because they are *close* to each other but A with Z precisely because they are *distant*: you can (and do) play it either way. By the time you invoke the various principles of association you can go from anything to anything whatever, as indeed, in the course of free association, people do, and are meant to do. Now this is not a criticism of Frazer alone, but of the entire empiricist tradition, of which he is a distinctive part, in so far as it tries to give an account of the actual working of the human mind. If the human mind really worked by association, we should all be suffering from a kind of semantic cancer – a kind of rapid growth of association in all directions, which would bring us from anything to anything. I have my private association because my life is what it is. So if I say a given word, that word would mean something to me because it had come to me in a context of certain experiences. But *your* life is different, and when you hear me saying the same word, it would bring up completely different associations. So, because your associations are yours and mine are mine, there is virtually no chance of our really communicating. If associationism explained the way the human mind really worked, there would be total semantic chaos.

Now the interesting thing is that there is no chaos. The surprising thing is that, semantically and verbally, people are dreadfully well behaved. People generally speak proper – they don't *behave* proper but they do *talk* proper. People generally observe the phonetics and syntax of their subculture. The orderliness of conceptual behaviour is very remarkable in any one society. Associationism fails to explain that order and this links up with the other criticism I mentioned: it doesn't explain moral order either. Why do people have strong moral compulsions and strong taboos – why did the priest observe that strange rule? Association is simply too undisciplined and too weak to explain all this. Associations are born free, but are everywhere in chains.

This problem of compulsiveness and order lay at the heart of the thought of another man who worked at the same time, who did get the question right, and who was far more influential than Frazer on the actual thinking of later anthropologists: Emile Durkheim. For Durkheim, the question of the enforcement of conceptual and moral order – the extraordinary discipline which people display in their thinking and conduct, and the discipline in any one society – *was* problematic, and he worked out an answer. This may or may not be correct but it is ingenious and powerful – namely, ritual. Whether valid or not, his answer underscores the problem, while Frazer's obscures it.

Ritual is a way of instilling conceptual order in people. Durkheim was willing to leave animals to David Hume, so to speak – associationism worked for them, the animal mind is just an accumulation of associations – but what makes humans human is religion. At the heart of religion is ritual: it is the undergoing of the same intense ritual experience which stamps the same compulsions on people. This then makes society possible twice over: by enabling people to communicate, and by engendering those shared compulsions, the inhibitions which make social and moral order possible. Now Frazer didn't fully see the problem. He really thought associationism could do the trick – and it can't. Associationism is too chaotic to account for the order which he had himself so painstakingly noted and assembled. The similarity of patterns he had found can be explained in a facile way by some kind of Jungian theory: they all come out from a great collective store, an enormous attic of shared furniture, dredged up by various groups in diverse ways, but still drawing on the same store. The orderliness which can (in a facile way) be explained by Jung cannot be explained by Frazer at all. Associationism simply cannot do the job.

So what is it that Frazer really did? I think his whole enterprise was back to front. He mistook the empiricist theory of the human mind – brought to its highest point by Hume, and restated in our century by Russell – for an actual account of how the human mind really works. But it doesn't work that way. What the empiricists *really* did was to codify, not how the mind actually does work, but how it *should* work. They set up a kind of model, a kind of prescriptive, normative model of how science works, of how we test theories: we break up everything into parts that are as small as possible, so as to prohibit and exclude the maintenance of circular belief systems. Having broken it up we then experiment and see which connections really hold. It is a kind of summary of the rules of scientific method. But, projecting this norm backwards on to the whole of humanity as an account of actual practice, and trying to fit the changes associated with a transition from magic to religion and religion to science into it, we end with Frazer's theory.

His vision is also mistaken in assimilating ancient liberties – the kind of tolerance found in the religion of an ancient city, arising from the fact that the religion is danced out and told out in stories but not codified in a theology, so there's no orthodoxy and hence no heresy-hunting – to modern ones. Hume expressed his admiration for ancient liberties by greatly commending the reply of the Delphic oracle in response to the man who asked which rites are to be observed. The oracle answered: in each city the rites of their city. The recipe was relativistic, tolerant, civic as well as being this-worldly.

Now the assumption that this is similar to modern liberties is deeply misguided, and people began to notice that in the nineteenth century. Hume had failed to notice it and Frazer didn't do so either. Nor did he notice that the kind of pressures in an internally organized and heavily ritualized society would be intolerable for moderns. Modern liberty assumes not merely the absence of the tyrant, but also the absence of excessive social pressures – the freedom to choose one's own associations, the freedom not to take part in ritual. Nor did Frazer notice the conflict between the social theory of religion which he implicitly assumes when he compares the ancient to the moderns, and the highly intellectualist, non-social theory which he assumes in his main theory of the evolution of the human mind.

These are his weaknesses. In professional anthropology he was replaced by Malinowski, who overturned him at both the crucial points: Malinowski rejected the contextlessness and he rejected the evolutionism, not by saying evolution did not occur, but by saying it does not concern us when we explain specific social structures and cultures. It is not our job to indulge in speculative history about the evolution of the human mind and human society in general; it's our job to compare, describe and analyse societies as totalities, along with the interdependence of their institutions and their cultures. There was still some room for theory after that. It wasn't quite clear what it was going to be, but it clearly was not going to be evolutionist.

Frazer's central ideas were overturned, but he remains as a kind of marvellous monument to the attempt to carry them out. Like Russell, he exemplified a Cambridge attempt to make Enlightenment ideas work for the data and problems of a later age. In anthropology he was not followed, either in Cambridge or elsewhere. (And at least one Cambridge anthropologist, Edmund Leach, had a strong distaste for him.) Still, as a literary figure, and as King Harold in the history of anthropological thought, as the man who worked out fully and with great elegance the implications of a single vision, he will continue to live.

References

Ackerman, Robert, *J.G. Frazer, his Life and Work*, Cambridge University Press, 1987.

Downie, R.A., *James George Frazer: The Portrait of a Scholar*, Watts, London, 1940.

Downie, R.A., *Frazer and the Golden Bough*, Gollancz, London, 1970.

Firth, R. (ed.), *Man and Culture*, Routledge and Kegan Paul, London, 1957.

Fraser, Robert, *The Making of the Golden Bough: The Origins and Growth of an Argument*, Macmillan, London, 1990.

Fraser, Robert (ed.), *Sir James Frazer and the Literary Imagination*, Macmillan, London, 1990.

Jarvie, Ian, *Revolution in Anthropology*, Routledge and Kegan Paul, London, 1964.

Kuper, A. *Anthropology and Anthropologists: The Modern British School*, Routledge, London, 1992.

Malinowski, Bronislaw, *A Scientific Theory of Culture and Other Essays*, Oxford University Press, 1944.

Stocking, George, *Victorian Anthropology*, Free Press, New York, 1987.

8

Pluralism and the Neolithic

The late Professor Gordon Childe considered himself to be a Marxist, and would no doubt have felt somewhat surprised if told that the central idea with which his work is associated, that of the Neolithic revolution, is something by way of a problem, not to say an embarrassment, for orthodox Marxism. Yet that is how the matter stands. To the extent to which Western thought is under the influence of Gordon Childe's idea, it was in a position to say to Soviet Marxism – but we are more materialist than thou! The ideas contained in the notion of a Neolithic revolution do really seem to implement the insight that human society is determined by its mode of production. The theory singles out the most important change in the way in which humans keep body and soul together, the transition from foraging to agriculture, and says – *this* was the crucial revolution.

The basic text for orthodox Marxist anthropology is of course Engels' *Origin of the Family*, which uses the ideas of L.H. Morgan. As Dr V.A. Shnirelman himself points out in a pamphlet which preceded and complements the volume under review,[1] although

[1] *Vozniknovenie Proizvodiashchevo Khozaistva* (The Emergence of Food-producing Economy). (Naauka, Moscow, 1989, 445 pp.). The earlier pamphlet is *Problema Perekhoda k Proizvodiashchemu Khozaistvu v Zarubezhnoi Etnografii* (The Problem of the Transition to Food-producing Economy in Foreign Historiography). (INION of the Academy of Sciences of the USSR, Moscow, 1987, 68 pp.).

Morgan and Engels did indeed locate the origins of agriculture and pastoralism within the period of 'barbarism', they did not see this shift as defining the boundary between savagery and barbarism, and did not posit any rigid connection between food production and the social order. This being so, it would seem that Marxism endows the social order with a very significant autonomy, while it is those of us who are impressed by the idea of the Neolithic Revolution who really link society to its economic foundation.

Given this difficulty, the criticisms to which the theory of the Neolithic Revolution has been subjected in the West must be most welcome from the viewpoint of Marxist orthodoxy. The criticisms stress that the revolution was slow and protracted, that it followed diverse paths, that it could hang in the balance for a long time, that it was reversible, that similar conditions did not always impel diverse communities in the direction expected, and that societies lying on different sides of the great divide could significantly resemble each other, while societies lying on the same side of it could be radically different. All this suggests that it wasn't a revolution at all, or that it was no single one thing, or that it was not decisive. All this would seem to exonerate Engels (and Marx, whose instructions Engels believed himself to be carrying out in writing the crucial text) from the charge that he failed to be a materialist, by failing to pay sufficient attention to one of the two great transitions in human history, when a change in the mode of production really did transform everything. The charge could be formulated as follows: Marxism comments on a lot of social transformations which did not really happen, at any rate not as a general phenomenon, but then failed to recognize the one which really did occur! The defence seems to be: but that one did not happen either . . . at any rate, not in any general standard form. There is no one revolution and it was not a revolution.

This is certainly one of the major themes, and the conclusion, of the book under review. The author concludes (p. 400), 'in itself, the emergence of a food-producing economy did not automatically lead to the emergence of new structures, which would enable us to contrast the societies of early agriculturalists and pastoralists with all hunters, fishermen and gatherers, without exception.' The form of production, he observes on the same page, does not constitute an independent variable. A deeper and subtler approach, he says, looks instead at productive forces as a whole, which jointly with productive relations do after all allow one to give a correct account of socio-economic development.

Those of us who, like the present reviewer, have ever been tempted by a materialist, but not at all by a Marxist theory, may reply as follows. The overwhelming merit of the notions of both agrarian and industrial production is that each is *independently* definable (without cross-reference to the social order which it is meant to explain, and so without circularity); moreover, it is exceedingly plausible to suppose that so radical a change in a productive mode will also be reflected in the social order which it sustains. At the very least, these changes completely transform the *problems*, whether or not they also lead to similar *solutions*. If it turns out that there is no such neat correlation between the economic base, so defined, and the social order, we shall soon notice it: the idea is at least clearly subject to testing and we shall learn something from its falsification.

The negative part of the argument, the refutation of this kind of lucid and non-Marxist materialism, can be taken as established by the rich documentation contained in this book. On this point there would seem to be a convergence between Shnirelman's book and one published almost simultaneously by Donald O. Henry.[2] One is happy to accept this conclusion. What is less compelling is the positive inference made from the negative premiss. As the Estonian philosopher Eero Loone has pointed out (but as many Marxists have failed to recognize), the historical materialist thesis concerning the determination of society by its mode of production requires, for the precision of its meaning, for its genuine rather than merely verbal content, that *both* the mode of production *and* the social residue, whatever it is, should be defined *independently* of each other. Unless 'base' and 'superstructure' are defined independently of each other, saying that the former determines the latter says little or nothing. This elementary logical requirement

[2] *From Foraging to Agriculture: The Levant at the End of the Ice Age* (University of Pennsylvania Press, Philadelphia, 1989); see esp. p. 236.

is not always respected. To say that a slave mode of production engenders slave-owning society, that the feudal mode of production leads to feudalism, etc., tells us very little. The danger of such tautological materialism is discernible, to say the least, in some recent French attempts to produce a Marxist anthropology.

The invocation by Shnirelman of some wider but unspecified idea of 'productive forces and relations' (pp. 400 and 404), as providing a better explanation of social conditions than mere 'foraging' and 'food-production' on their own, does not really give us an alternative theory. The elimination of the single-track Neolithic revolution, on its own, leaves the field wide open – even, for instance, for the playful neo-idealist or Veblenesque provocativeness of the last sentence of Donald O. Henry's book, a work with which otherwise Shnirelman can be expected to be in sympathy. The two authors cross-refer to each other. Henry suggests that 'had it not been for some Neanderthal driven to grinding pigment for ritual purposes, it is unlikely that most of the world would be sustained by agriculture now' (p. 236); in other words, had not conspicuous display on the part of foragers required and engendered grinding stones for pigments, agriculture would not have had the milling technology it needed, and we would still all of us be hunting and gathering.

It isn't so much that we do not know Shnirelman's alternative to be *true*: rather, for lack of specification, we do not really know what it is. Until Marxism can operationalize the notion of 'forces and relations of production' in a way which enables us really to pick out different species of forces and relation on the ground, until that notion ceases to be a mere shadow thrown by the very social organization which it is meant to explain, we shall not really be facing a properly articulated and testable theory.

At the end of the book (p. 404), Shnirelman does concede the point which leads others, including the present reviewer, to continue to be committed to the use of the notion of a Neolithic Revolution – namely, that food production opened up fundamentally new possibilities for human society. The paths of transition may indeed have been varied, lengthy and complex: but they led to a world with radically new problems and options. *This* was the big barrier. This admission, however, is combined with a reaffirmation of the view that the mode of production does not directly determine social formations, but only does so through some intermediate variables. These, however, by remaining unspecified or very loosely specified, deprive the position of precise content.

Moreover, even in this weakened sense, the Neolithic Revolution is only allowed to constitute a necessary and not a sufficient condition of further development. There is one kind of post-Neolithic society, namely nomadic pastoralism, which in Shnirelman's view (he had previously written a book on the origins of pastoralism), constitutes a dead end – as in his view do some highly specialized forager societies. The remark is highly significant, in that it squarely places the author in the context of the once very vigorous Soviet debate concerning the nature and existence of 'nomadic feudalism'. Shnirelman's final remark in the book excludes the possibility of such a social formation. He does not consider the more general and important question concerning whether Marxism is compatible with such dead ends at all. The promise of eventual salvation for all mankind would seem to require that all property-endowed societies, however seemingly stable, must in the end be unstable and contain the seed of their own destruction, so as not only to permit but actually to necessitate the emergence of 'higher forms'. The dead-end theory leaves some of mankind at the mercy of inherently *extraneous* and hence accidental salvation.

I have focused on the doctrinal issue which as it were provides the book with its theoretical backbone. The interest of the book is of course in no way restricted to this. Its conclusion concerning the diversity of 'Neolithic' processes is supported by a very thorough survey of the transitions to agriculture in the Near East, the Caucasus, Central and South Asia, southern China and south-east Asia and Oceania, Europe, Africa and America. Each of these regions receives a chapter. The author proposes seven primary centres of the great transition (the Near Eastern, two in the Far East, two in Africa, and two in America), and a larger number of secondary centres. One alternative way of summing up the book would be to say that it builds on the work of the great Soviet biologist N.I. Vavilov between the wars. But Vavilov, Shnirelman stresses, based his conclusion almost entirely on the data of biogeography. The aim of this volume is to reinterpret those conclusions in the light of subsequent archaeological work and a more sophisticated model of the interaction of society and the natural environment. The information used is very rich, and the argument is tight throughout.

At the theoretical level, one could reproach the author with the fact that his acute sense of the diversity of Neolithic processes is not matched by a similar sense of the possible diversity of earlier societies, which would then tend to cast doubt on the usefulness of the traditional typology and periodicization of Marxist theory, and the explanatory or even descriptive usefulness of its categories ('primitive community', 'early-class society', etc.), with all the heavy and questionable theoretical loading they contain. Do these terms really refer to societies which resemble each other in any significant way; do they possess explanatory power, and is there any merit in the developmental series which they imply or insinuate?

Shnirelman does not embrace what might be called the strong Sahlins thesis, which proposes the superiority of the life of foragers to that of agriculturalists, but he does embrace a weaker form of it which would make some foragers superior (in welfare and/or complexity of organization) to some agriculturalists. This does indeed constitute part of the case for demolishing the Neolithic Revolution, by insisting on the diversity of real processes, and the absence of a neat tie-up between food production and social development. Strangely enough, Sahlins does not appear in the bibliography of the book, though he is discussed in the shorter pamphlet published in 1987.

This book appeared in 1989, the year during which many of the conventions governing Soviet intellectual life were profoundly changed. This means of course that it was written much earlier, and did not fully benefit from the change of climate. The quality of the argument and documentation are such that one must hope that the book (and not merely the articles contributed by the author to *Current Anthropology* in 1982 and 1985) will soon become more widely accessible to Western scholars. Shnirelman is clearly one of the most interesting of contemporary Soviet scholars, who confidently deploys material from a wide range of disciplines, and one looks forward to his future work with eagerness.

9

The Highway to Growth

People, Cities and Wealth is a profound, original and exciting book, in which E.A. Wrigley, a distinguished historical demographer, provides a great mass of information and ideas relevant to the central question of historical sociology – what is the distinctive nature of the modern world and how did it come about? Demographers are, I suppose, less prone than other people to the illusion that a post-industrial society can in any very serious sense be identical with the society of the same name and language which happened to have preceded it on the same territory. Demographically, the changes are simply too tremendous to be ignored.

Professor Wrigley's first major point concerns the contemporary commentators on the great transformation. The conventional wisdom is that a set of thinkers, stimulated by the various changes they had noted, rethought the human condition and codified its terms. Admittedly, they often did so under the impression that they were analysing man and society as such, rather than recording the principles of a distinctive new order. Hobbes and Locke in politics, Hume and Kant in knowledge, Clausewitz on war, many others in ethics and aesthetics, set down the rules, or one possible set of them, of the new order.

Here Wrigley, concerned with those thinkers who thought about economics and population, takes a different view: what Adam Smith and his successors were doing was not explaining the new dispensation but, on the contrary, proving that it was impossible, that it simply could not happen. Wrigley had claimed something like this earlier about Malthus, whom he described as laying bare the mechanics of a world at the very moment when that world was ceasing to exist. In this book he extends this diagnosis to the other great British economists. We know now that they were wrong and that it did happen, but this does not mean that, given their very persuasive set of premisses, their reasoning was not entirely correct. It is difficult to find fault with their arguments; and this being so, one good way of seeking out the secret of the new world is to find the crucial gap in their premisses. If they proved it would not happen and it did, whatever flaw there was in the premisses may be a good clue to the secret of the new order. This is in effect Wrigley's own strategy.

Industrial or affluent society as we know it is not based on great wealth as such, but on the perpetual and sustained growth of wealth. Its mechanisms of social control and its political legitimacy hinge on this: the legitimacy of government depends no longer on the ancestry of the monarch or on the approval of heaven or on the general will, but simply on the attainment of an acceptable rate of economic growth. But, in the view of Smith, Ricardo and Malthus, no such society was possible. Wrigley sums up their view as being that 'Societies might reasonably expect to make progress to a plateau of economic prosperity well in advance of that attained in feudal times, but had no hope of indefinite progress.'

Just this, of course, is the difference between the eighteenth-century and modern conceptions of progress. We see progress as indefinite and continuous, the eighteenth century saw it as the attainment of a definite, but final or finite, improvement. This idea the founding father of economics shared with a historian such as Gibbon. The eighteenth century in its complacency might consider itself blessed in comparison with earlier periods, and even on occasion as superior to the ancients, but it did not see itself as part of some perpetual ascension. The economists added an important nuance to the conviction that there was a fixed ceiling to prosperity: they thought they had shown that this *must* be so. The principle of diminishing returns was bound to set in at some point, where a further injection of capital, or a further refinement of the division of labour, would no longer yield adequate returns and growth would come to a stop. The economists were impelled in this direction particularly by the importance they attributed to land as the main or only source of raw materials, by the obvious fact that the amount of available land is limited, and also by the belief that the division of labour on the land could be pushed less far than it could in industry.

All this throws interesting light on the relation of Smith and the classical economists to their intellectual offspring, Marx. Marxian optimism has always seemed to me to be the fruit of a bizarre extrapolation, whereby if one kind of economy was linked to the minimal 'night-watchman' State, then an even better one would be linked to no State at all, to an absence of coercion. The spurious harmony of the market would then be superseded by a genuine and unconstrained harmony, beyond all states or markets. But Marx evidently owed not only his long-term optimism but also his pessimism in the medium term to Smith, and more directly. He simply took it over together with the arguments sustaining it, but then attributed it, not to an inescapable and general human condition, but to the specific features of an ultimately transient social order. Wrigley sums this up as follows:

> *Capital* is . . . a commentary on the severity of the tensions which were produced by the uneasy marriage of industrialization and modernization . . . His message was clear. The marriage was intolerable and must be dissolved . . . The marriage proved more durable than Marx had expected . . . What had seemed inconceivable to Smith and intolerable to Marx developed into an acceptable commonplace. National product could rise without apparent limit, and be so divided as to assure most men of rising real incomes.

This passage also highlights Wrigley's crucial distinction, between modernization, which *preceded* industrialization and here refers to the process analysed by Smith and proved by him to have only a limited and finite potential, and industrialization, which refers to that quite unexpected injection of new resources that refuted the pessimism of the classical economists in its original form (though it was retained by Marx to establish, not the limitations to growth, but the doom of a particular social order).

Wrigley also shows that Smith already contains (though he does not put it in these terms) the Marxist theory of imperialism, normally associated with Hobson and with Lenin. Because of the ceiling on its deployment, a developed country would find its capital unusable at home and be forced to export it, and so commit itself to external trade and foreign investment, notwithstanding the less favourable social and political conditions abroad. There is only a step from this argument to the perception that the flag would follow trade, and whenever possible ensure an improvement in those conditions, in an attempt to protect the invested capital. In Smith's day, Holland had evidently reached this condition. Low local yields from capital and the near-euthanasia of the *rentier* forced almost everyone to engage in business, because interest rates were too low to allow all but very few to live off capital. The Dutch weren't rich because they traded abroad, they traded abroad because they were too rich to make much in the way of profit at home. In other words, imperialism is not the last stage of monopoly capitalism, but a much earlier stage of any old capitalism.

Wrigley's main theoretical point lies in this separation of modernization from industrialization, in the special sense he gives those terms. He admits to having considerable difficulty with the definition of modernization, recognizes that his use of the term is eclectic, and does little more than attach a label to the changes which transformed European society between the sixteenth and nineteenth centuries. An alternative definition might be to say that modernization is simply the process analysed and commended by Adam Smith, whatever that is, and the process moreover for which the classical economists' pessimism was demonstrably valid. It is this definition which really fits Wrigley's use of the term. But a less circular and less question-begging definition might be something like this: modernization consists of those aspects of the social transformation of Europe which have basically social roots and can be sociologically explained, on the assumption of a reasonably constant and commonsensically conceived natural environment and a technology corresponding to that conceptualization.

The definition of the second of the two crucial terms, industrialization, would then be this: industrialization is the name of the process which enables a modern society to break out from otherwise inescapable social constraints. This might be called the *deus ex machina* conception of industrialization. Wrigley does not define it in this way, but takes over the conventional use of the term as 'a synonym for sustained economic growth'. But this really amounts to the same: sustained (perpetual) economic growth is, for reasons conclusively established by Smith and his fellows, impossible, but industrialization is the name of the impossible process we now know to have occurred, in defiance of the considerations and expectations of the classical economists.

What exactly was this *deus ex machina*, or *machina ex deo*, which brought about the miracle? Wrigley's full answer is complex and subtle, not to say elusive, but a first and not altogether misleading approximation to it is simple: coal. What enabled the system to break out was the injection of powerful new forms of energy. The classical pessimism was based on a certain vision of agriculture as the main supplier not merely of foodstuffs, but also of many other basic necessities, a conception which envisaged it basically as the fruit of cooperation of *living beings*, animal and vegetable, without much aid from the mineral. Human and animal brawn and the growth of plants combined to yield an output, aided by only fairly small inputs of inanimate energy from sources such as watermills and windmills. It was the tapping of seemingly endless sources of dead energy which completely changed the scene, initiated the reign of perpetual growth, refuted Smith's pessimism and made possible the Marxian variant of it.

Here Wrigley's terminology seems to me doubly unfortunate. He writes that 'The mutation in the economic landscape . . . involved the substitution of inorganic for organic outputs.' The notion of an 'inorganic industrial system' is unfortunate first of all because it is a little strange to refer to fossil fuels as 'inorganic'. Moreover, it also cuts across another well-established sociological terminology: Durkheim's contrast between 'mechanical' and 'organic' solidarity. It would be awkward for a Durkheimian, persuaded by Wrigley's arguments, to have to say that the most complex forms of organic solidarity were based on the inorganic industrial system.

But the terminological point does not really matter too much. What Wrigley has in mind is clear: the transition from the predominant use of living energy to dead energy. What is also obvious is the central point he wishes to make, which hinges on this substitution: this great change in the nature of the social world was not something inscribed on the agenda of human society, and thus something humanity had the right to expect, but, on the contrary, it depended on something external to man and society, something contingent and accidental, namely the presence and availability of coal.

Such a position clearly distinguishes Wrigley from those evolutionist commentators on the great transition, who believed the destiny of mankind to have been ever encapsulated in the human or social essence, only requiring time to reach its fulfilment. But it also distinguishes him from a thinker such as Max Weber, who also believed the coming into being of our world to be contingent, but who believed that the contingency was brought about by unusual factors internal to human society. For Wrigley, at least one necessary condition was not merely satisfied contingently, but was also external to the human realm. Moreover, he appears to believe not merely that our actual fate was not inscribed in the destiny of societies, but that quite a different destiny was so inscribed, and correctly read by Adam Smith, Malthus and Ricardo, whose perfectly cogent accounts were only falsified as it were unfairly, by an extraneous intrusion. Smith and Co. were like clever readers of a detective thriller, who rightly guess the culprit on the basis of all the available clues, and only find their solution rejected in the last chapter by means of the introduction of new evidence, previously withheld from the reader. No self-respecting thriller-writer would stoop to such a device, though I suppose history can do what she likes.

Some aspects of Wrigley's conclusion I find attractive and some repugnant (which, needless to say, does not constitute an argument against them). The separation of the process culminating in the eighteenth century from what happened later in the nineteenth and subsequently, in other words the distinction between modernization and industrialization in Wrigley's sense, I find interesting and important. The switch to a production-oriented society, with an increased division of labour and good government, was something which did not depend on the radical technological explosion, which only came later. In fact I am prepared to go further and say that I suspect it depended on its absence.

No doubt the improvements which took place between the sixteenth and eighteenth centuries depended in part on technical innovation, and in part on social factors; but had the technical innovations been really high-powered, would they not have attracted the attention of those elements in society who would either have utilized them to strengthen their own political power, or taken pre-emptive steps against their disruptive social consequences, or both? The injection of powerful techniques into the Third World tends to produce authoritarian politics and nativistic fundamentalist movements. It might have had a similar effect in early modernizing Europe, and the movement forward might have been throttled by the very forces it unleashed. So early development may well have depended on the relative feebleness rather than the power of innovation. In fact, by the time the new world emerged in full strength, and its implications were properly understood, it was too late to stop it. It had been camouflaged by its gradualness, and that was made possible by the relatively non-disruptive nature of its techniques. But in any case, 'modernization' in Wrigley's sense of an economically favourable reorganization of society, which cannot on its own lead to perpetual progress, should indeed be distinguished from open-ended growth.

But when the second stage came, was it really dependent on the geological structure of the British Isles? Wrigley's case here is much strengthened by his principal evidence, drawn from a comparison of England with Holland. Why did industrialization not happen in Holland? Here of course the relevant theorist ceases to be Smith, and Wrigley switches from the classical economists to the sociologists who came later. For Smith there was simply no problem: Holland was a country which had pushed the possibility of economic improvement close to its limit, and was now banging its head against the ceiling, so offering a foretaste of what was to be the fate of England. But for the sociologists writing later, at a time when it was known full well that there was no such ceiling and that the sky was the limit, Holland is an exceedingly difficult negative case to explain. Why so far, yet no further?

For the sociologists eager to explain industrialization in terms of favourable conditions plus an appropriate ethos, rationality is a crucial element in that ethos: 'That Holland had reached a high degree of rationality in economic affairs seems indisputable. Nor was it just an urban phenomenon,' Wrigley writes. It is well known that the Dutch are so rational that reason comes out of their ears. They are even rational in the countryside: no idiocy of rural life for them. Their society also exemplifies most of the other features which sociologists favour as the preconditions of industrialization. None the less, mysteriously, the industrial revolution failed to take place in Holland: 'Rationality in economic life neither led to a take-off, nor plunged the population into misery.'

Rationality on its own appears to be insufficient to guarantee either the blissful liberal or the tragic Marxist fate, which the theory promises to early industrializers. Wrigley suggests that Holland was probably more fully modernized than England in the early eighteenth century, and needed the steam-engine more urgently than England did, so as to solve its drainage problem. Holland did indeed adopt the steam-engine eagerly when it became available, but neither invented it itself nor, suggests Wrigley, would have done so on its own.

He does not deny that in a scientific age (a term he does not define) inventions will in the main be forthcoming when needed. But he suggests that 'technological innovation in a pre-scientific age is far from automatic.'

It would seem that the early industrial revolution (in Wrigley's sense) occurred prior to the scientific age, whenever that is held to have begun. By the scientific age, Wrigley must mean not the mere presence of Newtonian science, but its sustained application to technical problems and the presence of systematic industrial research. So his thesis could be reformulated thus: modernization (a high division of labour based only on pre-scientific technology, plus good government) can only take humanity up to a certain point. Scientific technology can take it much further. But there was a gap lasting quite a few decades, between the attainment of the ceiling of modernization and the elimination of that ceiling by scientific technology. During this gap, economic progress and impetus were, however, kept going by the providential presence of coal in England, and a similarly (?) providential appearance in England of a set of inventions, which linked the coal to productive need. Later on, no doubt, technology ensured the supply of inanimate energy, quite independently of local conditions. But without these accidents that gap might well never have been crossed. It is the difference between coal and peat which, industrially speaking, separates English men from Dutch boys.

It seems to me that by the time the watershed between modernization and industrialization, so crucial for Wrigley, had been reached, the bases of the scientific age and its spin-off technology had been firmly laid. This was so even if the habit of systematically seeking out the required technology on the basis of science had not yet been institutionalized, and even though early technological innovation had been the work of freelance innovators, not yet linked to the high tradition of science. If the fortuitous inventions and fuel deposits had not then been available in England, would the gap not have been weathered there as comfortably as it was in Holland, according to Wrigley, and would not the growth still have come, albeit a little later?

Wrigley's approach by contrast seems to separate the coming of the scientific age from modernization, and by implication treats it as one further contingency. But was it not far more deeply implicated in the modernization process? Is there not something to be said, after all, for viewing the entire process of modernization and subsequent industrialization as one?

The earlier modernization in north-west Europe had something distinctive about its political and intellectual culture that perhaps makes it impossible to treat it as just another case of a commercial and production-oriented society, one which, it so happened, led on to industrialism, thanks to the availability of coal. One could say that the cultural features which made the earlier modernization rather unusual also made the subsequent scientific transformation rather probable. If all this is so, the conjunction of the two processes which Wrigley wishes to separate becomes rather less accidental than he would have it. All this being said, the analytic separation that he proposes, of economic well-being within the limits of a common-sense technology and the law of diminishing returns, and of a scientifically sustained growth which defies both, is clearly a very stimulating and important idea.

The outlook and range of ideas which lead Wrigley to this position have both strengths and weaknesses. The book displays an extraordinary and enviable mastery of the social, economic and demographic history of western Europe. Its deployment of the comparative method, in disentangling both regional idiosyncrasies and shared influences, is masterly. Over and above the rich and detailed source material, Wrigley has thoroughly internalized the ideas of Smith, Malthus and Ricardo, and he is extremely perceptive about Marx. It is the ideas and the critique of these masters which give his material its unity and interest. Its focusing of the comparative method, not on other pre-industrial civilizations, but on the England/Holland contrast, adds to the book's originality.

But there is also a price to be paid for this rather North Sea-centred vantage point. If Wrigley's remarks about Marx are perceptive and convincing, his comments on Weber are somewhat perfunctory, and other sociologists are largely absent. (Freud is twice mentioned as a commentator on the great historical transformation, though it is not made clear which of his ideas are meant to be relevant, and how.) Comte and Durkheim are absent from the index, and so are writers such as Joseph Needham or Mark Elvin, who can throw light on the availability and role of technical innovation in China. Given the importance, for Wrigley's argument, of the question of whether innovations are the slaves of social needs or are autonomous, this is a strange omission. (The autonomist view is central for Wrigley's argument.)

His most important question is, quite properly, a very ambitious one. Both the question, and the method employed in answering it, are summarized in the following passage:

> It is not what was common to all modernizing countries, but what was peculiar to England which then appears important. And what is explained is not simply why the industrial revolution occurred in England earlier than elsewhere, but *why it occurred at all.* [Emphasis added.]

Many of us will persist in thinking that what the modernizing countries shared is in the end more important than coal and James Watt as the differentiae of England. No doubt we then lay ourselves open to the suspicion that we harbour an irrational aversion to considering the world we live in, whose nature is our main preoccupation, to be the fruit of a mere accident.

The suspicion may attach to Wrigley, as it does to his hero Smith, that in the last analysis, and all qualifications contained in this book notwithstanding, he takes the cultural and political idiosyncrasies of north-west Europe too much for granted. Hence he underrates their continuous relevance throughout the two processes which he would separate. He rightly quotes Smith's observation that the most important effect of commerce and manufacture is that they 'gradually introduced order and good government, and with them the liberty and security of individuals, among the inhabitants of the country, who had before lived in a continual state of war with their neighbours and of servile dependency upon their superiors'. Smith was right about the crucial importance of this link, but egregiously wrong about the mechanics by which the change was brought about.

In a passage actually quoted by Wrigley, he suggests that it was the vanity of the lords which allowed them to be seduced into switching their conspicuous display from retainers to baubles, thereby transforming a personal nexus leading to dependency into the impersonal, anonymous and politically anodyne nexus of the market, which engenders no submission. So, it would seem, it was their vulgarity which emasculated them politically. They were certainly no such fools. If they made the switch, they did so because a moral and political climate prevailed in which liquid wealth was a far better lever of power than the old, highly illiquid investment in retainers, and where indeed the latter could no longer be used to much effect, or at all. Economic sense, and not the most childish vanity, eventually led to the clearances, which Smith did not foresee. Whether the factors making for this political climate were also linked to those which eventually made perpetual unrestrained growth possible is another question. Such a link would have to be firmly established if Wrigley's disjunction of modernization and industrialization were to be repudiated altogether.

Specialists will use this volume for its extensive treatment of demographic, urban and social history. I have not discussed these details and would not be competent to do so. But all non-specialists concerned with the central question of the emergence and nature of the modern world will derive great stimulus and illumination from its general ideas.

10

A Marxist Might-Have-Been

The study of ideologies is liable to concentrate on success stories: belief systems which have made a powerful impact. But perhaps negative examples also deserve investigation. There may be clusters of ideas which have all the merits required for success, but which have, perhaps because they saw the light of day too soon or too late, or in the wrong place or context, failed to make the impact which was their due on merit.

I believe that the work of Yuri Semenov belongs to this category. It is relatively unknown outside the erstwhile Soviet Union, and has had only a limited impact inside it. The historical circumstances were not propitious to it. Yet there is a good deal to be learnt from it.

Yuri Semenov is a Marxist philosopher and social anthropologist (or what would, in Western terminology, be described in these terms). He has combined teaching Marxism-Leninism in a technological institute with being a member of what had been the Institute of Ethnography of the Academy of Sciences of the USSR, and what is now the Institute of Ethnology and Anthropology of the Russian Academy. Within this Institute, he was a member of a department known as the section of Primitive Society, other members of which are scholars such as I. Pershitz, V. Shnirelman and O. Artumova. Semenov may be described as a general theoretician of Marxism with a special interest in that part of Marxist theory which deals with early society and the early history of mankind. But he is also much involved with what in the West would be called comparative historical sociology or macro-sociology, with issues such as the typology of societies, historical periodicization, the acceptability or otherwise of the notion of an Asiatic Mode of Production and its place in the Marxist scheme. He is not, and as far as I know never has been, a field anthropologist; nor has he been specifically concerned with the internal organization of any one society. He is primarily a theorist. He is very much at home in the tradition of Marxist classics and its predecessors, but at the same time, is very familiar with Western social theory and in particular with social anthropological theory. For instance, he has written a summary of the debate, in Western economic anthropology, between 'formalists' and 'substantivists', between those who would uphold the usefulness of formal economic theory in studying the economy of simpler peoples, and those who, by contrast, prefer to focus on the actual institutions found in such societies, without interpreting individual economic behaviour in terms of a supposedly universal economic theory. His account of this debate is a model of lucidity and objectivity, and its translation has appeared in English.[1]

Something should perhaps be said of the history of the Institute of Ethnography (as it was) and its role. It has had, successively, three directors: Tolstov, Bromley and Tishkov. These correspond more or less neatly to three stages of Soviet history, to Stalinism, Stagnation and Perestroika. The fate of Perestroika is undecided at the time when these lines are being written, and I shall refrain from speculating about it here. Tolstov was a hardline Stalinist; his reign ended in the late sixties, after the fall of Khrushchev, and he is not relevant to our theme. Bromley expressed the relative tolerance of the period of *Zastoi*.

There are two features of Yulian Bromley's reign at the Institute which deserve note. One is the *relative* liberalism of the atmosphere at the Institute during the period, which was the object of

[1] 'Theoretical Problems of "Economic Anthropology"', *Philosophy of the Social Sciences*, 4 no. 3 (1974), pp. 201–31.

envy among members of neighbouring institutes (neighbouring both in terms of subject-matter and of physical location – I have in mind, for instance, the two institutes of history). I do not mean that the place was liberal by Western standards and that discussions occurred in public in which Marxism was questioned. What I do mean is that a high proportion of people who by the Soviet standards of the day had multiple black marks against them (a Jewish background, a period of incarceration in the camps, a habit of 'taking their mouth for a walk', questionable orthodoxy, a tendency to be willing to have contacts outside the socialist world) did find employment at the Institute, sometimes after failing to obtain it elsewhere or losing it. Internal debates, sometimes bitter, about fundamentals of social anthropological theory, with possible implications for Marxism, were not unknown. A member of the Institute who applied to emigrate and became a refusenik was treated with great leniency by the Soviet standards of pre-Perestroika days, being kept on at his previous rank for quite a time and, when dismissed, reappointed, albeit at a lower rank. No attempt was made to harass other members of his family. Members of the Institute active in spheres not then much approved (the revival of Jewish communal institutions in Moscow, or teaching Hebrew) though not receiving the promotions which were their due on merit, were nevertheless kept on. More orthodox members of the Institute certainly felt that Bromley was taking a risk by adopting such a tolerant attitude (an attitude which might be considered normal in liberal societies, but which was unusual and possibly risky in the moral and political climate prevalent in Moscow at the time). A cynical or hostile observer might well say that a double game was being played, one securing for the man in question the approval of the outside world for his relative liberalism and tolerance, yet also securing him Brownie points from the local establishment for restraining a bunch of potential dissidents. The contract which seemed to operate between the Director and the dubious characters (by the standards then prevailing) seemed to run roughly as follows: '*You lot* don't rock the boat too visibly, but be productive in the scholarly line, and perhaps help me a bit with writing my books, and *I* will do my best to ensure that you can get on with your work, without undue harassment. Who knows, some of you might even, in the fullness of time, travel a little, though this perk, in the nature of things, is severely rationed.'

The second feature of the Bromley period was that he gave the Institute a new direction, namely that of the study of *ethnicity*, i.e. the study of ethnic culture and ethnic relations, and hence, by implication, that he made a bid for 'ethnography' to become the science specializing in the problem of nationalities.[2] This was an interesting move from a number of viewpoints. Social anthropology in the Soviet Union (under whatever name it happens to be practised) is facing the same problem it faces the world over, namely that, with the rapid diffusion of modernity, primitive communities are rapidly disappearing, so that the discipline is quickly losing its distinctive subject-matter. Distinctive ethnic cultures, on the other hand, are not disappearing, and by making *ethno*graphy the study of ethnic culture – Bromley was rather given to using this verbal argument – the subject was assured of a sphere of inquiry. By turning the discipline into the study of ethnic culture, the field of structure was by implication left to other disciplines, and the likelihood of conflict with Marxist theory diminished. Above all, the orientation of the Institute in this direction made it possible to claim that it was dealing with something supremely important, namely the problem of nationalities and ethnic diversity, and even conflict, in the Soviet Union. When the problem exploded with the liberalization under Gorbachev, it was possible to say both that the Institute had focused on the problem long before its importance had again become manifest, and equally, that it had been unduly complacent about it. At the time, of course, it would have been impossible to publish findings to the effect that conflict and disharmony were rife.

It would be difficult to defend the publications of the Institute on this topic against the charge of complacency, if this means the failure to spell out the explosive nature and force of irredentist nationalism and of national conflicts in the Soviet Union – but one can only add that the publication of such conclusions, at the time, is simply not imaginable. Granting this weakness which,

[2] See, for instance, Yu. V. Bromley, *Sovremennye etnicheskiye protsesy v SSSR* (Contemporary Ethnic Processes in the USSR), (Moscow, 1975).

given the political realities of the time, could not have been remedied, the work of Bromley and his Institute must be credited with certain merits. It asked what seem to me the right questions about modern nationalism, namely, what are the relative life-chances of members of various ethnic categories, and what is the relationship between ethnicity, educational opportunity and career prospects. In other words, ethnic sentiment is not an atavism emanating from members of primordial *Gemeinschaften*, but rather a sentiment characterising urbanized, educated, mobile members of an industrial society. Secondly, Bromley was clear about the *social* nature of the modern ethnic group, as opposed to any kind of biological definition of it, and his debate with the romantic erstwhile dissident, the late Gumilev (geographer, and son of the poetess Akhmatova) concerned this point.

However, notwithstanding the fact that his public stance was primarily that of a theoretician of ethnicity, Bromley was not really, for better or worse, by temperament or calling, a theoretician. Though he considered himself a Marxist (sincerely so, I think) I do not think he deeply internalized the elaborate structure of Marxist thought, or found it of absorbing interest. He was not a man of either theoretical or dogmatic temper, and in conversation was liable (as a heretic in the Institute privately observed with amusement) to make quite heterodox statements, not because he wished to defy orthodoxy, but simply because he had not noticed that he was doing so. Now the age of stagnation was not an age of faith (on the contrary, it was an age of the erosion of faith), but it was certainly not an age of open dissent either. The Marxist decencies were observed. But in order to observe them, you need to know what they are. As in Václav Havel's excellent play about the role of unintelligible Marxist jargon in running a socialist enterprise, you need to have someone about who really understands how the language works, with all its nuances and flexibilities as well as its rigidities – someone who is, by temperament and intellectual equipment, a theoretician. Yuri Semenov was such a man. To describe him as an ideological watchdog of the Institute sounds unpleasant, and it is most certainly not my intention to do so. Rather, it is my intention to describe him as a man with a deep and thorough understanding of Marxism, who had sincerely embraced it, who had a fine sense of its problems and potentialities, and who knew how to play with the intricate conceptual system it contained.

At an international conference at which they appeared together, Bromley and Semenov gave the impression of being a team. Theory and praxis were not united in a single person, as perhaps might be ideal according to Marxism, but they were present in this two-man team, one of whom embodied great political skill and energy, and the other supplied theoretical refinement and depth.

So this perhaps was Semenov's effective role: at a time when ideological zeal and conviction were in marked decline, when the concrete work of the Institute was oriented towards a field in which Marxism was hardly relevant (or an obstacle), but when open dissent was not yet tolerated, to help supply that element of theory which was still *de rigueur*. He may not have been the only one to help perform this task, but he did it well, with ingenuity, depth, scholarship and (I am persuaded) with sincerity. Had history gone in a different direction, had the climate been different, his theoretical output might have received great acclamation. Were this a just world, which it is not, we might yet have heard of Marxism-Leninism-Semenovism: the adjustments and interpretations which Semenov brought to Marxism would have been so appropriate and at the same time so inherently plausible, if only the world had gone in a direction in which it still seemed to be going, shall we say, in Khrushchev's day, and in which perhaps it still might have seemed to be heading, without absurdity, for quite a few years after that.

There are two problems within Marxism to which Semenov seems to me to have made interesting, ingenious and suggestive contributions. One is the problem of origins: how did the human race and human society begin, and how do these beginnings fit into the overall Marxist scheme? The other is the problem of the basic typology of human societies and of the periodicization of history. Let us call these the problems of genesis[3] and of entelechy.

[3] Semenov's ideas on this are found in *Istoriya piervobytnovo obshchestva. Obshchiye voprosy. Problemy antroposotsiogenesa*. (History of Primitive Society: General Issues. Problems of Anthropo-Sociogenesis) ed. Yu. V. Bromley, A.I. Pershitz, Yu. Semenov (Moscow, 1983).

Genesis

Marxism crystallized in the mind of its founder in the 1840s. At least one commentator, Richard Tucker, believes himself capable of locating almost the moment at which Marx invented Marxism, in a fit of Hegelizing, when he suddenly saw that the philosophy of Hegel contained, in coded form, the economic history of mankind.[4] This early formulation of Marxism, however, suffered from at least two handicaps: it preceded the publication of Darwin's ideas and it also preceded, by a greater span, the publications of L.H. Morgan. In other words, there was as yet neither evolutionary biology nor the beginnings of modern anthropology. These elements entered into the later formulations of Marxism, but obviously they could not be present in the earliest crystallization of the system, prior to their own existence. This being so, what exactly did the founding fathers of Marxism think about the very beginning of human and social things? The main answer, as far as I can see, is that they did not think about it much, or perhaps at all. They were not merely Eurocentric, they were also history-oriented. They were not much given to looking at man against the backcloth of biology. History was enough.

Still, the question does have to be faced. There must have been a beginning, and an overall theory of the development of human society cannot avert its gaze from the question of how it all began. But Marxism has a special need to face this problem. In the way it finally crystallized, it attributes 'primitive communism' to human beginnings, and the attribution is of great importance. It helps provide crucial evidence that communism is feasible and also helps to answer the question – why is it desirable? Marx operated with the concept of *Gattungs-Wesen*, somewhat awkwardly translated as 'species-being', or perhaps as 'species-essence'. Why is communism desirable, why is man alienated from his true essence when he lives in non-communist, class-endowed social formations? One answer, once fashionable among some at least of the adherents of Marxism and also proposed by

[4] Cf. R.C. Tucker, *Philosophy and Myth in Karl Marx* (Cambridge University Press, 1961).

its most eloquent critic, Karl Popper, ran as follows – Marxism eschews moralizing, it merely preaches, in the wake of Hegel, the recognition of necessity.[5] It predicts what *must be* and, because it must be and will come, it has the only kind of goodness which scientific thinking permits, and Marxism is nothing if not scientific – or so at one time its adherents liked to think. The trouble with this simultaneously scientistic and Hegelian interpretation is that it most certainly did not correspond to the real state of mind of ardently believing Marxists in the days when the faith was still ardent (which perhaps would not matter too much: could not a measure of false emotional consciousness be enlisted on the side of history?), but it also does not seem to correspond to the actual convictions of Marx, at any rate during his youth. He does seem to have believed that man did have an essence, that this was in conflict with class society in general and with capitalism in particular, that the true essence would come into its own again under communism and that this validated communism.

Now this is all very well, but it raises some problems. It may be all very well for the young Karl Marx: for him, as Heinz Lubasz has insisted, Aristotle was not a classical text but a living scientific authority, and one has to take Aristotle as seriously as Hegel if one is to understand how Marx's mind worked.[6] In other words, there were species and they had essences. But this is not a view easily acceptable to the modern mind. For one thing, many of us are nominalists and do not believe in essences. (Some, like Quine, may not be too sure of their nominalism, but are quite sure they do not believe in essences and see the repudiated ghost of Aristotle behind the very notion of meaning.) But, quite irrespective of any general nominalism, there is the problem of Darwin, whose doctrine establishes, if it establishes anything, that there are no stable, given species. So, even if there were things in the world which did have essences, nevertheless species, being unstable, cannot have them. So where is *Gattungs-Wesen* now?

[5] K.R. Popper, *The Open Society and its Enemies*, 4th edn (Routledge and Kegan Paul, London, 1962).

[6] H. Lubasz. 'The Aristotelian Dimension in Marx', *Times Higher Education Supplement*, 1 April 1977, p. 17.

So if mankind is to start its career with a generic essence from which it can then be painfully alienated, it must first of all be endowed with an essence, and moreover with the essence which this theory requires. That is the problem and, in a volume produced under the auspices of the Institute of Ethnography, with the Director as one of its three authors and Semenov as another, the problem is answered. The volume was clearly intended to supply Marxism with its missing Book of Genesis, missing in part because Darwin had published so late. The part of this volume which answers this question – how did mankind acquire its essence, and what was its essence – is Semenov's work, as the volume itself specifies.

Theoretically, it would be possible to credit communism not merely to early man but also to his prehuman ancestors, and to legitimate communism not as something specifically human but as something belonging to life as such. The idea is not inherently absurd. The one great philosophy primarily inspired by Darwinism, namely Pragmatism, does precisely this. It claims that the correct procedure in the acquisition of knowledge is not something distinctively human, but something practised by all life: trial and error, the elimination of mistaken theories or interpretations by life itself. Among contemporary philosophers, the two who are widely held to be the best – Popper and Quine – believe versions of this theory.[7] Popper has acclaimed the similarity of the method deployed by the amoeba and by Einstein.[8] The only difference between life in general on one hand and humanity on the other (or perhaps, more narrowly, literate or scientific humanity) is that the process of elimination of error in the first case has to use the brutal procedure of eliminating the carrier of the error, whereas among us the error can be eliminated, while its carrier can live to err another day. But that is a mere detail, though perhaps one of some importance to the carrier in question. The basic point is that the recipe for cognitive salvation, according to these theorists, remains the same throughout the history of life.

7 W. V. O. Quine, *Ontological Relativity and other Essays* (Columbia University Press, New York and London, 1969).

8 K.R. Popper, *Objective Knowledge* (Clarendon Press, Oxford, 1972).

So this continuity of salvation procedure in all life *might* be a way out of the problem. But it really is rather more difficult to apply this doctrine in the sphere of morality and social organization than it is in the sphere of the theory of knowledge. For one thing, it simply does not appear to fit empirically. Some animals are gregarious and some are not. Communalism is not endorsed, as you might say, by the consensus of all life (whereas the cognitive method of trial and error perhaps is, or at any rate, it is not wholly absurd to claim that it is). Some species which seem to exemplify that communalism most perfectly – notably the social insects – seem exceedingly unattractive as moral or social models for emulation. Invoking them would hardly strengthen the appeal of communism. So, whatever the pragmatists may have done in epistemology, in socio-political theory at least this option would seem to be out.

Semenov adopts the other strategy. Something special happened on the way to becoming human, in the course of anthropogenesis, which differentiates man proper from his proto-human ancestors. What was it? It is natural for Marxism to look at man as the tool-using animal: it is the deployment of tools which really differentiates him. It is *work* above all which lies at the heart of humanity, productive and intelligent work. But tools need to be invented, used, maintained. And here we come to the heart of Semenov's theory of why early man *had* to be communistic, why he could not progress along the path of tool-using production unless he became so.

Proto-human gangs or bands were both cohesive and haunted by domination and violence. The strong dominated the weak. These bands had to be cohesive if they were to survive in a rude environment, and above all if they were to survive inter-band competition and conflict, but the only method of ensuring internal cohesion open to them was domination. Cohesion was present, but it was *enforced* cohesion. But this kind of social order, rule by thugs, was not propitious to technological innovation and advance, to the invention and deployment and development of tools. The innovating intellectuals, as we know from our own society, are not always or generally also physically strong and aggressive. Perhaps they become thoughtful because they are gentle, or they become gentle because they are thoughtful. Whichever way it is, the thugs will take the fruits of their innovation from them, and thus the rule of thugs is not propitious for the advancement of early technology. What to do?

Answer: an egalitarian, sharing, communistic ethos emerges. This doesn't ensure that the innovators get a special reward for their innovation (such a theory might suit a *laissez-faire* enthusiast seeking vindication in the history of early man, but it wouldn't suit Marxism), but at least it ensures that those palaeolithic or whatever innovators benefit in some measure, alongside the other members of the band. Without a communistic ethos, there would be no advance into tool-making and humanity proper!

The problem is on the way to being solved, but it is not yet solved properly. We see why communism was *needed*; we do not yet see how it came about. Do needs engender their own satisfaction? To say that they do is brazenly teleological thinking, incompatible with true science. Things do not happen in this sad world because they are required, because their occurrence would be of benefit to someone, even to mankind at large. Believers in a benevolent deity who had a beneficent design for his creation might argue in this way, but such teleology has been exiled from science.

However, it has come back, thanks to that widely used deity surrogate, namely Natural Selection. And indeed, Semenov uses this. (Note that if this is the correct interpretation of Marxism, its full formulation was not possible till after Darwin.) Semenov invokes Natural Selection, operating not on individuals but on bands, in such a way as to favour those which happen to develop a communistic ethos, one which insists on sharing, so that technological innovators benefit at least as much as their fellow band members. Bands which, on the other hand, persist in using violence-based domination as the main agency of cohesion thereby lose in the technological race and are, in the end, eliminated thanks to their economic inferiority. Elimination of bands does not necessarily mean the elimination of their members; a band may disintegrate and its members, or some of them, may find a place in a better endowed gang more worthy of survival. It is important to note that the elimination operates on social communities and their spirit, not on individuals.

So we have seen Semenov finding the theory which explains why mankind had to acquire a communistic ethos which then becomes parts of its species-essence *and* avoid the trap of teleological reasoning by means of a version of Natural Selection. However, he is not yet out of the wood. Natural Selection has been used to avoid the danger of teleology, but it is itself not acceptable as a basic principle of sociology, as the mechanism which determines and governs the fate of human societies. If *that* is all there is to it, if that is the main mechanism which rules history, what has happened to Marxism, to the doctrine that the internal conflict of classes is the main motor power of history? If Natural Selection propels or selects societies, are we not close to some form of biologism or even fascism?

This danger in turn is avoided. Natural Selection did indeed play a crucial part in the first stage of human history proper, in the endowment of mankind with its communistic ethos, but thereafter it is no longer essential, perhaps hardly present at all. How so? The communistic *ethos* works internally, through internal compulsion, through *will* and *consciousness*. A new mechanism has been introduced into the world, indispensable – a tool-using species evidently cannot manage without it, for it needs to be communistic and social, and there is no way of achieving this other than through an internal constraint. This defines society, and once it is present, a new and properly social mechanism operates, different from merely external selection by nature.

This line of thought is fascinating and dramatic. Semenov encounters danger after danger – first teleology, then biologism – and avoids each only by falling into the next, which seems worse than the fate it is intended to avoid. Certainly, this last solution – intended to avoid biologism – may succeed in its aim: but is not the price worse than what it is meant to avert? We are now clearly in the presence of a marked form of *idealism*: humanity is defined in terms of the presence within it of consciousness and will, which endows it with its truly human character and determines its subsequent development! Semenov's language here clearly evokes Rousseau and his General Will, and Durkheim and his Collective Representations. It is presumably perfectly in order for a Marxist to echo Rousseau (who had after all exercised an influence on the founder), but Durkheim is a different matter. (Semenov quotes neither by name, but there can be no shadow of doubt about the resonance of their ideas in his argument and his prose.)

But fear not: the danger of idealism is in turn avoided, once again. The invocation of will and consciousness would indeed condemn the position to idealism, were they the prime movers or the ultimate, irreducible explanation. But, most emphatically, they are nothing of the kind. They do not initiate anything, nor do they terminate the chain of explanation. They are *at the service of* an economic imperative: the need to engender, enhance, develop, protect the invention and deployment and maintenance of tools! Consciousness and will, inner conceptual and moral constraint, in the style of Kant and Durkheim, are indeed brought in to explain how morality and humanity are possible – but only as servants, as instruments, of an economic need. The decencies of historical materialism are respected and observed.

But is that not a teleological argument? Is not a need invoked to explain the emergence of the thing which satisfies that need? Is that a permissible line of reasoning? We have of course been at this point before: teleology is avoided by the time-honoured, traditional method of using Natural Selection; and then biologism, by invoking inner compulsion; and then . . . and so on.

The circle is neat, complete and tight, but not, as far as I can see, vicious. This does not mean that the position is necessarily valid, but it is not inconsistent or incoherent. However, its elegance and coherence are not its only virtues. The position is presented with considerable eloquence and literary verve, and it is most moving, it seems to me, when it describes the inner condition of the early man caught up in this process. The new communistic inner compulsion is operative within him, but its nature and purpose are not yet fully clear and may cause bewilderment; moreover, perhaps it is not yet fully effective, and must need on occasion to be supplemented by the earlier instrument of social cohesion, namely *external* compulsion, mediated or sanctioned by menaces, fear, perhaps even terror. Given that the newly humanized hominid band is still surrounded by nasty enemies, whose cohesion has not been weakened by the transition to humanity, so that the old mechanisms are still working to the full, humanity in a single band may need to be reinforced, in extremity, by the use of the old methods, which in any case may have a tendency to survive, as old habits do . . . In the fullness of time, the new inner compulsion and its economic fruits will be sufficient both to ensure the cohesion of the newly human band, and to protect it from external enemies who have not made the transition; but that happy time is not yet. One must wait, and in the meantime the newly emerged humans may be haunted both by prehuman survivals (violence, domination) and by the unintelligibility and merely partial effectiveness of the new, inner sanctions.

Such is Semenov's account of the inner condition of very early man, pained by the survival of oppression and inequality in his own band, puzzled by the incomprehensibility of the new ethos and its dubious hold over himself and his fellow members. What a striking parallel with the mental state of at least some Soviet citizens (prior to Perestroika, of course), pained by the survival of oppression and intimidation, puzzled by the ineffectiveness of the new socialist morality, disappointed by its material fruits, at any rate so far . . . Of course, as long as humanity is present only in one band, as long as socialism is present in only one country or a set of them, as long as the fruits of a technology-friendly ethos have not yet fully arrived, it is all bound to be a bit painful. Patience is required. In brief: Semenov has not merely provided an elegant and ingenious solution to a problem which his fellow-Marxists have preferred conveniently to ignore; the solution he offers is full of powerful resonance for the Soviet citizen, pondering his condition.

Entelechy

The problem of the roots, nature and authority of the acquisition by early humanity of our shared species-essence is not the only one for which Semenov provides a solution which is virtually a model of ideology construction. There is another problem which has long haunted Marxist theory, namely that of the application or applicability of the canonical five or more stages of human history to the actual empirical material of history.[9] Have all societies really passed through primitive communism, slave society, the Asiatic Mode of Production (the inclusion of this item is of course itself a major bone of contention), feudalism, capitalism, socialism . . .

Semenov has in fact contributed significantly to the debate concerning the existence and historic location of the Asiatic Mode of Production. This problem has evidently troubled him over a long period and his persistent attempts at furthering its solution testify to an intellectual quest without dogmatism, just as his account of the history of the central debate in Western economic anthropology bears witness to his erudition and his capacity to sum up, with great fairness and accuracy, positions which are not his own and with which he disagrees fundamentally. But it is not his contribution to the specific problem of the Asiatic Mode of Production, but rather his handling of the more general problem of the status of social formations and their place in world history, which is of interest here.

Do the canonical stages of Marxist theory, with or without the problematic Asiatic Mode of Production, actually apply to concrete societies? During the first and very partial Thaw in the sixties, an influential and symptomatic book[10] appeared which reviewed the question, and the crucial essay in it observed that the *exceptions* to the law of stages, if that is what it is, appear to be more numerous than the cases of conformity with it. It is in fact exceedingly difficult or impossible to locate a society which is known actually to have passed through all the stages of social development which Marxism credits to the inner logic of social development, to the dictate imposed by the growth of the forces

[9] Semonov's ideas on this are available in English. See especially Y. Semenov, 'The Theory of Socioeconomic Formations and World History' in E. Gellner (ed.), *Soviet and Western Anthropology* (Duckworth, London and New York, 1970).

[10] *Problemy Istorii Dokapitalisticheskikh Obshchestv* (Problems of the History of Pre-capitalist Societies), ed. L.V. Danilova and others (Nauka, Moscow, 1968). See the first essay, by L.V. Danilova, 'Diskussionnye Problemy Teorii Dokapitalisticheskikh Obshchestv' (Contentious Problems in the Theory of Pre-capitalist Societies).

of production on the social organization and class structure within which they operate. So?

There is an interesting answer to this problem and Semenov offers it. Basically, it runs as follows. The law of stages, the applicability of the various stages and the sequence in which they are meant to appear, applies and is meant to apply not to individual societies, but only to *world history as a whole*. Too many expositors (virtually all of them, Semenov seems to imply) have uncritically assumed the wrong interpretation, which would turn the Marxist thesis into something like this – for any society, the development of that society will proceed from primitive communism via Asiatic society and slave society and feudalism to capitalism and then to socialism and communism. The correct interpretation – which of course raises its own problems with which Semenov then deals – runs, by contrast, as follows: these stages apply to mankind as a totality, to the global history of humanity, but not to the individual societies which compose it. What the thesis, when correctly interpreted in this matter, implies for individual societies remains to be seen.

This interpretation has some considerations in its favour and some which go against it. On the positive side, it is obviously the case that the theory had indeed been inspired, not by the contemplation of the fates of individual societies, but by reflections on world history. It emerged at a time when Europeans still tended to confuse their own history with world history as such. Against it there are various thoughts: if this is the correct view, why has it so frequently been ignored or contradicted within the Marxist tradition itself? Why was the Marxist community so frequently in error, without being corrected by its own intellectual leaders, who should have known better? If Marxism claims to be 'scientific', as it does, ought not the same scientific laws to apply in all similar cases, and in any case, how can a *single* unrepeated sequence also be a law? In the case of a unique sequence, how can we distinguish between a necessary connection, exemplifying a law-like necessity, and a mere contingent succession?

When I first heard this suggestion of Semenov's I held it to be ingenious, interesting and endowed with a certain inherent plausibility, but contrary to the real spirit and intention of the founders of Marxism. Since then I have become much less sure of this last point; it may well be that Semenov exaggerates the originality of his own interpretation, and that in fact it is more pervasively present in the Marxist tradition than one might suppose. For instance, it appears that a similar view had been put forward by the influential Soviet theoretician Bogdanov. Even more important, it is plausible to attribute such a view to Marx himself, at any rate in his youth. Roman Szporluk's penetrating book on *Communism and Nationalism*[11] argues that precisely such a view underlies *The Communist Manifesto*, which in Szporluk's interpretation is a coded debate with Friedrich List (though the only explicit internal hint seems to be a pun, when the authors of the Manifesto refer to the *listig* – cunning – German bourgeoisie). Szporluk's account of Marx's basic argument is this: the German bourgeois can never, never catch up with the British or the French, and List's advice to the Germans on how to do it is absurd, pointless and doomed to failure. Germany has no hope of ever going through the transition from feudalism to capitalism, which would seem to be a kind of exclusive privilege, an *initium*, of the English and the French. All the Germans can hope to do – and it is really a privilege and an advantage, rather than a deprivation – is to join in a wider, world-historical transition, in which, it would seem, the Brits provide the economy, the French the politics and the Germans the most advanced philosophy (exemplified above all by Marx himself). In other words, Marx in his youth intended to bestow on the Germans, without ever being solicited to this effect, that historic chance of stage-hopping which, very much later in life, he considered, granting to the Russians, at the insistent bidding of Vera Zasulich. It must of course here be said against the Semenov/Szporluk reading of Marx that, in his correspondence with Zasulich, he spoke of the possibility of stage-passing as a rare opportunity offered by history to Russia, so that, at any rate later in his life, he himself subscribed to the conventional interpretation of his own position, as a law-like generalization applicable to all societies, rather than a strange law

[11] Roman Szporluk, *Communism and Nationalism: Karl Marx versus Friedrich List* (Oxford University Press, New York and Oxford, 1988).

with only a single exemplification, namely human history seen as a whole.

But let us assume now that this interpretation is to be accepted – which of course has the advantage, from the viewpoint of defending Marxism, that individual societies are no longer expected to exemplify all stages, and so their failure to do so no longer constitutes a scandal – what are the problems it faces and how does Semenov cope with them? If individual societies no longer directly exemplify the slave-owning, feudal, or any other stage of world history, how do they relate to these stages? Or, to put it the other way round, how are these stages, or the social formations which define them, incarnated in the concrete life of mankind?

The answer offered is the following: mankind finds itself in a given stage or, if you prefer, the social formation defining a given stage is present, when the *leading* society, or cluster of societies of that particular time, exemplifies the social formation in question. For instance, mankind finds itself in the slave-owning period when the leading society of the time, which happened to be that of the classical Mediterranean world, is based on a slave-owning economy. How does one identify the *leading* society? It is the one which will engender the next higher stage in the sequence. This definition introduces an inescapable teleological element into the scheme, but Semenov does not appear to mind this. Moreover, it also means that one can only identify stages with hindsight, when one already knows where the next and higher stage actually emerged. These objections would not seem to be fatal to the scheme. But what it all means is that historical periodicization, and the attribution of a social formation to an age, is *not* done by some counting of societies, let alone of individuals, and deciding that humanity is in a given period does not hinge on whether the majority of societies live under a given social system, or when more men live under it than under any other. No: the stage is determined by the dynamics and direction of the system. It is the social *leaders*, collectively speaking, who decide. The collectivism is important: Semenov, though very Hegelian in spirit, knows only world-historical nations, not world-historical individuals. (At an international anthropological conference in the 1970s, the French Marxist Maurice Godelier described Semenov as a Hegelian, somewhat to the latter's embarrassment, given the presence of an entire Soviet delegation. At that time, a Soviet scholar did not care to be called a Hegelian in public. In fact, Semenov knows Hegel well and likes him, and his work is certainly not devoid of the Hegelian spirit – which is not to cast doubt on the sincerity and orthodoxy of his Marxism.)

The pattern of this historical leadership is interesting, in Semenov's scheme. There is a marked tendency throughout human history for blockages, dead ends, impasses or, to use the expressive Russian word he employs, *tupik*-s. So, for instance, ancient Asian society did not progress, and the breakthrough to the next stage, to slave-owning society, only occurred at the very margin of the old Middle East world, in the Balkan peninsula, where Dorian barbarians, iron-users endowed with an early form of class structure, came upon a peripheral element of ancient society. The same happened the next time round: slave society did not seem capable of the breakthrough to feudalism, which occurred only at its periphery, in north-western Europe, where a marginal part of slave society came into contact with a new wave of barbarians. Although Semenov does not spell it out in so many words, this passing of the torch of progress sideways, the interplay of the old periphery with new entrants, also occurred at the transition from capitalism to socialism, which occurred not, as those who anticipated it had supposed, at the very centre of the capitalist world, most ripe for the explosion and the transformation, but, on the contrary, at its edge, in backward Russia . . . In Semenov's philosophy of history, which stresses this tendency of the sidestepping in progress, the role of the *new* entrants, this ceases to be a difficulty and an embarrassment for Marxism, something which calls for special explanation, and becomes, on the contrary, just what one would expect.

There are of course some oddities or asymmetries in this system. The sideways passing of the torch of progress does not occur in *all* transitions. It cannot occur right at the start, in the first transition, from primitive communism to ancient society (or whatever the first stage was after primitive communism) for the simple reason that at the time when *all* societies were in the condition of primitive communism, there were not and could be no leaders, so no one was holding the torch and no one could hand it on. Moreover, that particular transition seems to have happened quite independently in a number of places all over the world, thereby, in Semenov's own account, confirming the scientific accuracy and depth of Marxism. (Perhaps: but in saying so, does he not implicitly revert to the 'law-like', multiple-application interpretation of Marxism, which in his main argument he repudiates?) The sideways passing also cannot occur in the very last transition, for the opposite reason: although there is, most emphatically, a leader prior to the transition who is holding the torch high, there will no longer be anyone to whom it could be handed, for with the coming of the final stage of communism there is only one global society left; there can no longer be either leaders or led.

But by far the most important exception to the sidestep rule of historical advance is of course the transition from feudalism to capitalism. The torch was not handed over to anyone on that occasion. The West Europeans, the French and the English, had been prominent under feudalism and they became quite specially prominent under capitalism. Societies and cultures remained fairly constant, and so did international leadership and pre-eminence. It was of course precisely this transition which was at the centre of all European sociological preoccupation, including that of the Marxists. It was this particular transition which led to the attribution of primacy to internal, endogenous factors, and to the shift from concern with international rivalry and conflict, to a preoccupation with *classes*, i.e. intra-social categories. This particular transition could hardly have had any other form: it is hard to imagine barbarian conquerors settling in the keep of the feudal baron whom they had conquered and promptly turning to commerce, finance and finally industry. It was this transition which had, above all else, inspired Marxism, and maybe it was indeed a mistake on the part of the founding fathers to try to assimilate all the other great transitions of history, whatever they be, to this model. Semenov does not really try to do the reverse but, basing his general theory on a supposed shared feature of the other transitions, he has to leave this one discreetly aside as somewhat untypical.

One might say this for the Semenovian interpretation of Marxism: unlike the interpretations prevalent earlier, it is no longer Eurocentric. It has the great merit of relating Marxism to the situation as it crystallized *after* the October Revolution, above all to the world in which expectation of an imminent proletarian revolution in the developed capitalist world was replaced by an international competition between rival social systems, and in which the homeland of the revolution had or claimed the leadership of the socialist bloc. Semenovian Marxism avoids Eurocentrism twice over: it pays at least as much attention to the great historic transitions other than that from feudalism to capitalism, which had so obsessed West European thought, and it is preoccupied with the problem of peripheral societies, and with the relationship between societies that lead the way to a new social form, and those which follow. None of this was at the centre of attention of those who originally formulated Marxism, but, by the second half of the twentieth century, it was not something which could easily be ignored. The system incidentally endows ethnic plurality, cultural and political diversity, and backwardness with a historic function: history still moves endogenously, but only if one thinks of all mankind – when one thinks of individual societies and ethnic collectivities, diversity acquires an essential function: it has a crucial role to play in making historical progress possible. Even backwardness becomes indispensable. In classical Marxism all crucial developments were endogenous, but this was assumed to mean internal to individual societies. Cultural plurality, the diversity of nations, the existence of backward societies were so to speak contingent, inessential accidents, which perhaps complicated history but made no difference to its essence.

Now, in the new scheme, all this is changed. Ethnic diversity has its role, the fact that the Revolution occurred in backward Russia is no longer a problem and an embarrassment, but a confirmation of a well-established historical trend, and the notion of a society being the leader and pioneer on the path to a new social formation acquires respectability and authority. This is a form of Marxist theory which can be linked to the international stance of the Soviet Union as the leader, or putative leader, of the socialist camp after 1945. Whereas it would have been difficult to seek much inspiration or guidance for the problems arising from this situation in the older formulations of the doctrine, this variant clearly contains suggestiveness, encouragement, the reinforcement of faith through the claim that what is happening is but one further instance of the mechanism which guides history, of the Cunning of Reason in action . . .

So this version is ingenious, interesting, plausible, reasonably compatible with the founding texts of the doctrine and, above all, richly suggestive and full of resonances for any thoughtful Soviet citizen, concerned with the condition of his country and willing to relate it to its official faith. All this being so, it would have deserved wider recognition and acclaim than in fact it received. *If* only the Soviet Union had continued successfully to lead one large segment of the international community towards a new social order, which in due course secured the recognition of its own economic superiority . . . and if the Soviet Union, in the period of Stagnation, had been a society in which anyone took an interest in the elaboration of Marxist doctrine, then this particular contribution might have been, if not acclaimed, at least granted sustained attention. But the period of Stagnation was not an age of faith, much less so than the previous age of Terror had been. Those in power had little interest in the theory which was supposed to legitimate their position, and those eager to change the system, either because of its inefficiency or its inhumanity or both, no longer sought clues or guidance within the ideology. The time for the refinement of Marxism had gone.

In the history of beliefs as in the history of other activities, it is not only the victors who are of interest. Much as I admire R.G. Collingwood,[12] I have never been able to bring myself to accept or even sympathize with his view that we can only reconstruct the logic of the thought of those who succeed. In history as in a football competition, the losers outnumber the victors, but their strategies and adjustments are not without interest. Semenov's interpretations of Marxism start out from the perception of problems which are indeed central and crucial for Marxist theory,

[12] R.G. Collingwood, *An Autobiography* (Oxford University Press, London, 1939).

and he solves those problems with ingenuity in a manner which makes his answer pregnant with meaning for the *bien-pensant* Soviet citizen of pre-perestroika days. The fact that this clientele was no longer receptive, that history moved in such a direction that the faith was eventually beyond all saving, is another matter. This does not really detract from the interest of that ideological enterprise as a display of theoretical skill of a high order.

11

War and Violence

What would a general theory of the role of warfare and coercion in human society look like? As an initial, stark hypothesis, I would propose a new law of three stages: at first, violence was contingent and optional. In a second stage violence became pervasive, mandatory and normative. Military skills become central to the dominant ethos. In the third stage, which we are at present entering, violence becomes once again optional, counterproductive and probably fatal.

In the forager stage of human society there is no *production* (*ex hypothesi*) and what is acquired is generally small in quantity and not easily storable. There being little or no stored surplus, the question of defending it and fighting over it does not really arise. It is possible to fight about other things: access to the hunting or gathering territories, access to females, or position in the internal hierarchy of the social group. But the relatively small size of foraging societies makes social positions less visibly worth struggling for – much less so than in more complex societies. Likewise the units available for mobilization are less formidable than they become later. In brief, though violence no doubt does occur, there is no reason to expect it to become the central organizing principle of society. The maintenance of the social structure does not positively require it, at any rate on any large scale, and the members and resources for large-scale violence simply are not available.

The situation becomes different in societies with systematic production and a stored surplus. Agrarian society can be defined by the possession of these two related traits – the production of food and other necessities and luxuries, and their storage – plus one negative trait: the absence of any sustained *growth* of the technological base. The social equipment is large but relatively stable; if innovations occur, which from time to time they do, they arise in isolation and not as part of some systematic programme of growth.

Between them, these two traits – the existence of a stored surplus and, all in all, the absence of technological amelioration – entail the pervasiveness of systematic coercion. There is no luminously self-validating principle of the division of the surplus, and no principle can be self-enforcing. The social structure is a system of roles, such that each role carries with it a definite entitlement to part of the stored surplus. The surplus must be defended against those who would wish to redistribute it in their own favour. Those who guard and control the limited surplus are in a position to enforce principles favourable to themselves and generally do so. Those who control the means of coercion can and do decide how the surplus is to be divided. Wealth can generally be acquired more easily and quickly through coercion and predation than through production.

The knowledge that this is so is reflected in the ethos of agrarian society. In medieval Spain it was said that war is not merely a more honourable but also a quicker way to wealth than trade. This principle is very widely, even if not universally, recognized throughout the agrarian world: specialists in violence are generally endowed with a rank higher than that of specialists in production. In Western Europe 'nobility' and the martial vocation were in effect equivalent.

A good deal obviously depends on how the means of coercion – weapons – are distributed. They can be distributed fairly evenly, or they can be concentrated under the control of one part of society. In the latter case, the unevenness or monopoly of the means of coercion can be geographically localized in one definite group, say at the centre of society; or alternatively, the right to bear arms can be the privilege of a territorially dispersed stratum. Various factors can influence the concentration or dispersal of the means of coercion. If weapons are both expensive and effective, centralization of power is the likely consequence.

Most agrarian societies are authoritarian. The main factor conducive to this conspicuous trait is the logic of the pre-emptive strike and the implications of the desirability of disarming, whenever possible, any potential rival specialists in coercion.

However, this principle does not operate in all circumstances. Sometimes it is difficult to disarm and coerce entire populations. Pastoral nomads constitute the most conspicuous example: the mobility of nomads, and above all the mobility of their wealth, makes it difficult to constrain them. They both escape and resist coercion. Their whole lifestyle – their work, after all, consists of the exercise of violence against beasts of prey or other shepherds who would raid their flocks – provides them with a permanent training in the exercise of violence and in the resistance to the violence of others. Though pastoral nomadism provides the most obvious example, similar conditions can also sometimes be encountered among peasantries, especially when they are located in difficult terrain. Such societies then develop, to use S. Andreski's useful phrase, a high Military Participation Ratio.[1]

However, societies so blessed with a wide military (and hence political) participation would seem to be in a minority among agrarian societies. Fairly centralized, hierarchical and oppressive societies, in which the elimination of rivals has led to the concentration of power, are rather more common. Note, however, that *neither* of these two great species of agrarian society is liable to lead to an ethos of *production*, let alone one of economic and technical *innovation*. The more egalitarian and participatory societies are, characteristically, not composed of atomized individuals: their political life would be far too unstable and volatile if they were. They tend instead to be composed of sub-units which, in the absence of centralization, maintain law and order

[1] S. Andreski (previously Andrzejewski), *Military Organisation and Society* (Routledge, London, 1954).

by means of a balance of power, by checking each other. The basic mechanism of these societies, to employ a term initiated by Durkheim and widely taken over in social anthropology, is 'segmentary'. The mechanism was noted by the unjustly forgotten French scholar Emile Masqueray[2] (though he did not use the term); Durkheim used his material and acknowledged it in a footnote. The segments in question can only control and enlist the support of their members by dominating and pervading *all* the aspects of their lives – their ritual, marital, economic and other practices. Or rather, this should really be put the other way round: it is primarily by defining and controlling access to rites, brides, land and so forth, in terms of group membership, that these units perpetuate themselves and make sure of the loyalties of their members. They are holistic even if not necessarily hierarchical, and the individualist spirit and innovation do not flourish in their midst. This aspect of segmentary society was highlighted (again, without use of the term) by Durkheim's teacher, Fustel de Coulanges.[3] So agrarian man seems to face the dilemma of being dominated either by kings or by cousins (and frequently, of course, by both). Either way, the imperative of maintaining the social order trumps the desirability of improving the productive process.

From the viewpoint of the members of such a society, their position in the power hierarchy is a *far* more pressing concern than economic performance. Social position, more than individual productivity or economic efficiency, determines a man's entitlement to resources. He lives in a hierarchy, not in a market. One of the most symptomatic traits of this kind of society is that it tends to allow or encourage economic enterprise only among sub-groups which have first of all been socially and politically emasculated, and thereby rendered politically and militarily harmless. This is achieved through stigmatization of one kind or another, and an exclusion from both rites and the right to bear arms. But it is not only kings who prefer to use stigmatized aliens

2 E. Masqueray, *Formation des Cités chez les populations sédentaires de l'Algérie* (Leroux, Paris, 1886, and Edisud, Aix-en-Provence, 1983).

3 N. Fustel de Coulanges, *La Cité antique*, numerous editions.

or minorities for financial and economic services: it is very characteristic of segmentary societies that they despise and have an aversion to the none the less indispensable specialist. The specialist, whether musician, magician or craftsman, is impure.

These societies have additional characteristics which are corollaries of the features already mentioned, and which in turn help perpetuate those basic traits: they tend to be both Malthusian and land-hungry and man-hungry. The need for labour power and defence power causes them to value offspring, or at any rate, male offspring. This in turn leads to a tendency for population to expand to a point at which it is vulnerable to harvest failure or other catastrophes. Jointly with labour, the most important resource is land: power and security are measured, above all, in terms of possession and control of territory and of manpower.

The logic of the elimination of rivals, on its own, should naturally lead to the eventual emergence of a unique universal empire, where all power is monopolized by a single centre, which does not tolerate the emergence of any opposition. In some parts of the world this has indeed happened from time to time. But there are also forces making for fragmentation and polycentrism. Slow means of transportation and communication oblige the centre to delegate the defence of distant frontiers to local representatives and power-holders, who are ineffective if weak, but who make themselves independent when strong. It is hard to escape this dilemma. This is what Machiavelli said about mercenaries: if weak, they fail you, and if strong, they turn against you.[4] You can't win. Central empires also find it difficult to subjugate peripheral areas of savannah or mountain, which then harbour cohesive participatory, segmentary communities, endowed with great military potential. Thus they constitute a kind of political womb, a source of new rulers who from time to time displace the old. The best account of this kind of situation is, of course, found in Ibn Khaldun.[5]

To sum up the mechanism which tends to turn coercion into

[4] N. Machiavelli, *The Prince*, numerous translations and editions.

[5] Ibn Khaldun, *Muqaddimah*, translated by F. Rosenthal (Routledge, London, 1967).

the pivot, the key determinant, and so the central value of agrarian society: it possesses an important, invaluable, but limited surplus, which, however, does not grow. This must needs be defended and divided. The groups which control the means of coercion also control the distribution of this surplus, and decide its fate, and naturally direct it in the main to themselves. Marx put forward a theory according to which, in a market society, those who have only their labour to sell, and are thereby reduced to powerlessness, will receive a share equivalent only to the minimum required for their self-perpetuation. This theory turned out not to be correct, but something close to it does seem to apply widely in agrarian society, to groups other than those endowed with coercive clout; they receive little above the minimum required for their maintenance and reproduction. Why should those who are in control waste resources in allowing them any more?

There is, however, one important qualification for this initial simple model. Elites in agrarian society contain not only warriors, but also a clerisy. The simplest, but wholly inadequate, explanation of its influence is that it is due to the cunning manner in which it befuddles the minds of its clientele, and thereby induces it to grant the clerisy a good share of the produce, influence and perks. But a much more powerful and relevant mechanism is also at work.

The effectiveness of coercion depends on the cohesion of the agents of coercion. Any single one of them is generally weak: to be really effective, it is necessary that there be a number of them, often quite a large number, and that they stick together and maintain discipline. But what exactly makes men stick together, especially in perilous situations, in which betrayal and abandonment of a group – if that group is about to lose – may be by far the best strategy? Among the considerations liable to induce an individual to remain loyal, one of the most important is the conviction that *others* are also remaining loyal to the group, so that it will continue to be a numerous, disciplined and effective force. If the others are about to desert, it is very wise to do the same; if no one else will do so, it is most unwise to constitute the one exception, who will then be conspicuously punished, by way of example to all the others.

But how does one know, in situations which often involve geographical dispersal and lack of quick and reliable communication, whether this or that group or leader will continue to attract loyalty? One good criterion is whether that group or leader or cause is, by the recognized standards of the culture, 'legitimate'. This consideration does not sway the individual waverer because he is necessarily a fanatical adherent of the locally held doctrines concerning what is and is not legitimate. It sways him because he thinks that others are also swayed by it, perhaps in the same opportunist spirit as he is, and so, in the interests of his own safety, he wants to stay on the 'legitimate' side because he expects it to win.

For this kind of reason, those who control the symbols of legitimacy thereby also in some considerable measure control the crystallization of social cohesion and loyalty, and thus exercise great power, even if they are not themselves direct possessors of weapons or practitioners of coercion. The Enlightenment noticed much of this, and saw the medieval darkness it was eager to leave behind as one dominated by thugs and humbugs. Hence it looked forward to the day when the last king would be strangled with the entrails of the last priest. Where the Enlightenment went wrong was in its inclination to see this entire situation simply as the fruit of human stupidity – of the lack of, precisely, 'enlightenment'. If only men thought and saw clearly, it taught, they would refuse to be subject to the tyranny of thugs and peddlers of mystification.

What the Enlightenment failed to see was that this situation was not the consequence of stupidity and befuddlement, but the inevitable corollary of certain basic features of agrarian society: the presence of an important but limited surplus, where expansion was possible, in the main, only through the acquisition either of more human subjects or of more land.

The principles validating this or that form of organization, helping the rulers to be cohesive and the ruled to be submissive, could not but be the work of humbugs, when seen from the outside: a genuine trans-social or trans-cultural logic butters no parsnips and validates no ranking. *Some* legitimation was necessary for the system, and *no* legitimation could be logically sound.

So, whoever formulated and applied the principles governing the cohesion and clustering of things was inevitably obliged to use logically defective reasoning: no genuinely cogent arguments could possibly do the job.

How did we escape this condition, for escape it we did? This is the single most important problem in theoretical sociology, and it is the question which largely engendered sociology as a systematic inquiry. It is hardly possible to answer it definitively in a limited space, or perhaps at all. But, in relation to our problem of the role of coercion and warfare, it is possible to offer a sketch of some at least of the relevant elements in the answer. The stability or stagnation of productive forces – which, all in all, applies to agrarian society, or constitutes a very reasonable approximation to the truth – was eventually replaced by a permanently growing economy. Growth on its own might not have achieved anything: it was always possible for the coercers simply to slice off a bigger part of the growing cake, even if this meant thwarting and suppressing those responsible for that economic growth. The thugs were not averse to killing the goose that laid bigger eggs, and quite often, this was precisely what they did. An improvement in technological power on its own may simply strengthen domination – as happens, for instance, in 'underdeveloped' societies when its rulers receive and simply appropriate technical aid.

But in Europe the process was taking place within a multi-state system, and the thugs were unable to use growth to strengthen themselves everywhere at the same time and to the same extent.[6] The various thug states were also engaged, as was their habit and joy, in conflict with each other. Those which had tolerated, or were for one reason or another obliged to tolerate, prosperous and non-violent producers in their own midst, suddenly found themselves *more* powerful – because endowed with a bigger economic base – than their rivals. Those rivals had at first seemed more fortunate by remaining undisputed masters in their own homes, having suppressed or expelled their own pacific

[6] See John Hall, 'States and Societies: The Miracle in Comparative Perspective', in *Europe and the Rise of Capitalism* (Blackwell, Oxford, 1988).

producers. But in due course they came to pay for their domestic strength by international weakness. So all the states in the relevant part of the world were in the end obliged to emulate the liberal path to economic prosperity, or at least some aspects of it, in the hope of augmenting their power and relative international position.

Later still the whole world tried to emulate them and parts of it succeeded, sometimes brilliantly. The last and most dramatic example of this mechanism could be observed in 1989; under the influence of a (this time, nominally secular) clerisy and its associated thugs, Eastern Europe had adopted, or been forced to adopt, an over-centralized system which – as became evident after some time – severely inhibited production and thus eventually undermined the power of those in charge of the system. Finding themselves economically outstripped, those in charge of it proceeded to dismantle their own erstwhile faith-inspired and thug-dominated system.

So, under the new dispensation, the relative attractiveness of production and coercion changed. It is no longer more honourable to become rich by warfare rather than by trade. As for being quicker – under conditions of potential nuclear warfare there are no longer economic gains to be made by violent conflict. Not much would be left to pillage. Victors in a nuclear war, if any, would be in no condition to feast in the banqueting halls of the vanquished, or to rape their women.

The entire shift from valuation of coercion to valuation of production was only possible because, rather surprisingly, indefinite, sustained, continuous technological and economic improvement *had* become possible. Under favourable circumstances, power had very occasionally moved from thugs to traders even in earlier periods: but as long as there was a kind of ceiling on economic development, the shift did not proceed too far, and either reached a limit beyond which it could not go or was eventually reversed. Some of the early theorists of economic liberalism, far from announcing the coming of an entirely new era, were pessimistic about the long-term prospects of the new dispensation, for this kind of reason.[7]

[7] See E.A. Wrigley, *People, Cities and Wealth* (Blackwell, Oxford, 1987).

So it was only *sustained and unlimited* expansion and innovation which finally turned the terms of the balance of power away from coercers and in favour of producers. In the inter-polity conflict, no units managed to survive and to continue to compete if their internal organization was harsh on producers and inhibited their activities or impelled them to emigrate. The process was brought to a completion when the technology of destruction became so powerful as to lead to Mutually Assured Destruction. Now, production and trade are not merely a quicker way to enrichment than aggression: they have become the *only* way for a society as a whole.

Does this mean that post-agrarian society will become and remain pervasively pacific? It is not obvious.

The peace-inducing consequence of high technology hinges on a number of assumptions, more or less valid for a time, but which cannot be assumed to be valid permanently:

1. The peace-engendering potential of the recent very powerful technology depended, paradoxically, on the superiority of offence over defence. Europe was given over to pervasive violence in the days when the baron's keep could generally resist aggression: this encouraged the baron to be aggressive when convenient and then enjoy the spoils in relative security. But modern technology makes destruction more powerful than any defences against it, without at the same time ensuring that no retaliation will be similarly effective. And the crucial fact seems to be that, while destruction is guaranteed, it cannot be so complete as to prevent retaliatory counter-devastation.

For some time yet this may continue to be the case. For instance, one of the most impressive and persuasive arguments against SDI was that not only was it expensive, but it was far more expensive than the eventual development of devices which would bypass and counteract it. Hence, a power which acquired a measure of immunity for a time would do so at great cost, while its rival would only need in due course to deploy a fraction of that cost in order to restore the old situation of mutual terror. This seems to be true at present, but can it be assumed that it will remain true indefinitely? There is also the possibility that the destructive power will grow even further and help ensure that a first strike would be so effective as to eliminate the danger of a retaliatory one.

2. The powerful destructive weapons were so complex and expensive that they could only be acquired in any large quantity by a very small number of superpowers. These tend to be endowed with at least relatively pacific populations: the new weapons could only be produced by industrial machines, whose members are not literally warriors in any old sense, but instead are highly-trained technical personnel, whose work and education incline them to lead inherently pacific lives. The authorities in the superpowers in question were also at least relatively rational and moderate: they were not, by temperament or ethos, committed either to a cult of wild risk-taking as inherently admirable and noble, nor were they, whatever their formal pronouncements, fanatical enough to fight for their belief system irrespective of risk. The number of superpowers remained small, and their rulers were at least cautious.[8]

All these assumptions may in due course cease to hold. Very destructive weapons may, like other industrial products, become ever cheaper and cheaper. The complexity of their production may diminish, so that they may become increasingly available by purchase, or even by local production, even to societies whose members are not pervaded by a relatively pacific, productive ethos. The sheer number of states capable of acquiring terrifying weapons will in due course rise exponentially. The larger their number, the greater the probability that some of them will lack that relative moderation and rationality, which inhibits either the use of totally and indiscriminately destructive weapons, or threatening to use them, when the prospect of effective victory, or of successful blackmail, is small.

Note that, while a large armoury may be needed if there is to be any prospect of victory and survival, a much smaller one will do for a determined blackmailer. He knows that his success will depend on the credibility of his threat. He will realize that his threat will only carry conviction if *he really does mean it*, whatever

[8] Cf. a remarkable survey of these issues by Carl Kaysen, 'Is War Obsolete?', *International Security*, 14 no. 4 (1990), pp. 42–64.

the cost to *him* if his bluff is called. He may well be willing to pay that price, even though he knows that, if his bluff is indeed called, he will himself perish, together with his enemies. As the proliferation of high-tech weapons proceeds, the probability of some of them being acquired by groups endowed with such a state of mind eventually becomes very great. The present increase in international terrorism offers a small but frightening foretaste, as yet on only a moderate scale, of such a situation.

3. The preceding argument hinged on the destabilizing and hence conflict-engendering consequences of developing technology: aggression will continue to trump defence, but the means of aggression will become increasingly cheap, widely available and so to speak portable; this diffusion will almost inevitably in the end lead to these means coming into the possession of someone inclined, through fanaticism or folly, to deploy them.

There is also a contrary argument. The unique victory of producers over the specialists in coercion, in modern times, hinged on economic and cognitive growth: no polity could be powerful unless it grew, and no polity would grow unless it protected internally, and eventually gave power to the producers. Can this crucial mechanism continue to operate indefinitely?

In our world, the Gadarene rush towards ever greater output continues to be feverish, so it is hard for us to imagine that it will at some stage come to a rest, or even be reversed. But, although even imagining such an eventuality clearly puts a strain on our powers of imagination, nevertheless we should attempt such a *Gedankenexperiment*, much as it goes against the grain.[9] I see no reason for assuming that there must at some point be a ceiling on further invention, or a new combination of elements to provide new outputs; but it does seem to me plausible to envisage a ceiling beyond which further improvements in the human material condition, though still possible, will no longer make much difference to human contentment, and hence will lose attractiveness. To put it in other words, is there not a point at which the marginal utility of further wealth declines to zero?

[9] See Fred Hirsch, *The Social Limits to Growth* (Routledge and Kegan Paul, London, 1977).

Once the satisfaction of material needs is fully secured, will there not come a point at which special joy is obtained only from 'positional goods', from changes in the relationships between men rather than through changes in the relation between men and things? No doubt, at present, men strive to secure changes in the relations between men *by means of* changes in the relation with things: they try to impress or dominate men by increasing their own material possessions. But it may well become ecologically imperative to diminish or perhaps to inhibit altogether this tendency, which in any case may be a hangover from days of material scarcity, and which may wither away of its own accord, once we lose the pervasive fear of material scarcity (if indeed we do). There are paths to prestige other than conspicuous display of possessions: for instance, conspicuous absence of consumption. Other societies have on occasion used such 'inverse', ascetic markers of rank and, strange as it may seem, advanced industrial society may in due course emulate them.

What would be the consequences of such a situation? My argument has been that, throughout the agrarian age, concern with power position inside a society was (quite rationally) incomparably greater than concern with economic productivity. Advancing the latter had little or no pay-off for those who achieved it. It was only aided by the strange and unusual mechanism which favoured producers over power-seekers, by eliminating entire collectivities which produced less or grew less than their rivals. It was this which in the end turned the scales and inverted this priority. In a re-stabilized world, if and when we reach it one day, the old and so to speak 'normal' priority may be re-established once again. Direct power rather than power-wealth will count. If it does, systematic coercion and hence its occasional overt manifestation ('war') may once again recover its pride of place as the key institution of human society. Coercion specialists rather than augmenters of wealth may once again become the rulers of society. It may be that their methods will be those of the Mafia, rather than those of large-scale inter-polity warfare, but that does not affect the principle of the thing. If wealth is neutralized, power and coercion will once again arbitrate among men and assign them their social location. Specialists in coercion may once again become the dominant stratum in society.

*

Social anthropology has a split personality. It has two faces, one megalomaniac and the other, by contrast, endowed with a kind of microscopic sensitivity. It sometimes likes to talk of man or society as such, in general; at other times to delight in mapping the most detailed texture of specific social situations. My first argument was clearly of the megalomaniac kind: it attempted to offer an overall theory of coercion, in the contexts successively of exiguous, of stable and of expanding resources, with a final speculation about the consequences of a possible re-stabilization. The conclusion of this very abstract argument was that systematic, institutionalized violence was optional in the first stage, mandatory in the second and much diminished in the sub-stage of the third we have reached at present, though the nature of the final condition is not yet clear.

But social anthropology also has its micro-contribution to make. Here, *ex hypothesi*, one generalizes less: what one can do is offer a *sample* of the kind of account available of the social role of violence *and* of the abstention from violence. The example offered here concerns the curious and rather widespread institution of the collective oath, as a legal decision procedure.

The collective oath is a very common institution, though details of it vary. It is, for instance, very commonly encountered among tribal Muslim populations, though it is by no means restricted to them. The idea is simple: if a member of group A accuses a member of group B of an offence (murder, theft, rape, say), then the justice or otherwise of the accusation is decided by requiring the accused and a determined number of his kinsmen (the number required is liable to vary with the gravity of the alleged offence) to testify solemnly, at a sacred place, to the innocence of the accused. If they do so he is deemed to be innocent; if they or some of them refuse to do so, or make a mistake while doing so, he is held to be guilty. His group then proceeds to provide the appropriate compensation or blood money to the accuser and his group.

The *prima facie* absurdity of the whole procedure leaps to the eye. In the kind of society in which this institution is found, loyalty to clan or tribe is held to be a powerful principle, stronger by far than any rather hypothetical devotion to abstract truth or justice. Yet the procedure in question turns those who are closest to the accused 'by blood' into his jury! Those who are most inclined to exonerate him become his judges! Clearly, the procedure is predetermined in favour of the dismissal of all cases. Being so blatantly loaded, it must be useless. Or so it would seem.

In actual fact, the procedure is neither predetermined nor useless. Its outcome was not always obvious. The procedure is or was much used and invoked, which rather suggests that it could not be altogether pointless. How is this possible?

One answer is available, internal to the cultures within which the institution is found, and also frequently taken over – rather uncritically, it seems to me – by external observers. This explanation runs as follows: the whole thing works because the participants are deeply imbued with fear of the supernatural and so hesitate to testify falsely, even when impelled to do so by the very powerful *esprit de lignage*. It is the Other World, and the fear it inspires, which compensates for the temptations of cohesion in this world.

This is not an adequate explanation, if only because it is in conflict with the empirical fact that perjury does in fact occur. The terror inspired by the transcendent does not appear to be sufficiently powerful to ensure truthfulness at all times on the part of the kinsmen-jurors (who, incidentally, may on occasion simply not *know* whether the accusation is actually valid). So what is the correct explanation?

The institution in question is generally found in social contexts where the central state is either absent or weak, and cannot or does not really impose its laws on the land. Groups within that population depend *on themselves* for their maintenance of order. But note: this is just as true for relationships *within* groups as it is concerning relations *between* groups. A central, law-enforcing agency is absent not merely to settle conflicts *between* groups, but just as much in connection with conflicts *inside* groups. Groups themselves either lack an internal agency capable of maintaining order altogether or have it only in a rudimentary, not very effective form. Typically, the tribal chief in such a society does not differ very much from ordinary tribesmen: his household may be a little bit richer and larger, and he may be endowed with a small tail of dependants who enhance his prestige, but all of it doesn't amount to very much: he has no real court, no army, no secretariat.

In fact, the whole distinction between internal and external conflict lapses in this kind of society. Characteristically, groups of diverse scales are 'nested', and they very much resemble each other in their function and manner of operation. Resemblance is vertical as well as horizontal: groups resemble not merely their lateral neighbours, but equally the sub-groups of which they are composed and the mega-groups they help to make up. For most of the time all these groups are 'latent': they are activated into a kind of corporate, visible existence, either by the occurrence of a conflict at the appropriate level or by one of those periodic rituals which remind members of who exactly they are, socially speaking. Some ethnographic observers have wasted a great deal of time trying to find the 'real' crucial unit, which should prevail over all the others on the analogy of the crucial unit (the national state) in their own society. When they failed to find it, they even indulged in a lament at its disappearance, and assumed that it must have been present earlier, prior to its decadence . . .

But it is precisely this 'nested' or segmentary quality of certain tribal societies, the fact that vested units of diverse scale are similar to each other in organization, ethos and formation, which is crucial in the explanation of the collective oath. Consider the group of the accused: it too is internally divided into sub-segments, even if, at the next level of size, it also constitutes an entire segment, in opposition to the unit of the accuser. Those internal segments are also unlikely to be in total harmony with each other: there are few families whose members love each other without qualification. The internal conflicts may be trivial or they may be grave; it is not easy to know just how grave or how trivial without putting it to the test. What people say in unserious, hypothetical situations hardly counts: they may exaggerate either their love and loyalty or, on the contrary, their griefs and resentments toward their kinsmen. What does count is what they do when they are asked to stand up and be counted.

Assume the group to be basically cohesive. All in all, they trust their accused kinsman and value his membership in the group. They may even be convinced of his innocence, and the conviction strengthens their determination to stand by him: they have no desire to encourage others to take the name of their clan lightly and go about indulging in ill-founded accusations against honourable members of the clan. It is precisely in such a situation – facing a cohesive, determined unit – that the accusing unit has least incentive to proceed to the next stage liable to follow the oath, namely the feud, and use violence to set right the wrong which one of their number has suffered. By accepting the verdict of the (successfully performed) collective oath, they can avail themselves of a means of retreat without loss of face. It was not fear of the cohesive clan which made them accept the verdict (perish the thought), not at all; it was piety and respect for the supernatural, for the saint at whose shrine the oath took place . . .

Assume the opposite situation. The lineage of the accused is internally divided and distrustful of the accused: they suspect not merely that he may be guilty, but also, more important, that his inclinations to commit the kind of offence of which he stands accused will in due course involve them all in a perilous feud with some powerful enemies, or worse, with a whole coalition of enemies. They may not yet feel willing to take the ultimate sanction and kill him themselves (though the notion of a special, praiseworthy kind of fratricide does exist in this kind of society); but it may not be a bad idea to teach him a lesson by letting him down at the oath . . . But once again, they can do so without loss of face by invoking piety and respect for sanctity as their principal motive.

In practice, of course, not only are most situations located somewhere in the middle of this spectrum, but it is also not really clear just how the matter stands. The demand that the oath be taken, and the implied threat of feud if either it is refused or its verdict not respected, puts a strain on the accused group. It *probes* for cohesion. Internal jockeying takes place, both in negotiations within it and between it and the accuser. Many conflicts are settled by agreement in the course of such negotiations, 'out of shrine' so to speak, before the oath actually takes place.

So what is of the essence of the procedure is not so much the fervour of the belief in the supernatural, and the conviction that magical punishment will be meted out to those who testify in support of a bad case. What *is* of the essence is that the testimony is public and solemn, and thereby provokes maximum opportunity, or even provocation, for public opinion to rally for or against those who are making out a case and those who stand accused. Misfortunes will sooner or later befall the area in any case, and the drought or flood or whatever it may be will fall on the just and the unjust alike. A party testifying on behalf of an implausible or unpopular case risks receiving the blame when the indiscriminate misfortune strikes, as eventually it will. Or rather: attribution of blame for the misfortune can provide a good justification for any potential hostile coalition against that group.

All this, in conjunction with the internal strains, may cause members of a group to hesitate before testifying. They will no doubt express it to themselves in terms of respect for the sacred and fear of the sanctions it may impose on them . . .

Should one admire or deplore this system? Modern states are not eager to strengthen local kin units and do not in general permit such a system to continue. Individuals and witnesses, selected for supposed access to relevant information, do testify; but collectivities are not allowed by the newly imposed national legal codes to affirm their cohesion and swear themselves or their kinsmen out of their predicaments. But was it a good system while it lasted?

It was a kind of compromise between *Realpolitik* and justice. It did not allow verdicts to go against large, cohesive and determined clans, however guilty. To that extent it respected the realities of power and turned its back on truth and justice. But at the same time, in all those very numerous cases in which power is more or less evenly balanced or, more important, where the power situation is unclear and the outcome of an eventual conflict uncertain, so that both parties stand to lose by escalation to an outright conflict – in all those cases the procedure is endowed with a kind of sensitivity to the merits of the case, to justice. It then becomes sensitive to firmness of conviction and to inner doubt, and provides them with the means of an honourable expression.

In this neat and formal, institutionalized form, collective oath is only to be found in tribal societies. But the underlying principle operates in many semi-anarchic situations, i.e. in conflicts where an over-arching sovereign is either absent or unable or unwilling to arbitrate, decide and impose his verdict. The reason for this may not always be that the sovereign is absent or weak; it may be rooted in the fact that the domain of activity in which the conflict occurs may not be, according to the ethos of the society in question, fully subject to legal and enforceable rules. The limits of state power may be defined not only territorially (the old polity could not assert itself in the desert or in the mountains) but also by functional zones: the modern British state, for instance, which has no trouble in dominating the Highlands, may be unable, or ideologically reluctant, to impose its will in an industrial conflict.

In many advanced societies this applies to prices and wages, and consequently there is no legally just and enforceable wage rate (though there may be enforceable minimal wages). Strikes have much the same logic as collective oaths. Very strong unions or very strong employers can indeed impose settlements contrary to the moral intuitions of the society. But more often neither side is in quite such a strong position. The effectiveness of a strike, or of the resistance to it, depends on the cohesion and/or conviction of the two sides. They will indulge in a poker game of bluff before a possible confrontation. They often settle 'out of strike', so to speak, but the incentive for so doing hinges on a strike remaining a real possibility. And until the strike actually takes place, one cannot be sure just how many will maintain their oath-taking position and for how long. It is the *collective* nature of taking a stand which has weight, and it needs to be put to the test from time to time.

Another dramatic contemporary example of the principle underlying the collective oath can be found in the United Nations and its voting procedures. There, once again, there is no world authority to enforce decisions, so that we are, in that sense, in an anarchic situation. But national representatives generally vote in blocs or clans, rather than as individuals. Hobbes was quite wrong when he claimed that the condition of pervasive latent war makes life 'solitary, poor, nasty, brutish and short'. At any rate, it is not solitary: anarchy leads to gregariousness and the formation of mutual support and insurance *groups*, whether they be called tribes or international alignments. Ibn Khaldun was closer to the truth when he maintained the very opposite of Hobbes's position, namely, that anarchy *and anarchy alone* led to social cohesion.

In 1956 three members of the Western clan committed an act of aggression reprobated and unsupported by their fellow clansmen; but they did so in the expectation that, when it came to the collective oath at the UN, group loyalty would override other considerations, and their fellow bloc members would (with whatever inner reservations) support them. Their fellows chose to act otherwise and teach the aggressors a lesson by *not* supporting them. A lesson so administered restored the authority within the clan of the reluctant co-jurors (even if it temporarily weakened the clan as a whole), in a manner in which a private sermon ('We'll support you this once, but you must have no illusions about our disapproval, and don't count on us in similar cases in the future') could not conceivably have done.

I have chosen an institution in which balance of power, cohesion, moral considerations and transcendent belief are all profoundly intertwined, and govern the deployment of violence in an agrarian society, and I have tried to show that the principles underlying this institution can be discerned in a wide variety of contexts. Thus, on one hand, anthropology can help us understand the actual subtle operation of violence and institutionalized and collective coercion, hedged in by rituals and procedures which are functional and not explicable by their official rationale: on the other, it can also help us formulate very abstract – and no doubt very contentious – generalizations about the role of violence and coercion in wholly different *types* of society.

12

Tribe and State in the Middle East

The typical Middle Eastern tribal quasi-state was based on a combination of the following elements:

1. *Segmentary-lineage organization*. This means in effect the existence of cohesive social groups that ensure order by joint effort. They have a high military participation ratio, to use S. Andreski's phrase;[1] in practice all adult males take part in organized violence and share the risks involved.

The most characteristic institution of such a society is the feud. An offence perpetrated by a member of group A against a member of group B is followed by retaliation by *any* member of B against *any* member of A. If peace is made and compensation paid, members of A all make a contribution and the members of the receiving group B all share it. The consequence of this kind of institutionalization of collective responsibility is that each group has a strong incentive to police its own members. No one else can do it for them and they will suffer if they fail to do it.

The corresponding negative trait of this kind of society is that there is little or no external or superimposed policing by some

1 See S. Andreski, *Military Organisation and Society*, 2nd edn (Routledge and Kegan Paul, London, 1968).

specialized order-enforcing agency, ideally neutral. The circular, self-perpetuating and self-reinforcing mechanism inherent in this situation is obvious: strong self-policing and self-administering groups result in a weak or absent central agency; a weak central agency results in the need for strong, self-protecting, mutual-insurance groups.

A vital aspect of segmentary society is *nesting*. Groups contain subgroups, which in turn contain other subgroups, whose relationship to each other is once again similar. There is no pre-eminent or crucial level of social organization. The balance of power operates *inside* groups as much as it does between them. The groups that appear in the literature as tribal confederations, tribes, clans or segments all function in roughly the same way. Conflicts are likely to arise at any level and then to activate the relevant groups. Otherwise they remain relatively latent, though they come together for festivals, pasture migrations and other occasions.

The self-image and self-definition of these groups in the Middle East is usually, but not always, genealogical and patrilineal. If group membership is a function of descent, and descent is counted in one line only, this automatically engenders a neat and unambiguous system of nested groups such as the one required by this kind of social order. When carrying out fieldwork in the central High Atlas of Morocco, I found that ordinary lay tribesmen, as distinct from holy lineages, possessed Occamist genealogies; that is, they did not multiply ancestors beyond necessity. The number of ancestors remembered (or invented) corresponded closely to the number of actually existing social groups, each of them requiring an apical ancestor for their definition.

The fact that these groups are not merely unilineal but also patrilineal may be held to be a consequence of the pervasive Middle Eastern and Mediterranean agnatic ethos or of the requirements of pastoral social organization. One interesting exception does exist in an area otherwise continuous with and similar to the Middle East – the Saharan Tuareg, who have a matrilineal ideology and had, in some measure that has never been properly explored, a matrilineal social organization. (They are also atypical in possessing a highly developed hierarchical ranking among tribal groups. This feature is also occasionally encountered elsewhere, though is less extreme forms.)

Contrary to popular belief, these groups are not always self-defined genealogically. Among mountain peasants the definition of groups, at any rate above the micro level of extended families, is often territorial rather than genealogical. Moreover, even when the definition is genealogical, recognized procedures exist for the reallocation of groups and individuals in defiance of what would be the commands of 'blood' (or of 'flesh' or 'bone').

What this kind of system of collective responsibility does require is unambiguous membership. When kinship is rectified by a recognized public ritual, the resulting situation still satisfies the needs of the system. So in a supposedly kin-defined unit it is common to find subgroups that have become effective kin by ritual rather than by blood.

2. *Weak, quasi-elective, or even fully elective leadership.* The commonest pattern is the existence of a chiefly segment or lineage, which is traditionally empowered to provide the leader for a wider group also comprising other lineages and segments. It is characteristic of this system that there is no clear and unambiguous rule of succession.

The consequence is that, at the demise of a given chief, the selection of the successor depends on the balance of power and prestige rather than on the simple application of a rule. The succession can go to son, brother, nephew or paternal uncle, and the terms for paternal uncle and son of paternal uncle are used in a classificatory way, embracing a wider category than would be implied in the English usage of these terms. Hence the succession may be determined either by an informal vote – it may go to the man whose potential for leadership is demonstrated by the support he receives from other segments – or by conflict, in which case the leadership potential is demonstrated by what one might call bloody praxis.

These societies are caught in a dilemma: they need leadership for the purpose of indulging in and resisting raids, and for external relations. At the same time, their internal organization is based more on a balance of power than on its concentration. A rough generalization is tempting: the more important the group's external relations, the more centralized and effective is its leadership likely to be.[2]

3. *Symbiosis of pastoral and agricultural populations*. This type of organization is especially appropriate for pastoralists and even more so for *mobile* pastoralists. The latter's mobility, and the fact that their wealth is on the hoof, makes them both inclined and able to resist or evade centralized government. Such organization is also frequently found, however, among sedentary peasants in inaccessible terrain. The political implications of such a location are similar to those of nomadic or semi-nomadic pastoralism. This kind of organization has much smaller prospects of survival among vulnerably located agriculturalists constrained by the limits of an oasis or dependent on irrigation.

Vulnerable agriculturalists and aggressive pastoralists are complementary and economically symbiotic.[3] In a barely governed or ungoverned condition, grain or dates are exchanged for meat or milk products, but the rates of exchange are unlikely to be determined exclusively by the principles of the market. The rate at which products are exchanged or handed over can be interpreted as some kind of cross between price, tribute, protection money and an insurance premium against failure of production. The pastoralists have an interest in not allowing their oasis clients to starve when the harvest happens to fail.

The setting up of a stable relationship between the two parties is politically delicate and may favour the emergence of a stable leadership, a strong chieftaincy or a tribal quasi-state. The agriculturalists have an interest in dealing with a single authority, which in turn has an interest in their own survival and in their taxable prosperity. They prefer this arrangement to being exposed to simultaneous and unpredictable harassment from a number of uncoordinated would-be exploiters, some of whom may be tempted by a one-time, destructive seizure of large booty, even if it diminishes the prospect of future and repeated tribute. After all, future tribute may go to someone else.

2 See A.M. Khazanov, *Nomads and the Outside World* (Cambridge University Press, 1984).

3 See also Ross Dunn, *Resistance in the Desert* (University of Wisconsin Press, Madison, 1977).

Both agriculturalists and pastoralists also have an interest in the availability and proximity of craftsmen and traders. From the viewpoint of an oasis proto-bourgeoisie the attractions of a relatively strong and stable protector are similar to those that it possesses for the agriculturalists. The pastoralists, by contrast, have an interest in access to a well-supplied, reasonably priced and safely accessible market.

4. *Complementarity with holy lineages.* An institution common, though not universal, in the region is the presence of status-differentiated holy lineages dispersed among the segmentary tribes. These usually claim descent from the Prophet. Their elevated status – especially if combined with abstention in principle from involvement in the feuds of lay tribes, exemplifying a kind of limited, role-specific pacifism – qualifies their groups, or at least their more prominent members, to act as arbitrators for the ordinary tribal citizenry. They also provide a kind of loose leadership, which, however, is dependent on the optional support of the led.

5. *External trade and pilgrimage routes.* A strong chieftaincy or tribal proto-state is likely to be located on trade routes, pilgrimage routes (the two are often combined) or, indeed, on a possible route for the hajj or pilgrimage to Mecca. Traders and pilgrims on the move need transport, accommodation and protection. Like locally settled artisans and traders, they prefer to deal with a single and effective patron rather than with a number of competitive ones, probably both unreliable and rapacious. Trade is often a necessity rather than a luxury. The general ecology and the extremities of climate and aridity impel social groups towards specialization. This in turn obliges them to trade; but the requirements of trade push the society towards some measure of political order.

6. *External ideological input.* For reasons not easy to grasp for an organizationally oriented social scientist, the Muslim world is pervaded by a reverence for the high-culture variant of Islam – egalitarian, scripturalist, puritan and nomocratic. This ethos seems to have a life and authority of its own, not visibly dependent on any institutional incarnation. In normal conditions this ideal is implemented, at most, in a relatively small part of Muslim society: by the urban scholars and by their socially well-placed clientele.

The ideal presupposes literacy and an ethic of abiding by rules rather than personal loyalty. Its often emphatic reprobation of claims to special mediation with the divine (the sin of *shirk*) makes it inappropriate for illiterate tribal groups. Those units have a great need for mediators practising arbitration between men in the name of mediation with God. None the less, the authority of the exclusive and unitarian ideal is widely respected, even by those who do not and cannot at most times implement it. From time to time this ideal is activated and becomes a powerful and effective sentiment; it then plays an important part in state-building.

7. *The wider political game*. The tribal territories of the Middle East are peripheral and yet internationally important. Before the appearance of oil wealth they were seldom important for what they produced or contained, but they did possess strategic, and sometimes symbolic, significance. This led outside powers to take an active interest in controlling them or denying such control to others. These powers were in rivalry with each other, and they fostered rivalries within the tribal regions. In the nineteenth century the nominally centralized Ottoman Empire, for instance, operated in the tribal regions of the Arabian Peninsula from two mutually independent bases, one in Egypt and the other in Iraq. Likewise, the British Foreign Office and the India Office could each have distinct policies of its own.

8. *The mercenary or* mamluk *option*. Tribal chieftains proper did not possess the resource base for creating professional armies and bureaucracies. Their armed forces were the tribe, activated by conflict or the prospect of loot or by inspired leadership. This characteristic was both their strength and their weakness. The tribal military unit was a pre-existing social group, endowed with cohesion by its shared experience and concerns and habituated by the normal conditions of its life to mobility, violence and frugality. The continuity between the social and military existences of the tribal armed forces often made them formidable; they did not need, like ordinary recruits, to be specially trained and endowed with an artificial *esprit de corps*. They arrived, fully trained and *encadré*, with recognized leaders and a familiarity with the terrain in which they were to be deployed.

Their weakness lay in the very same attributes. Their social organization predisposed them to fissiparousness as well as cohesion. The lack of a separation between their civil and military roles made them exceedingly responsive to pressures other than the long-term plans of the supreme command. Notoriously, they went home when it suited them, oblivious of strategic considerations. Seasonal obligations and customs meant at least as much to them as long-term strategy. Hence, any tribal chief whose domain came to exceed a purely tribal base naturally attempted to supplement and balance his tribal following by a professional, individually recruited armed force composed of mercenaries and slaves. To do so required no social inventiveness on his part; the model of such an organization was highly developed in the Middle East ever since the decline of the caliphate.[4] The *mamluk* system worked, and on occasion it worked exceedingly well.

Discussion of the Combination of the Elements

It is unlikely that the original inventors of the system were careful students of Plato's *Republic*. Nevertheless, in a Muslim idiom the underlying ideas constituted a remarkable implementation of Platonism. Social corruption and decline were to be avoided: members of the ruling elite were to be systematically trained from early youth in military and administrative skills and, at the same time, were to be profoundly imbued with a pervasive ethos intimately linked to the legitimacy of the state they served. They were to be cut off from the temptations of kin and wealth, which otherwise distract men from the performance of their political duty.

The fact that these elites were to be called slaves rather than guardians was relatively unimportant. The state owned them, but they owned the state. A meritocratic career pattern reinforced their commitment to the state and its service; their recruitment from geographically, ethnically, even religiously and

[4] See Patricia Crone, *Slaves on Horses: The Evolution of the Islamic Polity* (Cambridge University Press, 1980).

pigmentationally alien zones strengthened their loyalty or at any rate reduced their temptations. Like the tribesmen who made up the original power base of an expanding chieftaincy, they came from a rough background and were not habituated to the softening snares that weaken urban rulers; but unlike the tribesmen who came collectively, they were also severed from the seductions of kin links.

If the system did not last forever, its eventual decline was due to precisely the reasons Plato foresaw: this ruling guild, its cohesion originally forged not by the shared perils of the desert but by subjection to the common rigours of deliberately severe training, in the end succumbed to the temptations of honour, kinship and wealth. This was the order in which Plato expected the temptations to operate, as was to be reflected in successive degenerative shifts of the body politic. The actual decline need not be quite so neat. Hinduism is another remarkable kind of implementation of Platonism, though one that wholly surrenders to the principle of kinship, while retaining the rigid hierarchy of wisdom, coercion and production.[5] So the *mamluk* system is but one variant of Platonism. It fully deploys certain elements in the Platonic recipe: education, insulation, propertylessness and kinlessness.

From another viewpoint the *mamluk* system appears as an extraordinary attempt to produce bureaucrats ahead of their time. The traditional state is hampered in its centralizing tendency by the inveterate inclination of men to forge local and kin links, which lead them away from duty and obedience and cause the state to break up into autonomous regional units. It is only in the modern world that a number of factors – a general atomization of society, a widespread orientation towards work and vocation, the pervasive socialization of men by formal education rather than local community – have jointly turned virtually everyone into a potential bureaucrat. Men can now be trusted, on the whole, to perform their tasks in bureaucratic organizations without

5 This interpretations of the caste system has recently been interestingly challenged by Declan Quigley in *The Interpretation of Caste* (Clarendon Press, Oxford, 1993).

constantly yielding to the temptation to bend the rules so as to favour their own kin. We are all *mamluks* now. Traditional society did not have this advantage; for reliable bureaucratic performance it had to rely on slaves, eunuchs, priests or aliens.[6]

We may well ask whether, when the *mamluk* principle and its modification are brilliantly successful on a large scale, we can still talk about a tribal state. There would indeed be something preposterous about referring to the Ottoman Empire in its fully developed form in such terms; that was how it started, but it did not retain that form. The *mamluk* principle is an alternative to a tribal base, and pure versions of either one constitute the two end-points of a spectrum; societies located at the extreme ends are rare, and many Middle Eastern polities were located somewhere along the middle of this range.

We can put the question in another way. Given the emergence of the Ottoman state, is Ibn Khaldun's theory of Middle Eastern society, on which I have been relying heavily, still defensible as an overall theory of the Muslim world of the arid zone? My own inclination is to say *yes* and to offer the following argument: no doubt the two elements, the paradigmatic Ibn Khaldunian use of a tribal base and the rival one of a slave bureaucracy, could and did mix in diverse proportions in various Middle Eastern state formations.

The Ottoman Empire began as a cluster of typical tribal polities in Anatolia. It was only when one of them achieved outstanding success that two things happened: it acquired an atypical base, in the Balkans and western Anatolia and eventually in the Nile valley, of docile sedentary peasants; and the *mamluk* element came to display a kind of hypertrophy, eliminating the rival element. The two changes were no doubt connected. An extensive and taxable peasant base made it possible to sustain a non-tribal state apparatus, and the new base was ill suited for governance by tribesmen. The system then reproduced itself in an autonomous form in Tunis and Algiers and perhaps elsewhere.

In extensive areas, however, the Ibn Khaldunian formula, using the old elements, remained alive and well. It constituted the normal

[6] See K. Hopkins, *Conquerors and Slaves* (Cambridge University Press, 1978).

political condition of a large proportion of Middle Easterners despite the nominal Ottoman overlordship. It was signalling – perhaps not always wildly – to be let out. In due course it made its public reappearance, with Abd el Kader in Algeria, the Mahdiyya in the Sudan, the Wahhabis in the Peninsula, the Sanusiyya in Cyrenaica, the Rashidis in Ha'il, petty tribal chieftaincies in eastern Anatolia, the Ibadi imamate in Oman and the Zaydi one in Yemen. In extensive areas it had never really been hidden.

The way in which all these various elements combine in state formation varies a great deal. One can think of a number of possible scenarios. Tribesmen who herd their flocks in an arid hill range that also shelters an oasis, and who are governed, in so far as the term is appropriate at all, by a loose chieftaincy, may secure control of the oasis. They thereby provide the chiefly lineage with a dual base. Henceforth the chief divides his time between an oasis town base, whose prosperity he may enhance further by inviting craftsmen and traders to settle, and a seasonal chiefly progress among those of his kinsmen who have remained on the pastures. His more privileged wives remain in the town house while he fortifies his links with his tribal kinsmen by marriages, possibly short-lived, with daughters of segment chiefs. He balances the concerns of the diverse constituents of his chieftaincy, and he encourages the pastoralists to practise their depredations, not on his own subjects, but preferably outside. He has to balance the advantages of allowing his old supporters and kinsmen the benefits of both kinds of pillage against the advantages of receiving protection money by proscribing pillage. The optimal solution is to allow just enough pillage to retain the loyalty of the tribal segments and provide maximum encouragement for the payment of protection. Marginal pillage should equal marginal tribute in a finely tuned tribal chiefdom.

The chief has to guard against defections among the tribal segments by giving subsidies that can rival those promised by other similar chieftaincies, ever ready to seduce some of his following by offering better terms. All this takes money; so he himself is in the market for the reception of subsidies and arms from outside powers, which in turn are eager to use his strategic position either to ensure their own communications or to undermine the communications and claims of their rivals. Each outside power has its own local clients, but the alignments are inevitably unstable. Treachery is endemic.

Trade and pilgrimage routes are also tricky. Insistence on excessive security may antagonize tribal dependents and diminish revenue. The game is played out within the chiefly lineage as well; rival cousins, brothers and nephews enlist, and are enlisted by, external participants in this complex, never-ending game. New entrants appear with changes in the international scene, and some old ones are eliminated. Nothing, certainly not death, ever terminates the game; leadership in a segmentary society has a dragon's-teeth quality. I heard this complaint in Pahlavi Tehran: however many tribal leaders you kill, new ones always emerge from the chief's lineage. The killed or assassinated chief or claimant cannot return to compete another day, but his brother, son or nephew will.[7]

There is another possible scenario. Consider an alternative story in which all these elements are indeed present, but with one further participant: religious fundamentalism and revivalism. Islam is ever prone to reformation; it might even be described as the permanent Reformation. The faithful are frequently willing to respond to a preacher calling for a return to a purer version of the faith (assuming that they or their ancestors had ever really known it), a form unblemished by questionable and quasi-pagan practices. The community–polity equation impels the preacher to become a political figure as well.

Shi'i-s consciously re-enact the founding martyrdom of their special faith, but other Muslims are likely to re-enact or re-feel the original conflict between the establishment of the faith and the preceding – yet ever-present and menacing – age of ignorance. The enthusiasm evoked by such an appeal to purification may give the purifying chief the advantage of an extra element of cohesion among his followers and a special capacity to organize units far larger than those supplied by their own kin-based political language. This action may confer on him some of the

7 Madawi Al-Rashid, *Politics in an Arabian Oasis: The Rashidi Dynasty* (I.B. Tauris, London, 1991).

advantages that are painfully, and much more expensively, acquired by larger states through the revenue produced from their control of extensive agricultural territory and through the recruitment of mercenaries and *mamluks* with the help of that revenue. This special formula of tribe plus religious revival can lead to political fortune, particularly when combined with the good luck of an alignment with outside powers victorious in a world war. The faith-linked chieftaincy can then triumph over its main rival, whom in other respects it resembles. This is in effect the story of the Saudi victory over the Rashidis.

A different kind of tribal state can also arise, one based on the mutual complementarity of lay tribal leaders and holy lineages. In such a case the wider society is divided into a majority of lay tribesmen and a minority of hereditary saints. The saints are settled around one or more shrines, which are revered by all. The lay tribesmen comport themselves in accordance with the well-known rules governing a segmentary society: collective responsibility, diffusion of power, weak leadership (elective or quasi-elective) and wide participation by male heads of households in all political and other responsibilities.

The conflicts that inevitably arise between groups of all sizes are arbitrated or mediated at the shrines by the hereditary saints, who are determined by birth rather than chosen in any kind of human election. The shrines are strategically located close to the points of maximal conflict – at the border of major tribal segments or near pastures, which require seasonal reoccupation and periodic reallocation. The number of men of saintly birth is much smaller than those of lay birth but at the same time much larger than the number of saints required to preside over shrines and act as effective arbitrators. The real, so to speak operational saints are selected from the wider pool of latent saints by birth.

According to the locally accepted theory, this selection is made by God. In reality, *vox Dei vox populi*. The choice of the possessor of *baraka* is made by a drawn-out and tacit process, stretching over generations, in which the attribution of divine grace works through the bestowal of support on this or that saint by the lay tribesmen. It is this support that effectively endows some saints with charisma. He who is treated as a saint becomes one.

The respect he is shown enables him to arbitrate effectively and thereby display and prove his sanctity. The donations he receives enable him to entertain generously without seeming to count the cost and thereby, once again, to demonstrate his saintly status.

The lay tribesmen are obliged to feud, and the saints are obliged by the very definition of their role to abstain both from violence and from litigation, the latter being but the continuation of the feud by other means. By their comportment some saints attract special reverence. The respect they inspire in some of their clientele then makes them attractive to other potential parishioners; an arbitrator who is widely respected, and whose judgement is heeded, is of more use than one whose verdict may be spurned by the other party to the conflict. In this way a kind of quasi-state crystallizes. Violent lay elective chiefs and pacific hereditary saints complement each other in the system. An elegant, stable and satisfactory system of an internal balance of power can develop. In the central High Atlas a system of this kind persisted and provided cheap and satisfactory quasi-government for about three centuries.[8]

Two things deserve note in connection with the saints of Ahansal: the stability of their local power and their abstention at most times from wider political ambition. They did not in general intervene in wider Moroccan history. On only a single occasion did one of their number display a wider ambition. He paid for it by a horrible death, the occurrence of which, however, is denied by local tradition, which credits him with an occultation, to be followed by an eventual return in the hour of greatest need. So far, this prognostication has not been borne out. By an accident, most fortunate for the historian, his real death was witnessed by Thomas Pellew, an English renegade captive in the service of the then sultan, who in the end managed to return to England and publish an account of his adventures. The local faith in an occultation, faith that persisted into modern times, can on this occasion be corrected by independent external documentation.[9]

This kind of scenario, which might be called the Ahansal

[8] See Ernest Gellner, *Saints of the Atlas* (University of Chicago Press, 1969).

[9] *The History of the Long Captivity of Thomas Pellew in South Barbary* (London, 1739).

version, differs from the preceding variant, which could be called the Saudi pattern. A different type of Islam is involved in each of the two models. We are dealing with a tribal state in each case, but the religious cement is quite different. The social incarnation of Islam stretches out along a kind of spectrum, ranging from a scholarly, puritanical, egalitarian theology at one end to an anthropolatrous, ecstatic, hierarchical folk religion at the other. Either form can make a significant contribution to tribal state or quasi-state formation. Hereditary saints, based on the principle of *shirk* (mediation or refraction of the deity) and vehemently reprobated by the orthodox high theology, can provide that minimal centralizing agency, which, however, deals very satisfactorily with the political problems of extensive populations. It can do so without much in the way of coercive centralization, that is, without what we would call a real state. It can help regulate the complex patterns of seasonal pasture use in a complex ecology, requiring seasonal migrations of large flocks and human populations from the Sahara to high mountains, and it can help keep the peace between the transhumants and the sedentaries.

By contrast, puritan unitarian Islam can endow one leader with sufficient legitimacy to overcome tribal fissiparousness and help him set up a more effective state, in which the written requirements of the faith receive a more stringent implementation. Here the men of religion become bureaucratic, ideological and judicial servants of the state, rather than being equal, or more than equal, partners of the petty practitioners of coercion. The revered marabout arbitrates between segment leaders and helps fuse the segments into a kind of polity; the scribe-judge helps a sheikh to become an amir by providing him with the appropriate legitimacy and with a rudimentary bureaucracy.

The available forms of religious political cement are by no means exhausted by these two versions, the Saudi and the Ahansal types. Intermediate forms combining political centralization with the use of hereditary religious arbitrators are available. The traditional Yemeni state, for instance, fused the central authority of an imam – legitimated by the Zaidi version of Shi'ism – with local arbitration by Sadah families, sharing their authority (based on a hereditary religious standing outside the tribal segmentary system) with tribal sheikhs whose authority was based on leadership *within* the tribes and also with legal families.[10] An interesting and well-documented mixed form of this kind emerged in Cyrenaica under the impact of Italian colonial aggression.[11] The Sanusiyya combined the organizational form of a Sufi (mediationist religious order, or *tariqa*) with doctrinal commitment to a relatively reformist ideology, that is, to supplying a purer version of the faith to the ignorant and illiterate Bedouin. Reformist Islam is normally hostile to religious orders, but in tribal areas, devoid of an urban infrastructure, Sufi organizational principles provide the only available institutional tool capable of sustaining missionary work. The doctrine must compromise if it is to be endowed with the minimum of social underpinning. The preconditions of the only possible form of political organization at the time, given the ecological milieu, eventually impelled the Sanusi towards the Ahansal version, the insertion of saintly lodges at the crucial interstices of the segmentary system. There they could provide mediation and arbitration. The need, by contrast, to unite a wide area and invoke a religious legitimation more potent than that of the traditional pre-existing *marabtin-bil-baraka* (petty saints attached to small segments) also impelled them towards a more unitarian and scripturalist version of the faith.

There is a permanent tension between the two principles of legitimacy, the egalitarian scripturalist and the kin-based mediationist. The former is incarnated in the theologian scholars who, on their own, have little potential for state formation. They are

[10] See Shelagh Weir, 'Tribe, hijrah and medinah in north-west Yemen', in K. Brown et al. (eds), *Middle Eastern Cities in Comparative Perspective* (Ithaca, London, 1986) and 'Trade and tribal structures in north-west Yemen', in *Arabie du Sud: Le Commerce comme facteur dynamisant des changements économiques et sociaux* (Cahiers du GREMAMO, no. 10, Paris, 1991); Gabriele vom Bruck, 'Réconciliation ambiguë: une perspective anthropologique sur le concept de la violence légitime dans l'imamat du Yémen', in E. Le Roy and T. von Trotha (eds), *La Violence et l'état* (L'Hasmallan, Paris, 1993).

[11] See E.E. Evans-Pritchard, *The Sanusi of Cyrenaica* (Oxford University Press, 1949) and the posthumous collection of papers by Emrys Peters, *Bedouin of Cyrenaica*, edited by J. Goody and E. Marx (Cambridge University Press, 1991).

neither well organized nor skilled in coercion. They can, however, provide a monarch, or a chief aspiring to become a monarch, with both legitimation and a bureaucracy. The tribal segments, the social base of the second and rival principle of state formation, are inherently well trained in the exercise of violence; but they normally lack legitimacy in the eyes of the wider Muslim society. In fact, their normal life constitutes a kind of paradigm of moral illegitimacy. They are seen as licentious and ignorant, neither willing nor able to live the good Muslim life. This, given the socially pervasive intensity of commitment to Islam, is no trivial matter. Only those who succeed in combining into large and powerful units in the name of orthodoxy can then spoliate those remaining sinners who remain fragmented and who failed to join the snowballing movement of revival.

The *mamluk* system can be seen as an extreme version, one that endeavours to dispense with the kin or tribal element altogether and stand it on its head. Individuals are recruited into the state service in an atomized manner and are torn out of their kin background by being technically slaves and/or of non-Muslim origin. Sustained religious and military training, which is *not* tribal, becomes a means of inducing a surrogate *'asabiyya*. One can look at the *mamluks* either as an artificial, education-produced tribe, or one can see them as the result of turning a religious elite, normally ineffectual politically, for once into a coercively and politically effective body. There are *mamluks de robe* as well as *mamluks d'épée*. When the system works well, individuals within it can successfully perform each of these roles at various stages of their career – they can be soldiers in their youth and cleric administrators later. Thus, they really live up to Plato's ideal of the Guardians.

What in general are the prospects of building a social and political order, a framework within which men may work creatively and enjoy the fruits of their labour with some degree of security and where both civilization and stability are present? In these respects, how does the Muslim Middle East compare with Europe?

Consider the pair of the most celebrated commentators on the two systems, Ibn Khaldun and Niccolò Machiavelli. What the two share, apart from their greatness, is a marked inclination towards dispassionate analysis instead of pious moralizing. Ironically, it is Machiavelli, whose notoriety comes from an alleged cynicism, rather than his Muslim counterpart, who more frequently abandons *Wertfreiheit* and slips into moral concern and expressions of regret. Ibn Khaldun's detachment was far more complete.

Their accounts of the problems of social cohesion and of order deserve juxtaposition. They were not quite contemporaries; Ibn Khaldun died in 1406 and Machiavelli was born a whole generation, or to be precise, sixty-three years later. The lifetime that separates the death of one from the birth of the other contains at least one momentous event, namely the fall of Constantinople and hence the definitive emergence of the Ottoman Empire. This event makes a considerable difference, one that is reflected in their thought; Machiavelli ponders on the Ottoman state, and Ibn Khaldun could not yet do so.

Nevertheless, their two worlds were not so very distant and can usefully be compared. Machiavelli, much impressed by the Ottoman Empire, considered its strength, like that of the empire of Alexander, to be due to the weakness of civil society in the East. Once you defeated the centre society could no longer oppose you, and the rest fell into your lap. How different from Europe, where barons might initially help you by betraying their overlord, but they would cause you perpetual trouble even if you succeeded in defeating their king. This argument has of late earned Machiavelli the rebuke of being the initiator of the 'Orientalist' heresy of Western denigration of the East. It is true that Machiavelli did not notice that, in the Middle East, tribes will also cause you trouble, even after you have defeated and replaced the sultan. The distinctively Middle Eastern path to political fragmentation eluded him.

An extraterrestrial observer, investigating the political life of man at that time and using the works of these two thinkers as his main texts, would probably come to the conclusion that the political prospects of the Middle East were far better than those of Europe. The sadness and pessimism that intermittently and irresistibly burst through the otherwise cool prose of Machiavelli's accounts were only too well founded.

In Ibn Khaldun's world, sketched out in the earlier part of this essay, there were three effective principles of political order: the natural cohesion of tribal life; the principle of military administrative slavery; and religion. No single one of these was perfect or exempt from eventual decay; but, in various forms of combination with each other, they held out some hope of at least a measure of political stability, temporary peace and effective government. A tribal coalition, endowed with unity by religion, could set up a state; a state that was guided and served by the religious scholars could function, upholding right and suppressing evil, and both observing and enforcing that fundamental entrenched political constitution already contained, as it were legally prefabricated, in the faith itself.

Logically, Muslim states need no constitution because religion already constitutes and provides the entrenched clauses of moral and political order. Religiously trained slaves of the state could endow the state with strength and operate the famous circle of equity, in which civil society, though disenfranchised, could produce sufficient wealth to sustain the state and so receive the required protection in return.[12] Thus, some degree of fusion of both civilization and cohesion was possible, even if the basic human dilemma – the conditions of cohesion and of civilization are mutually incompatible – could not be overcome altogether. Urban and tribal virtues cannot come together, one being born of the city and the other of the tribe; but carriers of each set of virtues, tribesmen and scholars, can occasionally combine and jointly set up and run a state.

These elements are present in a far lesser degree in the Italy and Europe observed by Machiavelli. Let us take each of them in turn:

Tribalism. Machiavelli notes that the only people in Europe who still live as the ancients did are the Swiss. By this he means that a society with an exceedingly high military and political participation ratio, and one that is firmly committed to a religion

[12] See Lucette Valensi, *Venise et la Sublime Porte: La naissance du despote* (Hachette, Paris, 1987).

sustaining civic virtue, is consequently free from outside interference and is fairly egalitarian internally: 'The Swiss are strongly armed and completely free' (*The Prince*); 'The Swiss . . . are the only people who today, with respect both to religion and to military institutions, who live as the ancients did' (*The Discourses*). This clearly corresponds to what Ibn Khaldun means by tribal *'asabiyya*; natural cohesion emerges when a group is bound to administer and defend itself. The military implications of this situation, the joint presence in one international system both of *'asabiyya*-endowed participatory units and of urban ones, are precisely those Ibn Khaldun had postulated for all mankind. In war the Swiss beat everyone, and no one, not even the French monarchy, could win without their help: 'The French are no match for the Swiss, and without Swiss help feel no match for anyone else' (*The Prince*). The armies recruited from urban civil societies, such as the Italian, are useless; Machiavelli notes that they only win if for some reason the rival army runs away.

Machiavelli was mistaken in supposing that the Swiss were the only armed, participatory self-governing communities left in Europe. He was close enough to the truth, however, for though some are also found elsewhere, they are marginal. Montenegro or the Scottish Highlands escaped his attention. But in early modern Europe barbarians, whether as a threat or as a salvation, were indeed in short supply. As late as the eighteenth century, Edward Gibbon, wondering whether the fate of Rome might also befall Augustan Europe, noted this with a touch of surprise: Europe had run out of savages.

Slaves on horseback. For some reason or other, Europe had lost the institution of slavery. Especially in Italy, the regrettable principle of a free labour market developed and flourished in a sphere of activity for which it is especially unsuitable – the market for military service. The consequences were disastrous, and Machiavelli comments on them at length and with feeling. Mercenaries are useless, he says. In danger they desert you; in victory they become your masters. It is in fact hard to say whether it is their success or their failure that spells the greater danger for their employer. How about auxiliaries, the armed forces supplied by an ally? The disadvantages that attend their use are at least as great. What is to be done? Civic societies supply armies that win only when the enemy happens to flee; mercenaries and allies turn against you when they prevail. In despair, the only advice Machiavelli is able to give is that of deploying *mixed* forces. Presumably, the hope is that not all of them will betray you at the same time.

The Muslim world was better endowed: on one hand, a kind of generalized and pervasive Switzerland without cuckoo clocks, full of free rural communities, surrounded virtually all states. It provided and ever-present reservoir of natural political and military talent; the future, Ibn Khaldun predicted in his autobiography, belonged to the Turks and the Arabs because of their populousness and cohesion.[13] The relatively small territory of the central Alps could hardly match the expanses of Central Asia and all the mountains and savannah of the Middle East. The future may belong to Turks and Arabs, but it does not belong to the Swiss. The *mamluks*, drawn in large measure from the Caucasian and Central Asian reservoirs, and later from the Balkans, were the Switzers of the Muslim courts. 'Where are my Switzers? Let them guard the door,' cries the king in *Hamlet*. But soon he announces, 'The doors are broke.' Claudius would have been much safer with janissaries. The *mamluks*, produced according to the Platonic recipe of sustained training, deep indoctrination and meritocratic promotion, were clearly superior to the opportunistic, treacherous and volatile mercenaries, whose suspect motivation was bound to turn them into unreliable supporters.

Religion. The contrast is just as unfavourable to Europe if we turn to religion. Ibn Khaldun was clear about the great political potential of faith. Religious enthusiasm, when superimposed on the natural cohesion of participatory groups, engenders large units and a more effective discipline. Ibn Khaldun did not greatly discuss the micro-structural services provided by petty saints, though he was familiar with them; but he was explicit about the services religion could provide in helping to enlarge the political unit.

13 See Ibn Khaldun, *Le Voyage d'Occident et d'Orient*, translated by Abdesslam Cheddadi (Paris, 1980).

By contrast, the role of religion in Europe, according to Machiavelli, is dismal. In *The Prince* he first declares that there is no point in discussing ecclesiastical principalities: 'I shall not argue about them; they are exalted and maintained by God, and only a rash and presumptuous man would take it on himself to discuss them.' But the temptations of rashness and presumption quickly become too strong for him, and he goes on to describe how the political astuteness of three successive popes for a time made the Papal States great. In *The Discourses* he is more explicit and damning: 'Owing to the bad example set by the Court of Rome, Italy has lost all devotion and all religion. It is the Church that has kept, and keeps, Italy divided . . . Italy . . . has now become the prey . . . of anyone who attacks it. For which our Italians have to thank the Church, and nobody else.' The Swiss, says Machiavelli, are the only European people to maintain the ancient virtues; but if the court of Rome were to move to Switzerland, the Swiss would soon be brought down in utter disorder. This ingenious experiment has never actually been tried.

So there are no tribes (but for the blessed Swiss), no corps of well-trained servants of the state, no socially effective and inspiring faith. What hope, then, can there be for Italy or Europe? In the tribal urban complex of the Muslim Middle East, by contrast, the blend of tribal cohesion and urban civilization is at least periodically revived. Faith and virtue are doomed to an eternal return. One could hope for some peace during the stable periods before the wheel of political fortune turned once again. To the north of the Mediterranean, however, there seems to be no hope at all.

On the evidence available at the time, such a conclusion would have been entirely reasonable. History has turned out rather differently. It is not part of this essay to speculate about how Europe, and in the end even Italy, broke out of the impasse. The manner in which a new centralized bureaucratic state came about, one in which everyone was turned into soldier and bureaucrat and became a *mamluk*; the way in which the relationship between state and civil society was transformed, so that civil society took part in politics and the state took part in the economy; the manner in which religion recovered its social potential in a new form – all this is another theme.

But it is appropriate to look, at least briefly, at the subsequent fate of the world of tribal politics in the Middle East. There are many who hold that the Ottoman Empire makes Ibn Khaldun's account inapplicable to recent centuries. I do not believe this to be so. Under the surface the world of Ibn Khaldun continued to function; it re-emerged as the empire declined. It only came to an end when new military and administrative technologies were imported and tilted the balance of power in favour of the state. The subsequent new order has a number of conspicuous features: civil society continues to be weak in face of the state; political conflict within the state apparatus, even when nominally ideological, is generally a matter of the rivalry of patronage networks, often with a regional or quasi-communal base. This is a kind of tribalism in a new milieu and idiom. In marked contrast to other parts of the world, in the Middle East religion has retained or enhanced its capacity to act as a political catalyst. Secularization is conspicuous by its absence. Politics is frequently fundamentalist. Strong religion, a strong state, weak civil society and the fragile *'asabiyya* of quasi-kin, quasi-territorial patronage – that seems to be the heritage.

13

The Maghreb as a Mirror for Man

The Maghreb has given the world one of its greatest social scientists – perhaps *the* greatest. It is hardly possible to approach the question of the contribution of North Africa to our understanding of human society without beginning with Ibn Khaldun. In this astonishing fourteenth-century thinker, we find both echoes and contrasts of the dominant themes of European social thought. The contrasts are specially illuminating, arising as they do from the distinctive nature of the North African social experience.

If one were to single out one issue which, more than any other, pervades the European preoccupation with the foundations of the social order, it would be the opposition of *Gemeinschaft* and *Gesellschaft*, of community and society. This is not just a theoretical contrast: these terms inspire nostalgia, fear, hate, ambivalence. On one hand there is, it is claimed, the organic collectivity, the brotherhood of men, whose diverse activities intertwine with each other to form a network of sentiment and understanding, and which create a seamless culture and sense of solidarity; on the other, the voluntary association of autonomous individuals, linked only by freely chosen contracts, negotiated in the light of rationally assessed conduciveness to private and lucidly defined aims. This confrontation, or something very much like it, is not absent from the thought of Ibn Khaldun; on the contrary, it is absolutely central to his entire vision. But the manner in which it makes its appearance is altogether different, and the difference is profoundly significant.

First of all, in Europe, the opposition appears as a *succession*. We *moved* from status to contract. In the beginning, there was *community*. Later, it was replaced by *society*. It is this transition which preoccupies European thought, morally and emotionally as well as intellectually. Was it a boon and liberation or a catastrophe? This question continues to polarize the feelings as well as the ideas of Europeans.

In Ibn Khaldun, the great polarization appears not at all as a succession, but as an *essentially* synchronic phenomenon. The two social forms are not merely present at the same time, they *have* to be present at the same time; they need each other; neither of them can possibly manage without the other; they are complementary. The human social condition is scarcely conceivable without their joint presence. As each is indispensable, and in any case the world is not moving from one to the other, Ibn Khaldun does not waste too much time debating their relative merits. Of course, he is acutely aware of their respective strengths and weaknesses, but his attitude is far more clinical, detached and dispassionate than that of latter-day commentators. He would seem to be a stranger to the near-hysterical adoration or repudiation of either the Closed or the Open Society.

In his scheme, there is first of all the cohesive, rustic, self-administering community. The powerful commitment of its members to each other and to their community is forged by the insecurity of a rustic world in which no central authority keeps the peace. Without cohesion, survival would be impossible. The cohesion imposed by this natural imperative enables members of the community, in other words tribesmen, not merely to govern themselves, but also, when opportunity arises, to govern others. Tribal life is the school of political virtue, and it is the only such school. (There is an exception to this principle of which Ibn Khaldun is aware, but which he does not fully incorporate in his thought: the *mamluk* system, which in effect implements the Platonic recipe – train your rulers very very hard, from childhood onwards, and deprive them of wealth or kin so as to free them from temptation.) The absence of specialization is the corollary of tribal political virtue. The tribesmen are cohesive because they resemble each other and distrust anyone who is distinctive; much later on, Emile Durkheim was to name this kind of cohesion, based on similarity, 'mechanical solidarity'. This cohesive but unspecialized community is quite incapable of producing the material and cultural preconditions of a full and civilized life, although at the same time it aspires to possessing them and positively *needs* them.

These economic and cultural needs can only be satisfied by those agglomerations of specialists and middlemen known as cities. The city is born, as in Plato's *Republic*, of inflated needs, of the development of desires in excess of the human minimum: but – and this is an important difference between the two thinkers (and the societies they reflect) – in Ibn Khaldun this extra need is not restricted to the city and its inhabitants, but pervades the society as a whole. Society as a whole, not just the city, needs the city. The cohesive rustics, though incapable of satisfying their needs from their own resources and capacities, nevertheless share those needs.

The urban population, by contrast, which can and does satisfy those additional requirements, both among its own number and among others, does however pay a heavy price for its economic and cultural competence, for its *civilization*. Its own specialization and diversity, and the fact that it depends, for the protection of its activities, not on its own cohesion (it has none) but on superior political authority and extraneous force, means that it is politically and militarily emasculated. It is atomized and incapable of corporate action. It is doomed to be ruled and to be excluded from participation in government. It needs rule, but cannot itself satisfy that need.

Society needs both order and government on one hand, and the arts and crafts and cultural skills which make civilized life possible. The essence of Ibn Khaldun's superb interpretation of his own world (which he believed to be the human world in general) was that each of these two indispensable ingredients is indeed supplied, but by distinct parts of the overall social body.

Government is the gift of the tribe to the city, and acceptable economic and cultural conditions are the gift of the city to society at large. Neither element could manage on its own. Each is indispensable. It is good to be clear about their merits, but it would be fairly pointless to moralize about them too much and commend the universalization of either one or the other. The coexistence of the two elements leads to a cyclical political process, a collective version of the circulation of elites, a rotation in the wheel of fortune: rulers weakened by the benefits of urban life need to be replaced in a political *Stoffwechsel*, by a new tribal invasion, introducing a new dynasty with a revived tribal power base. But this merely rotates the personnel and does not alter the overall structure.

Ibn Khaldun was not destined to make an impact on European thought till the nineteenth century. By then Europeans were preoccupied with the changes which were so conspicuous in their own society, and increasingly curious about societies which had not undergone the same changes or had followed a different path. The founding fathers of Marxism, for instance, were interested in the material which had begun to flow from Algeria after the French conquest, partly in pursuit of documentation concerning their idea about the absence of private property in archaic and/or Asian societies.[1] But in due course Engels evidently stumbled on and took over in its entirety Ibn Khaldun's vision. In his 'Contribution to the History of Primitive Christianity', published in *Die Neue Zeit* in 1894/5, well after Marx's death, Engels in fact succinctly sums up Ibn Khaldun, though without naming him. No doubt the content of de Slane's translation reached him, very probably through the Russian scholar Kovalevski, who had been received by Marx in London. Engels stresses that the conflict between opulent and lax city dwellers, and envious and puritanical tribesmen, leads to a revivalist revolution, legitimized by religion, but which in the end changes nothing, other than a rotation of personnel. How different with us, where religious camouflage of social conflict nevertheless leads to real change! So Engels, using Ibn Khaldun, by implication proposes a dual philosophy of

[1] See *Marxisme et Algérie. Textes de Marx/Engels.* Présentés par René Gallissot avec la collaboration de Gilbert Badia (Paris, 1976).

history, one granting progress to the West but consigning the East (and Arabs specially) to cyclical stagnation.

While there can be no serious doubt that Ibn Khaldun's ideas influenced Engels, the interesting thing about Alexis de Tocqueville is that he seems to have reached some of the same ideas, but to have done so independently. He makes the very same crucial point about the indispensability of cities, in the context of discussing French strategy in the conflict with Amir Abd el Kader in Algeria.

> The Arabs have a greater need of cities than they themselves realize . . . no society, be it even half-civilized, can do without cities. It can do without villages but it cannot do without cities. Nomadic peoples escape this necessity no more than others, in fact they are even more subject to it.[2]

The point had apparently been suggested to Tocqueville by remarks reported to him, which had been made by tribesmen in negotiations concerning the exchange of prisoners. The Arabs, while remaining loyal to Abd el Kader, nevertheless complained bitterly about the conditions to which they were reduced by being cut off from trade by the French. What use are our flocks, they said, if we have no access to towns in which we could purchase what we need but cannot manufacture ourselves? Herds for them evidently had, above all, exchange value.

Tocqueville also approaches the issue which was later to become central for scholarly concern with the Maghreb, namely the internal mechanics of social control and cohesion within the rural self-governing unit, something which constituted the basic datum for Ibn Khaldun, but whose inner dynamics he had not examined in detail. Tocqueville vacillates between on one hand seeing parallels between the centralization attempted in Algeria by Abd el Kader and that achieved in France in the fifteenth century by Charles VII, and on the other, the great difference between attempting such centralization in a tribal and in a feudal society.

[2] Quoted in *Alexis de Tocqueville, De la Colonie en Algérie*. Présentation de Tzvetan Todorov (Editions Complexe, Brussels, 1988), p. 81.

Centralization in a segmented society is harder than it is in the kind of society we know in Europe.[3]

This theme came eventually to predominate. One of the most crucial and influential passages occurs in Emile Durkheim's classic *De la division du travail social.* But behind Emile Durkheim, there is the most unjustly half-forgotten Emile Masqueray, and his *Formation de cités chez les populations sédentaires de l'Algérie.*[4] It was Masqueray who, in his study of the three main Algerian Berber groups (with a side glance at central Morocco), assembled the material which was due to lead to the theory of 'segmentation'. Durkheim grants him a footnote,[5] which in fact he has to share with Hanoteau and Letourneux, the compilers of Kabyle customary law. But Durkheim owes Masqueray a great deal. Durkheim formulated the idea of segmentary social organization, in which groups are not merely composed of similar subgroups and resemble their neighbouring groups, but in which they also resemble the larger groups of which they are part. In his articulation of the model Durkheim uses the Kabyles as his example. Durkheim proceeds to comment on the collective control of property, which he exaggerates, and which for him is merely a corollary of the lack of individualism in this kind of society, which concerns him less than it did the Marxists.

Two lines lead from Masqueray and Durkheim to the present. The more famous one, at least in the English-speaking world, leads from Durkheim to the late Sir Edward Evans-Pritchard, through whom 'segmentation' became one of the most widely used terms in the vocabulary of social anthropologists. Evans-Pritchard applied the notion in his study of the Nilotic Nuer and of the Bedouin of Cyrenaica, the nearest he came to working in the Maghreb. In his hands, it became a widely used theory concerning how social order can be maintained in the absence of the state. Egalitarian, highly participatory social groups (at any rate, as far as male heads of households are concerned) maintain

[3] Tocqueville, pp. 65 ff.

[4] Ernest Leroux, Paris, 1886; republished with 'presentation' by Fanny Colonna (Edisud, Aix en Provence, 1983).

[5] *De la division du travail social,* 10th edn (PUF, Paris, 1978), p. 152.

internal discipline through their opposition to other similar groups, to whom they are collectively responsible for possible misdeeds of their own members. Internally, order is likewise maintained by the opposition of subgroups. The feud, the collective oath, the collective payment and reception and distribution of blood money, are the natural forms of legal relationships in such a society. The balancing act between groups is repeated at a number of levels of size, as many as correspond to possible points of conflict. This produces the characteristic 'nesting' effect, with groups being parts of larger groups which organizationally, functionally and terminologically resemble them, so that there is no one crucial and pre-eminent level or unit. 'Balanced opposition' is found at every level. Groups have only weak leadership, which in fact, and sometimes in law, is elective and depends on the support of the led. Groups are only activated into effective cooperation by conflict, though they are periodically reminded of their existence by ritual. The balance of power and the activation of cohesion by external threat, which is only *a* principle of order maintenance in other societies, here becomes *the* pre-eminent one and very nearly the only one.

The other line of influence leads directly from Masqueray to Robert Montagne, whose *Les Berbères et le Makhzen* (Paris, 1930) is specifically concerned with Morocco and whose debt to Masqueray is as evident as Evans-Pritchard's to Durkheim (and more fully acknowledged). The British social anthropologists were more concerned with the mechanics of tribal order maintenance than with tribe-state relations, whereas Montagne was concerned with both. In connection with the former problem, his theory of the crucial role of moieties, of *leff*-s, resembled the Durkheim/Evans-Pritchard theory, except in so far as it failed to include the 'nesting' effect, the operation of the same principle of 'balanced opposition' at quite diverse levels of size. On the other hand, he added an important and fascinating theory concerning the oscillation of these societies between two forms, the participatory egalitarian model on one hand and, on the other, the ephemeral emergence of strong chieftaincies. He also had much of interest to say about the relationship of both tribes and chiefs to the state. Masqueray and Montagne, both of them, were also directly influenced by Ibn Khaldun and can be considered to be of his intellectual lineage. Montagne influenced the American anthropologist Carlton Coon and thus, through him, David Hart.

The idea that early, or should one rather say stateless man, is a collectivist rather than an anarchist is of course a very widespread one, and it would be absurd to claim a North African origin for it. Nevertheless, Ibn Khaldun and his successors (both those who read him, and those who were influenced by the same North African material) provide one of the most concrete and realistic illustrations of the point. They show Thomas Hobbes to be wrong: the life of pre-state man is not solitary, poor, nasty, brutish and short. Rather, it is gregarious and cohesive, relatively well-off, human and participatory, and with about as good a chance of longevity as that of his centrally governed contemporary. The state itself is born of the cohesion of the stateless community, and atomization is the consequence of political order, rather than of its absence . . .

In due course the notion of segmentation, with a somewhat modified content, also migrated from social anthropology to political science, and was used to characterize and hopefully to explain the kind of political system in which rival patronage networks struggle for control, cutting across social stratification, and using ideology only in the most nominal, perfunctory sense. This approach is visible, for instance, in John Waterbury's influential study of the Moroccan political system, *The Commander of the Faithful*.

With the end of colonialism this entire tradition, or cluster of traditions, came to be subjected to sustained criticism. Robert Montagne no doubt constituted the summit of French colonial ethnography and sociology in Morocco, and so his ideas suffered from their association with their author's political position. His final book, written not long before his death, *Révolution au Maroc*, predicted the failure of Moroccan nationalism, and it was almost immediately refuted by events. Yet though his specific prediction was mistaken, that cannot be said of his supporting analysis. He used the right reasons for the wrong conclusion. He argued that the ideological nationalists could not succeed because they ignored the social realities of the Moroccan countryside. If one reformulates his question and asks why it was that the traditional centre of authority prevailed over the leftist radicals, one can still obtain a good deal of illumination from that volume.

But all this is relatively specific debate, and a matter of the past. During more recent decades, anglophone social anthropology underwent a new and curious mutation, within which two themes can be discerned. One of them is the conviction that the subject should be the study, not of social structures, but of systems of meaning ('cultures'). The other is the passionate desire to atone for the sins of colonialism. The two themes have a curious link. It is held that the study of social structures involves seeing other people's social organization in one's own terms, and was in fact used both as a means of domination and as a ratification of that domination. The clarity and objectivity to which this kind of anthropology aspired were spurious. By contrast, if we start out from the basic equality of all systems of meaning, and try merely to convey one system to members of another, we shall both refrain from claiming or endorsing inequalities *and* we shall get our method right. The 'interpretive' method guarantees inter-cultural equality; inter-cultural equality demands the interpretive method.

Is it just an accident that many of the most influential practitioners of this hermeneutic-relativist turn, whether in its early and moderate form (Clifford Geertz) or in its more extreme version (Paul Rabinow, Vincent Crapanzano) worked in Morocco? Be that as it may, the curious consequence is that very specific issues, concerning the nature of order maintenance in the Moroccan countryside, are argued out in the context of an extremely abstract and elusive general issue, concerning the very nature of society and the possibility of understanding it. Is order maintained (or was it) by groups of patrilateral cousins mutually frightening each other into restraint? – a good concrete question – is argued out in the context of whether there is an objective way of describing societies, or whether such objectivity masks domination, and the correct procedure is to transmit alien meanings through eccentric and obscure literary devices. It should be added that not all critics of the theory of segmentation are motivated by wider and abstract concerns: scholars such as Abdallah Hammoudi or Henry Munson or Dale Eickelman have been led to criticize it for quite concrete reasons.

This is not the place to settle either the wider or the narrower issue, if indeed they are to be settled definitively at all. All I have tried to do, with brevity and as much objectivity as I can summon (given that I have my own strongly felt viewpoint on these questions), is to summarize the issues and sketch the history of the debate. I have omitted scholars whose work does not directly relate to his debate (Fatma Mernissi, Jacques Berque, André Adam, L. Rose, H. Geertz, Raymond Jamous, Ken Brown, D. Seddon, Elaine Combs-Schilling, Vanessa Maher and many others).

But it may amuse Moroccans, and Maghrebins generally, to see how their own society has been used as a (political and philosophical) projection test by the wider scholarly community. One can only await their own verdict with impatience.

14

Lawrence of Moravia

Alois Musil (1868–1944) is known to Western anthropologists only as the author of *The Manners and Customs of the Rwala Bedouin* (1928). It is the standard, and to this day probably the best, ethnography of the North Arabian bedouin, extensively used (with acknowledgement) by subsequent writers on the subject, such as, for instance, Michael Meeker in *Literature and Violence in North Arabia* (1979). There is also an important later study of the Rwala by William Lancaster, *The Rwala Bedouin Today* (1981). Apart from this, little or nothing is known about Musil in the West. Two Austrian biographies have been published (Erich Feigl's *Musil von Arabien: Vorkämpfer der islamischen Welt*, Ullstein, Berlin, 1988, and Karl Johannes Bauer's *Alois Musil: Wahrheitssucher in der Wüste*, Böhlau, Vienna, 1989), and there is some writing in Czech about him, notably some biographical essays and a bibliography, which appeared on the occasion of the centenary of his birth in 1968, a year during which, however, other and more dramatic events in Prague were bound to distract attention from the Musil celebrations.

The two biographies in German are not independent of each other: Feigl, a journalist, published first, but acknowledges help from Bauer, the historian, who presented his dissertation in 1985 and later reworked it as a book. The two volumes overlap to some extent, both in material and in interpretation. The print, photographs and scholarly apparatus are better in Bauer's book; the crucial map of Musil's travels is more legible in Feigl's, which also fits more easily into a pocket. Neither of the two authors appears to have mastered Czech, which is probably a necessary, though perhaps not a sufficient condition for interpreting Musil's *pensée intime*.

The fact that Alois Musil is so little known is strange, in so far as he is one of the most remarkable men of our century, whose life is profoundly significant in a wide variety of ways. First of all, most dramatic, though perhaps not in the end most important, he was the T.E. Lawrence of the other side in the First World War, of the Central Powers. He was probably a more effective and successful soldier than Lawrence, not merely because he attained higher rank – Major-General, or sub-Field Marshal – but because he achieved more, with smaller means and much less support. Musil aimed to stop the North Arabian tribes and sheikhs from fighting each other or the Turks, and if possible make them resist the English and their allies. In this he seems to have succeeded: the very fact that the Turks held out in Medina right to the end of the war, the fact that the little trains went on chugging along the Hejaz railway (on occasion to be pillaged by Lawrence's men), the fact that Lawrence's successes came so late in the war and did not greatly affect its outcome – all this bears testimony to Musil's success. The two men knew of each other. Lawrence noted that strange things were happening, that an Austrian, as he described him, was advising the Turkish General Staff in Damascus. Lawrence added wryly that he hoped that the Turks made better use of Musil's expertise than the English made of his own.

Musil had an opportunity to express his views on Lawrence in 1935 in a talk on Czech radio, after Lawrence had killed himself on his motorbike. The title of the talk included the word 'legend' and was not uncritical: Feigl observes that it disproves the widely held view that obituaries are never truthful. Bauer quotes from it more extensively. Musil refers to Lawrence's defective mastery of Arabic, the fact that, though he did indeed constitute the right flank of the (British) army in Palestine and Trans-Jordan, he had never set foot in Arabia proper and was unknown there, that gold rather than his charisma secured him followers, and that they deserted him as soon as the gold ceased to flow. Musil clearly did not admire the opponent whose fame had so very much exceeded his own. But he did greatly respect him as a writer, and thought that in his genre – which he did not define – there had been nothing as good since the Napoleonic Wars.

Who then was this 'Austrian' who did so well and yet remained unknown while Lawrence became a legend, and how did fame elude him? It is a fascinating and significant story.

Alois Musil was not ethnically Austrian, though he was, as long as the Empire lasted, an eminently loyal and indeed devoted subject of the Habsburgs. He was the son of a Moravian peasant; they must have been solid yeomen, as the family tree can be traced back to the beginning of the eighteenth century. To this day, there is manure in the yard of the family house, now inhabited by Alois Musil's aged last surviving nephew, and the nephew's wife complains bitterly that the apple harvest, unbought while imported apples are on the market, clutters up the living-room. He was a second cousin of the incomparably more famous Robert Musil, the author of *The Man Without Qualities*. The two men knew each other and corresponded, and there is a significant connection between the man who wrote ironically about 'Kakania', as Robert derisively christened the Austrian Empire, and the man who tried to save it. Much of Alois's life seems to come straight out of Robert's great novel. But Robert Musil's branch of the family – the two men shared a great-grandfather – had risen in the world into the middle or upper-middle class, acquiring a 'von' in the process (which, however, Robert did not deign to use), while Alois's family remained on the land, still peasants, albeit solid, prosperous ones. Alois, who had populist sentiments, later in life observed that a nation depends on its peasantry, for they are close to the land. Characteristically, the ascension of Robert's branch meant Germanization, while Alois's remained profoundly Czech in culture and spirit.

Like many other peasants' sons in the area, Alois entered the Church, having decided on this course as a secondary schoolboy. His vocation was serious; his call was to scholarship as well as to faith, and it was this calling which, oddly enough, was to lead him to high military rank and achievement. The days of military religious orders and of soldier-monks are long past (even if a recent Archbishop of Canterbury did win the MC), but the link between the two spheres is interesting: it was the faith which inspired the scholarship, and that in turn proved to be of military value. Musil's initial patron in the Church was the famous Archbishop Kohn of Olomouc, like Musil himself of rustic Moravian background, but a converted Jew, who refused to pander to anti-Semitism by changing his name. The no doubt apocryphal story circulated that when Franz Josef signed the decree naming Kohn an archbishop, he asked anxiously, 'Ist er wennigstens getauft?' ('Was he at least baptized?') Kohn was later obliged to resign by the Pope. Musil for his part was accused of innovation *in articulis fidei*.

The peasant's son who became a priest had a theological preoccupation: monotheism. This concern was to remain the dominant theme of his life. Among the Arabs, he chose the name Musa, and he named his home in the Czech lands Villa Musa. His faith may have assured him of the validity of monotheism, but this in no way inhibited his curiosity and his sociological theorizing about its social roots. Theology led to the Old Testament, interest in Old Testament society to Hebrew, then to Arabic, and a concern with both the geographical context of Old Testament events and the societies inhabiting the region in Musil's own time. This was not idle curiosity: Musil became convinced that the *desert* provided the clue to the origin and even the maintenance of monotheism. Pastoral nomads had not been converted to monotheism; it was their spirit, their lifestyle, which had engendered it.

As an Old Testament scholar, he explored the toponymy of the Bible. For instance, he became convinced that the real Mount Sinai was somewhere east of Aqaba, a volcanic hill unrelated to the mountain now so named. This seems to make sense: people fleeing from Egypt were hardly likely to ascend an arid and high mountain located on the way back to Egypt. A site east of the Gulf of Aqaba is far more plausible. At about the same time as Malinowski was absorbing the philosophical ideas of Ernst

Mach, which then helped him to transform anthropology from a speculative-historical-genetic discipline into a synchronic-social one, Alois Musil was similarly switching from a concern with the Arabian desert as the locale of the Old Testament to an interest in its current inhabitants: at the centre of his interest were the roots of monotheism in social experience rather than in revelation. It was really the same movement of thought: the social role, not historic origin, provides the real explanation. But Alois Musil merely practised this insight, without turning it into a theory. He was indeed accused of producing naturalistic accounts of biblical miracles. Robert Musil like Malinowski studied Ernst Mach for his doctorate: it is a small world.

The expertise acquired in the course of trying to understand both Old Testament and modern bedouin society – on the assumption that the two resembled each other – turned out to have mundane consequences. Prince Sixtus of Bourbon-Parma (whose sister Zita was the wife of the Crown Prince and so, after 1916, the last Austrian Kaiserin) was eager to undertake an adventurous trip in the Middle East; the ratio of romance to the pursuit of political influence in his motivation is something open to speculation. Nominally, and under a pseudonym, the Prince was the leader of the expedition. But the expedition also needed a trustworthy scholar/guide, and who was more suitable than the man who by then had a very considerable reputation both as explorer and scholar? The British had also tried to recruit him no fewer than three times. Had he agreed to the British propositions, he might actually have been, not Lawrence's Austrian counter-image, but rather, so to speak, Lawrence himself. By 1906 Musil was sufficiently well known as an Arabian explorer cartographer to be asked by the British Foreign Secretary, Sir Edward Grey, to draw the boundary between British-occupied Egypt and Ottoman Palestine. Musil obliged, thereby causing some trouble much later in the century: the Israelis built a hotel on the west side of Eilat (a resort which certainly did not exist in Musil's day), the Egyptians claimed that it lay on their territory, and Musil's map proved their point. Before Musil, there was of course no clear boundary.

But he did not join the British in the war. Instead, through his now established connections at the Habsburg court, he became an *éminence grise* in the Hofburg. In due course there were murmurings about the influence of that Czech priest. Actually, there were at that time two Catholic prelates, connected with each other, who had such a position: Musil, and his friend and fellow scholar Pater Schmidt, head of the Austrian anthropological school, also preoccupied with monotheism and well known for his views concerning monotheism as the original religion of mankind, only lost or diluted by a kind of degenerative religious development. This he combined with some kind of Babylonian-centred diffusionist theory. Father Schmidt was naturally pleased with Alois Musil's ethnography, which seemed to confirm his own more general views.

When later there were bitter allusions to a Habsburg Rasputin, it was not entirely clear whether Musil or Schmidt was meant: perhaps both, as they acted in concert. There is something bizarre about Alois Musil being so described: this sober, unbelievably hard-working, puritanical priest, passionately attracted by the pure, mediationless forms of faith, could hardly be further away from the wild and woolly *man of God* of the Tsarist court. Rasputin had made a significant contribution to the destruction of the Romanov empire, whereas Musil had done as much as any man to save that of the Habsburgs.

By personally establishing a 'Pax Austriaca' in the desert between Palestine, Syria and Iraq, he protected the flanks of the Turkish armies opposing the British coming up from Basra and Egypt. The tribal politics of the period are most complex, though we know a lot about it thanks to the work of scholars such as John Kelly, Madawi Al-Rashid and Joseph Kostiner. Musil even contemplated a bedouin invasion of Egypt across Sinai, which would have been a kind of mirror image of Lawrence's later dash to Damascus. His achievements were despite, rather than with the help of, the Turks: Enver Pasha disliked or distrusted him and hampered his efforts. From his own viewpoint, he was probably right: Musil did not seem to care too much for either Turks or Prussians, and envisaged some kind of Austro-Arab Middle East. As is evident from the documentation of Bauer's book, he did not mind fibbing in his reports to the Germans, so as to mislead them about the situation in the peninsula. The duplicity was reciprocated. At the very same time, it seems, on the testimony of Musil's own book in Czech *Mezi Šamary* ('Among the Shammars', 1931), that Enver Pasha instructed him, Musil, to negotiate peace between the Rashidis of Hail and the Saudis, he also directly instructed the Rashidis to go on fighting the Saudis as allies of the British and as traitors.

Musil was close to action in the complex warfare between the various tribal quasi-states, notably between the Shammar and the Saudis. He gives a vivid account of the death of the British agent attached to the Saudis, based on a report made to him directly by (as he describes him) the black Ibrahim an-Nodeli:

> This revolver I took from the Englishman at Adzhrab. He had a big white hat and fired the gun. He fired seven shots but none of them did any harm . . . they fell in the sand without exploding . . . We threw ourselves at the defenders of the gun and drove them off. The Englishman did not run away but remained with the gun to the last moment. Seeing himself abandoned he looked for his horse, but this had been taken by the fleeing defenders. He ran on foot, sinking into the sand. I urged on my mare . . . suddenly a shot, my mare falls and I with it. I followed the Englishman on foot. I am used to the sand and he is not, and I am barefoot and he is in boots. I soon caught up with him. He stopped, turned, and raised his hands about his head, smiling. I shot at him and hit him in his side. He fell to his knees and again raised his hands . . . I drew my sword and split his head. He must have been about forty years old. His clothes and hat Saud ibn Subhan sent to Medina.

Musil characteristically repeats the story deadpan, without comment.

He does not name the man who literally stuck to his gun, was deserted (and robbed of his horse) by his companions, and was murdered, smiling in a big white hat, by his captor. Obviously this was Captain Shakespeare, agent with the Saudis at the time. This it appears happened on 22 January 1915, and Musil reported it first directly to Vienna, in a letter to Baron Burian, the new

Foreign Minister, dated 27 February 1915. What seems to be the very same story is also recorded in a report sent on 28 June to the German Ambassador in Istanbul, which is now in Bonn in the German archives concerning the First World War. In this version he is concerned to play down the importance of the little battle: there was no victory of the Rashidis over the Saudis, only over a segment of Shammars who had gone over to the other side, and the English were not involved: the unfortunate European gunner, he says, 'was presumably a Dutchman from Batavia, a mercenary in the service of Feysal ben Er-Rashid'. In this report he explicitly says he was present at the fighting at Adzhrab, the location previously given for the English officer's death. The British refer to this engagement as the Battle of Jarrab. For some reason it was important for Musil to discourage the Germans from thinking that the English were involved, and that the Saudis had been beaten. Bauer reproduces both the reports, without, however, commenting on the fact that they evidently refer to the same episode, or noting the deliberate discrepancy between them, or discussing the possible motives for it.

Musil's activity in the desert, important and dramatic though it was, did not constitute his most crucial attempt to change the course of twentieth-century history and save the Empire. The episode which marks the high point of his influence, and which naturally holds the greatest fascination for the Austrians, is the secret attempt by the Austrian Empire and its dynasty to save itself by means of a separate peace. The Empress's brother, whom Musil had guided through the desert, was also a Bourbon (acutely conscious, as he observed in a letter to Musil, of having no fewer than fifty-six sovereign rulers among his ancestors – one wouldn't have thought there were enough thrones and time-slots for so many, but presumably the little sovereign principalities in Italy make this just about possible), and he was well enough placed through his connections to send out feelers to the Allies about the possibility of a separate peace, which might save the dynasty. This was an exceedingly delicate operation, for obvious reasons: the basic idea was to save the Danubian monarchy from dismemberment by means of betraying the German and Turkish allies.

In brutal terms, the proposition made to the Allies was: you let the Habsburgs continue to have the Danube valley, and the French can have Alsace-Lorraine, and the Russians can have Istanbul. In a letter which may or may not constitute supporting evidence for Musil's complicity, he remarks that the loss of Istanbul would be less disastrous for the Turks than the loss of the holy places of the Hejaz.

Poincaré did not choose to keep this feeler secret: once it was out, the initiative naturally had to be disavowed. It is not only the case that treason never prospers, for if it does, no one dare call it such – it is also the case that if it fails, no one admits to having attempted it. This being so, what actually happened is a matter of dispute and speculation among historians: the Empress Zita, sister of Musil's friend and travelling companion, Prince Sixtus, lived on for such a long time that it gave her plenty of opportunities to comment on these intrigues, but she contradicted herself so often that, as Bauer observes, her testimony is worthless, and inspires the suspicion that, to this day, there is an attempt to obscure the truth.

Musil's own testimony, on the other hand, seems plain: by 1917 it was obvious to the new Emperor Karl and to Musil himself that the war was lost and that something like this had to be attempted, and Musil drafted some of the crucial letters connected with the affair. The two priests in the Hofburg were leading theoreticians of monotheism, and field research inspired by this concern led not only to crucial assistance on the ground, on the flanks of the Mesopotamian and Palestinian fronts, but also to the secret diplomacy of war.

It is this mixture of high scholarship, high society and high politics, all in the service of saving Austro-Habsburg culture and polity, which makes Alois's life seem to come straight out of his cousin Robert's novel. The two men knew each other and corresponded. It is hard not to suspect that the celebrations and intrigues described in *The Man Without Qualities* were indeed inspired by Alois's Orientalist Society, founded to promote Austrian influence, commerce and culture in the East: the founding committee contains *tout Vienne* – the Crown Prince, the Mayor of Vienna, Freiherr von Škoda of the Škoda works, *und so weiter*. Here we find all the elements of the Collateral Campaign of the novel.

Musil failed in both his grand designs: no separate peace was arranged which would have saved the Habsburgs, and while Lawrence and his bedouin did in the end reach Damascus, Musil and his never reached Suez. The fact that history is unkind to losers is only part of the explanation of Musil's lack of fame: whereas Lawrence had a genius for publicity, while pretending to flee from it (a flair at which he was rivalled only by Musil's fellow-Austrian, Wittgenstein), Musil in his old age genuinely avoided it and retired into scholarship. Though his cartography and his ethnography of the Rwala appeared in English, his account of his adventures was published only in Czech and so remained unknown to the international public. They are written in a straightforward deadpan style, and their political-military context, though obvious enough, is not explicitly stated: the travels are conspicuously, almost provocatively presented without any explanation of why he was there in the first place. Lawrence's tortured intensity had a literary appeal; Musil's simplicity of style – he practised simplicity, apart from valuing it – led in the end to his being treated as an author of travel adventures for Czech youth. Musil's life did indeed belong to the *fin de siècle*, but his style does not: there is no tortuous obscurity, and I have yet to find a sentence in his work which is not simple and clear.

So, notwithstanding Musil's efforts, whether in the desert or in secret diplomacy, the Habsburg Empire was not saved and was, on the contrary, dismembered. Feigl blames the narrow ethnic chauvinism of the first post-First World War republican Austrian government for helping to drive out Musil from Austria and Vienna, by a decree facilitating the dismissal of all 'non-German-Austrian' employees from the state service. There was no intention to implement it against Musil, but, not surprisingly, given his achievements, he resented even having to fill out any forms or seeing his standing to be *sub judice*. Feigl accuses this decree of as it were anticipating and even surpassing Hitler's Nuremberg laws in their eagerness to restrict employment opportunities in the newly reduced Austria to Austro-Germans. The scholars in Vienna, however, wished to retain him, while those from Prague hoped to entice him there. Whether through push or pull, Prague prevailed. However, a protest was heard in the new Czechoslovak parliament in February 1919 against the appointment of the man who had served with such distinction on the other side. Musil, however, had powerful supporters, above all the new president, Tomáš Masaryk.

There is a great irony in this: during the very time when Musil was endeavouring, at two quite different levels, to save the Habsburg monarchy, Masaryk was doing his utmost to destroy it. Masaryk's strategy during the war was to persuade the Allies of the importance of the Czech contribution to the war, so as to secure independence as a reward, and if only Musil had responded favourably to the British overture, and had been as effective on their side as in fact he was on that of Austria, Masaryk would no doubt have invoked his achievements. As it was, they had to be played down, and this, together perhaps with the simplicity of his literary style, accounts for Musil's obscurity. Despite his involvement on the wrong side, the Czech foreign minister contemplated taking Musil along to the Versailles negotiations, but desisted in the light of the consideration that the British would have him arrested. This does not sound plausible: Musil was not guilty of any war crimes, and did the British have either the power or the inclination to arrest members of *allied* delegations to Versailles?

Masaryk, on this occasion as on others, was generous, and did his best to aid Musil after the war: apart from assistance in securing the chair of Arabic at Charles University, he also introduced Musil to Charles Robert Crane, the American patron of scholarship (whose family incidentally supplied Masaryk with his American daughter-in-law). This eventually led to the American publication of the one book of Musil's which causes him to be known among Western anthropologists. It is dedicated to Masaryk, and expresses gratitude for his encouragement; it was printed in Prague. The book is also illustrated with a portrait of Musil in bedu dress, described by the caption as a Rwala sheikh, Musa. George Sarton, editor of *Isis*, reviewing the book, concluded from this that the learned sheikh Musa must have assisted Musil in his inquiries. He did indeed. Musa was Musil.

Musil and Masaryk had been diametrically opposed to each other in their wartime efforts: otherwise there was far more to bring them together than to separate them, and it is reasonable to suspect that they had a strong sympathy for each other. Both were Moravian peasants by background, both had risen from this background to become professors, both had initially gravitated to Vienna. Both were tough and brave, both were Hanáks, natives of the Haná plain of southern Moravia, and both conspicuously lived up to the Hanák reputation for stubbornness and vigour. 'Hanáci držte se' (Hanáks stand fast) was a saying even in the *K. und K.* army. It is plausible to suspect that the logic of the path which had led them to their respective and opposed stances in the war was similar: each of them was a puritan, with a strong sense of the connection between monotheism and genuine morality, and each experienced a strong attraction to direct, unmediated religion, in which a deity imposes moral obligation on the individual without the assistance of too much ritual or mediators. This attitude led Masaryk to leave the Catholic Church, and in the end to oppose the Empire which had been linked to it (notwithstanding the fact that, by then, the link was less than firm), and to idealize the Hussites who, without abolishing clergy or ritual, at least insisted on the equality of believers, lay or clergy, in ritual. It was this which made them into *Utraquists*. All this led Masaryk to a philosophy of history which connected the authoritarianism of Church with that of the Empire, and found the meaning of history in overcoming both of them, thereby justifying the establishment of a new state, which he liked to see as a revival of the Hussite inspiration. Masaryk only turned against the Habsburgs late in life, after hesitation, and in exceptional circumstances: there are good grounds for suspecting that the overall philosophy of history he invokes – history as the progression from authoritarian states and churches to liberal democratic ones – was in part a rationalization for a political decision only reached ambivalently, and not shared at the time by most of his compatriots.

Musil clearly had what *au fond* were very similar sentiments about religion, even though they led him, theologically and politically, in quite a different direction. He idealized not the Hussites but the bedouin. He thought that he found in them that direct relation to God and the moralism, rather than ritualism, which

Protestants value. The nationalist or Masarykian vision of the Czechs is that of suppressed Hussite Protestants, the Marranos of the Reformation: the nation was, as Friedrich Schiller put it, driven to Mass by force. If this interpretation applies to Musil, then he found an ingenious way of sublimating his Moravian Brethren sentiments: as a Catholic scholar, he studied and adored the bedouin. The reasons he had for admiring the bedouin could hardly be more relevant to the religious dilemma which had divided Europe:

> Divine service is different among nomads and settled people. Nomads have no sacred places, no images, no priests, not even rituals. In their religion they closely resemble the biblical patriarchs. In friendly conversation I asked my brother Nuri, prince of the Rwala – 'How is it that you have no places dedicated to the service of Allah?'
>
> 'Musa, we cannot have them . . . it takes us five years to camp again in the same place . . . Is not Allah present everywhere? . . . We pray to him in foreign lands and serve him without sacred places or a temple.'
>
> 'Have you no picture or object which would represent God?'
>
> 'We have none. As you have said to me, God is spirit. How could one represent spirit?'
>
> 'Have you no mediation between yourselves and God?'
>
> 'God is my father, I am his son. Is there need of mediation between father and son?'

The bedu sheikh, if this is an accurate account of his feelings, should make an ideal member of the Moravian Brethren. This account of a remembered conversation between Musil and his main patron and 'brother', sheikh Nuri of the Rwala, is taken from an unpublished final work of Musil's, 'Ze Světa Islámu' (From the World of Islam), on which he was working when he died, and which has never been either published or translated. A short fragment, which includes this conversation, was published as part of the Czech catalogue accompanying the exhibition held in Moravia on the occasion of the centenary of Musil's birth in 1968. The as it were Protestant, anti-mediation, anti-ritual, and anti-graven-images sentiments could hardly be clearer: it would seem to be the nomads, whether at the time of biblical or contemporary patriarchs, who tread the correct path in religion. It is interesting to reflect that three south Moravians were, during and after the end of the century, meditating on monotheism and morality: Tomas, Sigmund and Alois (in order of age). Tomas was led to a theory of history which postulates a secular transition from authoritarian states and churches to liberal ones, and it made him leave the Church and develop an idealization of Hussites; Sigmund thought he found the origins of monotheism in Egyptian court intrigue, and of puritanism in acceptance by underdogs of a monotheism rejected at court; while Alois stayed in the Church, but gave vent to puritan Protestant sentiments in his idealization of the bedouin whom he turned into a kind of specially pure Protestants.

Feigl claims that Musil was hostile to Zionist political aspirations, not indeed from anti-Semitism, but from concern with the impact these aims would have on the indigenous population. Bauer offers more evidence on this point, and the situation seems more complex. Max Brod wrote to Musil about this at Masaryk's instigation, but unfortunately the reply does not seem to have survived, though we do have the text of an article of Musil's in *Prager Presse* of 24 September 1921, on the occasion of the Zionist congress in Karlsbad earlier that month. In this he affirms that 'this great hour' of the Jewish people interests him as an orientalist and as a man, and that he has sympathized (*mitempfinden*) with the strivings of the Jewish soul since 1895. It is true that he is clear about the problems: he warns the Jews that they have only enemies in Palestine (whether Muslim or Christian, whether Arab or English or French), and so repeatedly commends unity to the Zionists, if they are to achieve the end of a 'free and complete national life in their homeland' (*Heimat*).

The advice he offers to the Zionists, in another article ('The New Europe', 3 June 1920) is interesting. The Zionists should waste no thought on the founding of universities, they should first work on the establishment of *basic* schools. This is very much the Czech speaking: the correct strategy for national revival is the concentration on elementary education, which is the basis for all else. One easily imagines Musil echoing the Masarykian slogan of *drobná práce* – work on the details, on the base, slowly, thoroughly, patiently.

Some advice also comes from Musil the orientalist rather than the Czech: he does not think the revival of Hebrew is a good idea. Better repeat the post-Babylonian practice. Those who returned from the exile used Hebrew for religion, but Aramaic for daily life. Arabic is no further from Hebrew than Aramaic, so why not respect this precedent and thereby gain the advantage of easy communication with neighbours? Musil does not think it likely that European colonists will take to agricultural work in Palestine: the place is too hot. He recommends instead an accurate (*genau*) study of surviving Jewish agricultural communities in long-forgotten Mesopotamian villages, with a view to applying the findings to the education of immigrants. 'The strength of a nation lies in its peasantry.' This would also assist, he adds, the fusion of colonists with the indigenous Sephardim, and so further understanding between Progress and Orthodoxy.

Musil's love-life has, at least so far, excited or justified less curiosity than Lawrence's. Bauer reports a persistent rumour among orientalists that Musil had secretly married a bedu girl, but suggests this may originate from an episode reported by Musil himself, that a sheikh had offered him his own daughter in marriage and his wealth in inheritance, given that he had not been blessed with a son. This is a curious story for Musil to tell without comment, as customary law would make it hard for the father to ignore the prior claims of patrilateral kin, whether to girl or property. Under normal circumstances, a sheikh would hardly get away with such a design. Musil himself makes this point about customary tribal law very firmly and explicitly in his book (in English) on the Rwala.

In his old age, Musil's most important relation seems to have been to a secretary, Anna Blechová, who was deeply devoted to his work. As she herself reports, not without humour, he observed to her – 'I knew how to work even before you came to me, but it was you who taught me how to slave away.' She does make one intriguing remark: she notes that in his final years (he died in 1944), though preoccupied with world politics, he 'did not fully anticipate the developments which took place'. Is this a discreet hint of a political alignment not held acceptable at the time these lines were written? There may be more to be found out here. One might add that though Musil was a puritan in most ways – he once reproached one of his disciples for indulging in the luxury of a weekly bath – he did like taking wine, including champagne, along into the desert, and was, it appears, a connoisseur.

So Musil constitutes an exceedingly complicated, paradoxical and difficult case for those who would damn all Western observers of the East as inspired by the need to misrepresent and to dominate. Which side was he on, in this Manichean conflict? As a Czech-Moravian peasant he was not a member of an imperial race. Was he colonist or colonized? He served an empire which was also the ally, not enemy, of an *Asian* empire, the two trying to prop each other up and failing jointly. Both were archaic and non-national. The Asian empire in question was none too kind to its own Asian subjects, in turn. He was, it is true, eager to enhance the Habsburg influence in the Middle East, and hoped to secure for it a kind of protectorate over the local Catholics. He would not have minded the establishment of an Arab state in the peninsula friendly to 'us'; in this he resembled Lawrence.

But in the end, on the crucial matter concerning where truth is to be found, and where the honour for its discovery is due, there was nothing Euro-chauvinistic about him. Quite the reverse. The great insight, for Musil, is the work of Semites, and not of Greeks:

> The traces of the Old Testament Ark of the Covenant led to the inner desert . . . I was eager to enter the psychic life of true Semites, unmixed with alien elements, not subject to alien domination, and so never directly subject to an external enlightenment . . . the familiarity with the psychic activity of true Semites in their homeland was very profitable for me, for it had to show me the reasons, why it was just the Semites who bestowed the three monotheisms on the world. Why did the Semites solve mysteries, whose significance escaped even the greatest Greek thinkers? Why was it just the Semites, who created no philosophical schools, who enriched the ancient world with insights which are, even for us, the source of ever new conjectures? I could only answer these questions in the Arabian desert.

So the crucial truth was discovered by Semites, both in ancient and modern times, and it was bestowed on them by their life in the desert and not by some capricious revelation. It is timeless, springing from a way of life, not from a specific source. A posthumous Czech article asked, plausibly enough, whether Professor Musil had been a Muslim? The proper question might have been – was he not some kind of generic monotheist, a secretly undenominational Unitarian? He thought the bedouin were monotheists but barely Muslim, only learning about their formal religion during the period he was investigating them. But they were being converted, according to him, not from some pagan polytheism, but from a kind of natural, primordial monotheism. They had learnt it from their life, not from preachers. He has some difficulty with their addiction to a faith in *jnun*, and he would need to maintain – though as far as I know he never actually said – that *jahiliyya* is an unwarranted projection by urban Muslims on to the bedouin, who in their natural state were never guilty of it. Truth is to be found in purity, simplicity, monotheism, and these emerge in the wilderness. Ibn Khaldun had taught that the desert engendered virtue, Musil thought it brought forth truth. *Extra solitudinem nulla salus*. How could a vision dependent on a special form of life be universally valid? He does not seem to have pursued this question. Perhaps virtue alone brings truth, and we should all seek virtue in simplicity. In his old age in Moravia, his lifestyle was certainly populist. He assiduously tended his numerous fruit trees (he planted no fewer than 5,000), and made sure of proper land use, when he was not engaged in scholarship. Was it atonement or consolation he sought on the land? Among the Arabs he had been a vicarious populist, but unlike others of that ilk, he sought purity rather than tradition. This Moravian puritan can hardly be even suspected of wishing to denigrate or dominate, or of lacking respect for those from whose spirit and condition he was so very eager to learn.

15

Anthropology and Europe[1]

Those who worked on the creation of the European Association of Social Anthropologists are to be warmly congratulated. By coincidence, their labours were crowned with success at the very moment at which Europe was also being reunited, and Eastern Europe liberated. It will not be possible, and ought not be possible, to see the creation of a *European* association of anthropologists in isolation from the tremendous events which have changed the political and cultural map of Europe.

The birfurcation and reunification of Europe has in the past played a major role in the development of social thought. Since the Middle Ages, the bifurcation of Europe has occurred twice. The first time round, it was the consequence of the break-up of the medieval religious unity of Western Europe, brought about by the Reformation, confirmed by the acceptance of that deep division at the Peace of Westphalia in 1648, and the enthronement of the principle of *cuius regio eius religio*. Henceforth the Counter-Reformation was to share Europe with the Reformation.

The end of the wars of religion was, I suppose, the first occurrence of *détente*. Henceforth, the two systems were to indulge in

[1] Delivered as the opening speech of the foundation meeting of the European Association of Social Anthropologists in Coimbra in 1990.

coexistence and compete by peaceful methods, at least most of the time. In due course, it became fairly obvious who had won. The principle of economic growth was not yet formally recognized as *the* foundation of social and political legitimacy, but in effect it was already operating. The commercial and Protestant societies of north-west Europe were surpassing the southern lands which under Counter-Reformation tutelage were reimposing, perhaps in a harsher form, the old values and social principles.

Reflections on this inequality are known as the Enlightenment and constitute the effective commencement of modern social theory and investigation. The Enlightenment gave direction and meaning to the French Revolution. The fact that the Revolution led first to terror and then to dictatorship provided further food for reflection. Evidently, social *rattrapage* could not be achieved quite so easily by the simple application of reason to society, which had been the Enlightenment recipe. A more sophisticated understanding of the social material which was to be transformed was required, it appeared.

Of these diagnoses of the failure of the French Revolution, of the attempts to do it better the second time round, Marxism was certainly the most influential and probably the most elaborate and best orchestrated. It incorporated the knowledge available in their time to the founding fathers, and thus presented itself as the culmination of current wisdom. Ironically, when it succeeded in possessing itself of a state, and eventually a whole cluster of states, it succeeded, once again, in bifurcating Europe. Yalta was a kind of Westphalian peace, confirming that 'cuius regio eius socio-economic system'. The social theory, born of the consequences of the north–south division of Europe, ended by imposing an east–west one.

Once again, the two systems had to compete in peace. This time, they weren't even persuaded of the need to do so by a very prolonged bloody war with each other. They had indeed fought a bloody war with a third party, but the main thing which persuaded them of the need for peaceful competition, and induced them to abide by its rules, was the fact that weapons by now were so terrible that an outright conflict would have destroyed both parties to it, and there could have been no victor.

This time, the outcome of the peaceful competition made itself felt and visible much more quickly – and more quickly than virtually anyone anticipated. For one thing, vindication by economic success had not earlier been a recognized principle, and for another, economic growth was now incomparably more rapid, and relative failure became correspondingly more conspicuous. The majority of the population were no longer peasants living in self-contained communities, capable of maintaining production even when relatively isolated from the outside world. Now the great majority, either side of the new curtain, were urbanized and industrialized, and the severing of communications appears to have had a disastrous effect on productivity. So the Bolsheviks failed to emulate the achievement of the Jesuits. *This* division of Europe lasted a mere forty years, or at worst, seventy.

The reunification of Europe in 1989 is an event comparable with the French Revolution and the Reformation in its significance. It has been quite wrongly compared with 1848. To my knowledge, Metternich did not, in 1848, instruct Windischgratz, Radecky and Jelacic not to use any force against the rebels, and warn them that they must expect no support from him if they did so. The uprisings of that year had come from below and they failed; those of 1989 were triggered off and inspired from above, and they succeeded. They were the consequence of, to my mind, a wholly unprecedented recognition by the leaders of an ideocracy that their ideology had failed.

What matters about the momentous events of that year is not simply that Europe had been reunited, but that it was reunited in terms of a new perception of social reality. That perception does not as yet possess a clear outline. What it rejects is obvious; what it endorses less so. Perhaps it will never acquire a sharp outline: perhaps it is of the essence of the social order which prevailed in the peaceful competition which had lasted forty or seventy years, that it is not and never will be based on a coherent vision, but, on the contrary, will embody an untidy pragmatic compromise. Perhaps the End of Ideology thesis is vindicated after all. The theory born of the malaise of the first great bifurcation of Europe has both failed *and* engendered a new bifurcation, and that has now come to an end. We will have to rethink it all, even if the fruits of our thoughts will not provide material for a new grand ideology, even if the time of such ideologies is over. We shall see.

A social science such as anthropology cannot remain indifferent to these changes. It is, after all, rooted in them. Social anthropology, at any rate as practised in Britain and in what may be called the intellectual sterling zone, is linked in its origins to the history of European thought and its internal divisions. British social anthropology, as a formal profession with its own guild, its very effectively imposed standards, its idiom and its shared paradigm, really goes back to Bronislaw Malinowski and the functionalist revolution and the replacement of Frazer by Malinowski as the model anthropologist. This transformation, which took place between the wars, was most intimately connected with another interesting bifurcation of Europe, one not identical with those mentioned so far, but not unrelated to them. This is the division between individualists/universalists and romantics/holists.

Ever since the late eighteenth century, European thought had been divided between two traditions, the individualism exemplified by a line running from Descartes to Hume and Kant, and a romantic collectivism which arose in reaction to this, at first anticipated by Vico, but becoming really influential through the work of thinkers such as Herder and Hegel. The former tradition culminated in a vision in which the ultimate court of appeal for cognitive and moral claims was the individual consciousness, which judges whatever claims were made upon it by confronting them with its own data, or setting them against its own inescapable inner structure. This was, if you like, the Protestant doctrine of the sovereignty of conscience, articulated in secular, or semi-secular, philosophic dress. By contrast, the romantic tradition, which arose in opposition to the Cartesians and empiricists, insisted that intellectual and moral life was a team game, that it was practised by entire and ongoing collectivities, and that intellectual life, in all its aspects, could only be carried on in terms of a set of shared ideas and practices preserved by a community, rather than excogitated by isolated individual minds. Real knowledge was a communal good and could not be privatized.

Both these traditions were liable to be in opposition to the remains of feudalism and baroque absolutism, but on behalf of different contestants: one on behalf of a liberal individualism, an open society, and the other on behalf of the newly emerging or re-emerging ethnic collectivities, affirming the new principle that political units should be based on 'nations'. The confrontation between the two trends was, for fairly obvious reasons connected with its history and composition, most sharply articulated in the Habsburg Empire. A dynastic state closely linked to the Counter-Reformation, to faith and hierarchy, was challenged by both the liberals and the nationalists. The liberals found their ideology in an atomistic individualism, which was empiricist in its theory of knowledge: it can be no accident that the most eloquent and profound formulations of liberalism in our century come from Vienna, from the work of men such as Hayek and Popper, and that so many modern formulations of empiricism are rooted in the work of Ernst Mach. The nationalists, on the other hand, found their idiom in some kind of romantic celebration of the communal life of the village and of a shared but idiosyncratic, rather than universal, culture.

This was the confrontation. The individualists had an acute sense of the need to validate claims in the individual's experience, which was not to be taken in by self-sustaining and woolly mythologies; the romantics, on the other hand, were acutely aware of the pervasiveness and unity and interrelatedness of *culture*. The individualists saw society and culture as the mere summation of individual aims and strategies; the romantics saw the way in which a culture spoke and acted *through* individuals, who found their true fulfilment in it, and they also had a fine sense of historic continuity.

Most of the participants in the debate took part on one side or the other. It is well known that every philosophical baby that is born alive is either a little positivist or a little Hegelian. By and large, the babies that appeared conformed to this division of the world, and located themselves on one or other side of the big divide. But not Bronislaw Malinowski. Therein lies his uniqueness, and it is connected with the manner in which he established a new discipline and a new profession.

Through his entire background, his father's interest in Polish dialects, his long sojourns in Zakopane and observation of the *gurali*, his involvement with the littérateurs of the turbulent and romantic modernist movement, through all this he was receptive to the sense of culture and a sense of its unity. East European nationalist and populist ethnographers did not go into the villages in order to test ideas about the early history of mankind: they went there to observe, record, codify, protect and strengthen a national culture. Love rather than theoretical universality inspired them. But if, with one part of his background, Malinowski belonged to the romantics, he was also a person whose dissertation was devoted to neo-positivism, to Mach and Avenarius. He was acutely sensitive to the Machian tendency to replace inferences to unobservables by constructions out of observables, and the two themes in Mach which specially struck him were, on one hand, the need to relate ideas to their experiential base, and on the other, where such a base on its own was inadequate, to invoke the functional needs of the organism as an explanation of this trespass.

It is the combination of these two elements which engendered the distinctive Malinowskian functionalisms in anthropology. The romantic hypostatization of culture was retained, but was justified in quite a new way by an empiricist epistemology. The sense of culture as an independent reality was detached from a worship of history: on the contrary, history was subjected to a severe empiricist critique. In primitive societies, where records are lacking, the historical speculation indulged in by the observer, on the basis of local beliefs and customs, was condemned as being, as it often was, speculative and untestable. It was replaced by the most characteristically Malinowskian treatment of beliefs about the past as *charters* of current practices, which was as neat an example of the implementation of the Machian principle of replacing inferences to unobservables by functional services within the observable as you could wish to find. The nationalist and populist practice of immersion in a culture, for the love of that culture, was turned into the main methodological tool of the new science, and endowed with a positivist rationale. The East European romantic moved from the Carpathians to the Trobriands, did much the same thing as before, but provided new reasons for so doing.

This served his scientific career: his holism and his positivistically based anti-historicism (no speculative, baseless reconstructions of the past) enabled him to overturn Frazerian anthropology at both its central points – its magpie-like, contextless method of collecting data, without bothering about the place they occupied in their cultures, and its assumption of an evolutionist explanatory schema. But it also suited his political predilection, his cultural nationalism and his political internationalism.

He was not the only Central European to react against the excessive use of history by nationalists: in a neighbouring Slav culture, T.G. Masaryk in effect defined his general position, which he called 'realism', as the avoidance of an exaggerated historicism in the pushing of national claims and formulation of policies. The difference between Masaryk and Malinowski was that the former went only part of the way in moderating, but not altogether abjuring, historicism, whereas Malinowski was uncompromising and total in replacing invocations of the past by invocations of present, synchronic function; and Masaryk did it all in the field in which the issue had arisen, in politics and social theory, whereas Malinowski so to speak sublimated it all into social anthropology. The suspicion of the current, political uses of the past, which must have arisen from his observation of the political practices which surrounded him, was displaced, and reappeared as a methodological principle in the dispassionate investigation of simpler societies . . .

There was, in a sense, no historic necessity for Malinowski to be the first one to link the cult of intensive, as it were immersive fieldwork with an empiricist justification. His predecessor and senior at the London School of Economics, Edward Westermarck, in many ways exemplified the same mixture as did Malinowski: as a Finnish Swede, he had more cause than Malinowski to detach himself from local ethnic romanticism. (It is not entirely clear why Malinowski did so – there was nothing in his background which would push him in such a direction – but the fact is, he did.) Westermarck, like Malinowski, was attracted by British empiricism, and much given to the practice of fieldwork: but he continued to be magpie-like in method and evolutionist in theory, and the fusion of empiricist philosophical background and fieldwork practice did not in his case, as it did in Malinowski's, engender the new functionalist style.

It was thus that the characteristically British style of social anthropology was born: the blending of the field research practice born of East European populist nationalism with the philosophical premises supplied by radical empiricism . . . This paternity has continued to be dominant till this day: the basic profile of the profession and its paradigm has not really changed. Levi-Straussian *structuralisme* provided new reasons for continuing the old synchronicist idiom, based on questionable analogies with linguistics: what works for phonetics does not work for society. It also favoured a shift of attention, away from social structure to culture, a shift in any case encouraged by the end of colonialism and the erosion or inaccessibility of structures. The late intrusion, or return, of Marxism to anthropology did not really mean that anthropologists found Marxism useful; rather it meant that Parisians who were Marxists anyway decided to attend, for once, to some ethnographic facts. And finally, there came the interpretive or hermeneutic twist in anthropology.

This was linked, with a curious time lag, to decolonization and to the expiation of European colonial guilt. The argument was that the lucidity sought, and sometimes attained, by Malinowskian anthropologists, in constructing models of alien societies, was itself a tool or a form of domination, and that its practitioners were insufficiently worried about the manner in which they were imposing their own vision on their material. Clarity of style and thought were themselves declared suspect. Descartes had led to Kipling: not Kipling, therefore not Descartes. Clarity was henceforth to be abjured and replaced by an awareness of the fact that there is indeed an investigator, whose own culture imposes itself in the very concepts he uses, and that he must lay himself bare before he can dare present his findings. If his findings are clear, then he is probably a positivist dominator. Atonement for the sins of domination is best displayed by laying bare one's soul, and the soul had better be a complex and tormented one, externalizing itself in correspondingly tortured prose. The impoverished masses of the Third World may find consolation in the thought that their erstwhile oppressors and exploiters are now suffering the agonies of obscurity of style.

This kind of hermeneutic turn in anthropology, especially in its later and extreme avatars, is simply idealism in a new idiom: the assumption, not always applied consistently, is that conceptual constraints, not physical or economic ones, are what really make societies into what they are. This method is objectionable for various reasons, including precisely the fact that it prejudges the question of the relative importance of conceptual and coercive constraints, in favour of the former. It is claimed, for instance, that it is what the state *means*, rather than what it does, which really matters. In small print, we then also read that, after all, it could not be what it is (and hence, presumably, mean what it means), if it were not also capable of coercing . . . Or again, practitioners of this style justify the tortuousness of their own presentation by the fact that the world has become more complex since the days of the first generation of Malinowskian functionalists. It has indeed: but to say this is to concede that an external social reality is after all available for exploration and characterization – for you have just characterized it. So the *other* cannot be quite so excruciatingly inaccessible – which is *also* claimed . . . It can also be said against this movement that, ironically, it does not really advance the understanding of the role of 'meaning' in social life, by using it as an irreducible ultimate category, as a means of self-titivation rather than analysis.

There is a further and perhaps most important objection to this kind of vision. It pretends, in the name of expiation of past sins of domination and inter-cultural inequality, to establish that all forms of cognition are equal, that the explication of one in terms of another is inadmissible, and so it encourages a certain style, in which indulgence in the exquisite torment of inability to transcend the chasm which separates the investigator from his object replaces any attempt to say anything very coherent about the object. But this affectation of cognitive equality is indeed nothing but an affectation. *The* central fact about our world is that, for better or for worse, a superior, more effective form of cognition does exist. It was, inevitably, born within the womb of one culture, for anything must begin somewhere; but it is perfectly obvious by now that it is not linked to any one society, culture or tradition, but accessible to all mankind, and, as it happens, it appears that it is implemented most effectively at present within cultures within which it had *not* originated . . . But the simple fact is that a form of knowledge exists, known as science, which appears to possess a number of astonishing characteristics: it grows continually, it is open-ended, yet at the same time there is an extraordinary degree of consensus among its practitioners, a consensus *not* imposed by coercion; it transcends any one culture, and is liable to undermine the favoured beliefs of all of them; and it is being universally, though perhaps not wholeheartedly and consistently adopted, for the simple reason that it leads to exceedingly powerful technology, such that those not possessed of it become helplessly weak and subject to a humiliating 'relative deprivation'.

This is the central fact of our world. Those who, in the pursuit of an exaggerated and somewhat belated expiation, would deny it, consequently start out from a premise *so* far removed from the actual reality of our situation that their thought can be little other than self-indulgent delusion. We cannot change facts, even if inter-cultural equality were incompatible with a given fact. Sartre, for instance, was wrong when he argued that it was legitimate to deny facts, so as to save a French working-class suburb from despair. Likewise, we are not entitled to deny blatant facts, even *if* it were the case that this is a precondition of saving Bongo-Bongo from despair or humiliation. But in fact, it is not anything of the kind. On the contrary, inventing an absurd philosophy in the interests of pleasing the natives of Bongo-Bongo is, in reality, an insulting, offensive act of condescension. We do not lie or commit self-deception on behalf of those whom we respect.

Perhaps this self-indulgent subjectivism had deep social roots. Mankind has, in the matter of *belief*, passed through a number of stages. First there was a period when humanity had rituals and legends, but no theory, no theology. Then came a time where, for some cultures at least, the centre of gravity of religion shifted to theory, to *doctrine*. Finally there came a time when the unique knowledge separated itself from any claims to a transcendent source or authority, but came to refer exclusively to *this* world, and to be validated by procedures and forms of inquiry unambiguously of *this world*. This in turn engendered a world of sustained cognitive and economic growth, one within which social arrangements came to be legitimated largely by the fruits of such growth, but no longer by any overall vision of things.

The thinkers of the Enlightenment, who supposed that because revelation offered one social vision, therefore science would offer another one, only this time the *right* one, were mistaken. Revelation offers one vision and science offers, not another, but *none*. Some noted it, and called it the End of Ideology, but even they got it a bit wrong. They supposed that post-ideological man would be a person of sound pragmatic common sense. Perhaps indeed he is, in his professional and business dealings; but in his private life, he may be wildly self-indulgent and uncritical. He is used to being surrounded by gadgets with intuitively obvious controls; he more or less expects a similarly user-friendly universe, and he may well be most receptive to the slogan that *anything goes*. The 'post-modernist' outburst of subjectivism in the humanities and social sciences may be a reflection of this rather wider mood, of the, as it were, Californization of the West. If so, we may have to learn to live with it for a long time.

The newly created *European* Association of Anthropologists is liable to become the forum in which, once again, the previously separated segments of Europe will interact. Last time round, in anthropology, if I read the situation correctly, East European love of ethnic culture, and the desire to record and save it as an integral whole, blended with Western European empiricism as a method, *and* with ideas borrowed from biology, so as to engender, in the first instance, the functionalist school, and then the whole tradition which followed it. What will be the eastern and western elements this time round, assuming that a fertilization will indeed occur?

It is impossible to predict the crystallization of ideas before it happens: if one could predict it, it would already have happened. One can perhaps make some negative observations: East Europeans, after forty or seventy years of sustained dictatorship, will hardly be tempted to embrace a form of idealism which insists that coercion is essentially conceptual. They know only too well that, though it may manifest itself conceptually, the point at which it applies its lever to recalcitrant subjects is far more earthy and brutal. Nor are they likely to embrace eagerly the doctrine of the equality of all belief systems: they know that what brought them liberty was, precisely, the fact that the doctrine of social organization, of social and other knowledge, to which they had been forcibly subjected, turned out in the end to be manifestly, conspicuously inferior to its rival. So it is *not* the case that *anything* goes. Don't try to tell an East European that Marxism will do just as well as anything else, simply because anything goes.

For these various reasons I would not expect, at least logically, the intellectual reunification of Europe to favour the present mood of indulgent hermeneutic-subjectivist excess. But logical expectations are not always fulfilled, and my prediction may well be falsified by events. We shall see.

16

The Coming *Fin de Millénaire*

Out of the oil-smooth spirit of the last two decades of the nineteenth century, suddenly, throughout Europe, there rose a kindling fever. Nobody knew exactly what was on the way; nobody was able to say whether it was to be a new art, a New Man, a new morality or perhaps a reshuffling of society. So everyone made of it what he liked. But people were standing up on all sides to fight against the old way of life. Suddenly the right man was on the spot everywhere; and, what is so important, men of practical enterprise joined forces with the men of intellectual enterprise. Talents developed that had previously been choked or had taken no part at all in public life. They were as different from each other as anything well could be, and the contradictions in their aims were unsurpassable. The Superman was adored, and the Subman was adored; health and the sun were worshipped, and the delicacy of consumptive girls was worshipped; people were enthusiastic hero-worshippers and enthusiastic adherents of the social creed of the Man in the Street; one had faith and was sceptical, one was naturalistic and precious, robust and morbid; one dreamed of ancient castles and shady avenues, autumnal gardens, glassy ponds, jewels, hashish, disease and demonism, but also of prairies, vast horizons, forges and rolling-mills, naked wrestlers, the uprisings of the slaves of toil, man and woman in the primeval Garden, and the destruction of society. Admittedly these were contradictions and very different battle-cries, but they all breathed the same

> breath of life. If that epoch had been analysed, some such nonsense would have come out as a square circle supposed to be made of wooden iron; but in reality all this had blended into shimmering significance. This illusion, which found its embodiment in the magical date of the turn of the century, was so powerful that it made some hurl themselves enthusiastically upon the new, as yet untrodden century, while others were having a last fling in the old one, as in a house that one is moving out of anyway, without either one or the other party feeling that there was much difference between the two attitudes. (Robert Musil, *The Man Without Qualities*, translated by E. Wilkins and E. Kaiser (Secker and Warburg, London, 1953), volume 1, p. 59)

The old remark claims that history repeats itself: first as tragedy, second as farce. In this case it might be the other way round: the first time it was, unquestionably, fun. It was good to dissolve the over-confident certainties of the nineteenth century, and *fin de siècle* modernism did just that.

This time round, however, it is not obvious that there still are any certainties to be undermined. Scepticism or the overturning of truisms by now has an inverse or boomerang effect: by undermining the criteria of all rational criticism, it confers *carte blanche* on any arbitrary intellectual self-indulgence. Total relativism ends by underwriting cheap dogmatism. If anything goes, then you are also allowed to be as utterly dogmatic as you wish: the critical standards, which might once have inhibited you, have themselves been abrogated. What could there be to check you? He who tries to restrain you, in the name of fact or logic, will be castigated as positivist, or imperialist, or both: after all, objectivism was at the service of domination. Total permissiveness ends in arbitrary dogmatism.

The *fin de siècle* was liberating, the *fin de millénaire* may be wilfully destructive. We should be wary of some of our self-appointed liberators. This mood may not be dominant, but in some spheres within the humanities, social sciences, philosophy, it makes so much noise that one might well think it was. Because we disavow world domination, we must also abjure the law of non-contradiction. It seems a curious inference. Still, it does have a kind of bizarre logic: Europeans had listened to philosophers who told them that their own pre-eminence was also the triumph of reason on earth. So perhaps the termination of that eminence should also bring the disavowal of reason. The reasoning is self-centred, either way.

No doubt, the state of mind is similar to the mood described so eloquently by Robert Musil, but it is now a century later, and this time it is the end of a millennium, not just a century. With the approach of the year 1000, Europeans anticipated the end of the world, but it failed to materialize. My suspicion is that, with the coming of the year 2000, they do not expect the world to end, but this time it will happen. In any case, I do not wish to contribute to the dissolution of the world by joining in the repudiation of all order, consistency and objectivity. The principles of the current version of this terminalist mood are as difficult to pin down as were those of Robert Musil's day: we have the names, such as post-modernism, but it is less than easy to find out what the devil they stand for. I want to try to identify the elements which go into this witch's brew.

Unquestionably, one element in this mood or climate is the yearning for post-imperial expiation. During the preceding age of faith, the West had dominated the world: now, many of those at home in it wish to atone for what had been done, and even more, for what had been thought. The sins of thought are in a way considered more heinous than those of deeds. They added insult to injury, and the insult lingers on when the injury has passed into history. When the West dominated the world it was not content with this achievement alone, as perhaps some past conquerors might have been: it was not enough to be the victor and to benefit from domination. A theory was constructed which, in a manner humiliating for the losers and victims, ratified that domination, and made it a consequence, not of a possibly contingent victory, but of the decree issued by the very process of history, of evolution, of the nature of things. A great Chain of Being placed victors about the vanquished.

During the period of its triumph, the West believed in progress. This was its theodicy, the new justification of the ways of God, or the world, to man. The meaning of life was to be found in successful upward striving. The domination of the victors was due to the fact that they had progressed further than all others along a path prescribed for all mankind. The obverse of progress was backwardness, so that the victims were not merely losers, but also damned and condemned by the verdict of cosmic process.

This was the permanent slur imposed by industrial colonialism on its victims: they were human, but somewhat less so than those who had proved themselves by ascent to higher rungs on the evolutionary ladder. Domination was a sign of election, of a higher station along the Chain of Being. This evaluative and philosophical loading of the notion of backwardness was heavy and, in due course, a neologism had to be invented to enable one to speak of it without, it was hoped, retaining the emotive charge. This of course is the origin of the word 'under-development'.

It is perfectly understandable that one should wish to get away from such invidious ranking. But why should it oblige one to go so far in the opposite direction, to end with total relativism? The underlying reasoning seems to run as follows: suppose there were objective, universal, absolute truths – suppose, for instance, two plus two always, *always* made four, come what may, in any culture, in any context. It seems harmless enough, and indeed, most of us normally believe just that. But wait: suppose that someone, somewhere, denies this piece of arithmetic? Suppose, worse still, that there is an entire community which jointly denies it, at least on some occasions?

A collectivity united in a belief is a culture. That is what the term means. More particularly, a collectivity united in a false belief is a culture. Truths, especially demonstrable truths, are available to all and sundry, and do not define any community of faith. But errors, especially dramatic errors, are culture-specific. They do tend to be the badges of community and loyalty. Assent to an absurdity is an intellectual *rite de passage*, a gateway to the community defined by that commitment to that conviction. And now the trouble begins: if we persist in calling this eccentric belief *false*, we are castigating a whole culture. We are excluding it from humanity, or at least, we are consigning it to a lower level, in virtue of being backward, retarded, fit for colonization. This is no longer to be tolerated. So what is the alternative? To recognize that all cultures are equally valid, that they carry their own norms of validity with them, and that to judge and damn them from the outside in the name of putatively universal norms (which, in reality, are tools of domination and exploitation) is wrong. So: respect for others entails relativism.

This seems cogent enough, and many find it so. Unfortunately, there is a lot that is problematic about this position, practically and theoretically. For one thing, the beneficiaries of this relativism, in a significant proportion, probably the majority of cases, do not seem at all eager to benefit from it. On the contrary, they are only too eager to acquire technology, which brings economic and military power with it. Second, those other cultures were in very many cases far from relativistic or inter-culturally egalitarian to begin with, internally. Their ranking of internal castes, under whatever name, may have been very far indeed from conferring equal respect on all diversity. Their vision of external barbarians may well have fallen short of universal reverence for all the cultural products of the human spirit. So our ecumenical relativist, eager to respect all systems of truth and value in the interest of not spurning any humans – *humani nihil alienum* ('nothing relating to man is alien to me') – finds himself committing the very sin he would avoid, at second hand: the cultures he endorses (or very many of them) themselves commit it, so that by endorsing them, he pledges himself to spurning that which they spurn, within or outside their own borders.

Furthermore, whether or not it is acceptable, the relativistic strategy only has meaning in a world of reasonably identifiable, separable cultural islands. You can do in Rome as the Romans do, if you know, more or less, what the boundaries of Rome are. But our world in fact is not remotely like that: it consists of overlapping cultural units, in rapid change, frequently undergoing fission or fusion. The choice is not between the rites of Rome and those of some other city, but rather between opponents in an internal dispute within Rome. The relativistic recipe does not help you choose, even if you believe in it, because it only provides a recommendation on the assumption of the availability of clear, given units. These are simply not available in modern disputes. So relativism is useless, even if it did not have other defects.

Let us leave its defects and consider the roots of its popularity. Apart from the pursuit of expiation, there is what one may call the American weakness. America (perhaps jointly with other European settler societies in regions where the indigenous population is small or non-existent) has a specially strong and rather distinctive tendency to absolutize itself. Notoriously, those who declared the USA independent found their own moral and political intuitions self-evident, humanly and universally, and they said so brazenly, in a document perhaps more frequently quoted and reproduced than any other secular text in the history of humanity. For reasons of great interest and importance, a certain individualism and a rational attitude, which normally only prevails under successful industrialism, had already come to dominate the North American colonies, even when they were only associations of free farmers.

In other words, America was born modern: liberalism was not its dissent, but its orthodoxy. Many theorists have noted this basic paradox. But it has certain consequences: European liberal societies have a fairly vivid recollection of the *ancien régime* which they have overcome, and hence of the historic relativity of the new values. Americans do not. They may have beaten George III but they have no clear sense of what kind of society he represented, even if the ancestors of current Americans were fleeing not from Stewarts or Hanoverians, but from Romanovs or Habsburgs. So liberal rational individualism, for them, represents not *a* human condition, but *the* human condition.

That of course is an illusion. An individualist who holds it self-evident that he is free to seek happiness, choose his own aims and convictions, and treat government as a public convenience, is not man as such, but an unusual kind of man. When, in the course of more or less advanced education, this is recognized, the discovery is liable to be at first bewildering and then intoxicating. The discovery of a profound diversity in human visions comes as a stunning surprise. It can be felt as a great liberation, but also as a moral insight, whose denial implies contempt for others and so deserves severe reprobation. When superimposed on and fused with the desire to expiate domination and assumption of superiority, relativism seems to be a morally binding revelation, and its denial appears as Politically Incorrect. So here we find an extensive and eager clientele, the consumers of facile relativism.

There is still another social source: the failure of the social sciences. In 1945, when America inherited world leadership and the White Man's Burden (now in the form of aid to underdevelopment), this was accompanied by the hope that the required effort would be assisted by sociological understanding. Talcott Parsons adapted Weberianism for the purpose of understanding a world undergoing the travails of industrialization; the men around him considered him to be the Newton of sociology, and themselves the Royal Society. Natural science was technical and its language unintelligible to outsiders. So social science must be similar, but all these men really achieved was the development of an impenetrable jargon, but one not endowed with any other merits. The expected Newtonian principles never emerged. They wrecked the prose style of the social sciences, but made no cognitive breakthrough. What to do?

Unable to offer any precise or powerful generalizations, but needing some professional revelations to justify their profession, many of the social sciences fell back on showing how societies (allegedly) construct their respective worlds. 'The social construction of reality' has become a key phrase. It enables them to claim that they have something important to tell us which we would otherwise be without. It vindicates many of the social sciences, by constituting their particular contribution to human knowledge. They tell us how we make our world, when previously we had thought, naïvely, that it existed without us. But this also made all such socially created worlds equal.

My favourite example of *sitting* is an example of how this works. Suppose you tell someone to *sit down*. No problem, no mystery there, nothing is hidden, nothing requires explanation, you might naïvely suppose. How wrong you are. A man who sits down *knows* he is sitting down. He possesses the *concept* of sitting, which he shares with other members of his culture, and which as it were guides and inspires his performance. Without the concept, there would be no action, only an inert physical state.

What does *sitting* mean? Placing one's *bum* in steady contact with a *chair* – so two further concepts are immediately and inevitably involved. The notion of a chair is associated with rank – there are people in whose presence you may not sit down first – and with the cultural boundary between chair-using and rug-using societies. There is an association with authority-conferring chairs – Chairs, thrones, *ex cathedra* authority. All scholarly, religious, political hierarchy and authority is implicitly present.

As for *bum*, its associations are at least as potent. The boundary between those who may and those who may not bare their bums is the boundary between children who are not full moral persons and adults who are. Between the latter, baring a bum is a very significant sign of either privileged intimacy or membership of a nudist club. Bums are comic, rude, dirty and sexually stimulating, hence dangerous. Their absurdity is a safety-valve, releasing some of the tension engendered by their intense desirability. Hence they are intimately linked to the aesthetic, moral, kinship boundaries of an entire culture. So every time you sit, you *ipso facto* employ a concept which in turn links you to an entire cultural-moral universe, its values and its tensions and its conflicts. Without that universe, your act would not be what it is, it would only be a dead, meaningless physical condition, rather than a part of a life: but your act, by reaffirming the concept, sustains that universe, whose concepts are linked to each other in a living totality. This two-way interaction has been called 'structuration', and this word is meant to explain how society both is and is not the mere sum of the individuals composing it. It is made up of individual acts, but it also permeates and defines *them*.

Pieces of prose like the one above are not untypical of a good deal of current social theory, though my attempt may not be up to the highest standards of the genre, and I do not expect to receive much acclamation for it. But this style does not merely provide the practitioner with prestige, and a product all his own which he can offer: it also has another role. The fact that all these worlds are socially constructed makes them an option, a historically specific system of ideas, carried by a distinctive, non-universal community. This means that they possess only a restricted and not an absolute validity. Nothing is, but thinking (collectively, by a whole culture) makes it so. This argument can be used to erase the validity of any fact or affirmation: but of course, it can also be used to establish and validate any favoured claim. So, all hostile characterization of favoured groups can be dismissed at a stroke, without any tedious and arduous investigation into their empirical foundation. This is 'deconstruction'. Likewise, however, favoured convictions are automatically underwritten, their authority derived from the support they give to the collectivity in question. This ease of both legitimation and delegitimation, at will, is very much part of that *fin de millénaire* conceptual permissiveness and antinomianism, the vaunted liberation from previous empirical or logical strait-jackets.

The argument to validity from favoured interests was of course anticipated in some versions of Marxism, which escaped the relativism implied by some of its own doctrines by formulations such as the claim that whatever aids the liberation of the working class is *ipso facto* true (in the words of one contemporary guru). Late Marxism had made its own significant contribution to the mood. Once, long ago, Marxism was endowed with a lot of positive views, with true consciousness as it were, and it only had its theory of false consciousness as a relatively minor appendage, to explain, for instance, the failure of the Germans of Marx's youth to see the truth, because they sought consolation for their then weakness in philosophical fantasy. As ever more of the doctrine of Marxism was refuted by history, and true consciousness shrank asymptotically to zero, the theory of false consciousness correspondingly expanded to take up the vacated area. So it became the much vaunted specialism of terminal Marxism, its practitioners indulging in exactly the kind of thing that Marx and Engels had ridiculed in *The German Ideology*: they consoled themselves for their own political impotence by prancing about in a philosophical cloud-cuckoo-land.

There was another movement which was rather fashionable a couple of decades or so ago, known as Ethno-methodology, which had its own distinctive style of achieving this antinomial permissiveness. It had been founded by a man who shared, allowing for nuances of spelling, the name both of a pop singer and of a chain of cheap restaurants, which somehow had a certain appositeness. The central gimmick of 'Ethno-methodology' was the invocation of the following dualism: our statements are claims to truth but they are also made by concrete people, usually with aims in mind, in definite social contexts. Practitioners of this style focused on the latter aspect and allowed it to trump the other consideration. Thus evidence or procedural propriety could not be invoked, as these were after all but moves in a game, made by an interested party, and it was legitimate for his rival to make other moves. The fact that a critical question elicits a contradiction or an error in your own position does not matter. A critic's question was a move made by an opponent, and can be explained and discounted as such: this characterization is treated as a valid delegitimation, but also a licence to disregard all customary procedural proprieties.

This type of device was also prominent in psychoanalysis, within which the motives are more important than evidence in interpreting the significance of an affirmation; in Freudianism this is a corollary of the alleged role of the Unconscious, whereas in Ethno-methodology it was made to follow from the social role of discourse. In each case, claims to genuine truth are smuggled in at the end (you cannot really do without them), but only at the discretion and under the control of the practitioner. I do not know whether Ethno-methodology is still practised, or whether it has been the victim of the planned obsolescence which is inherent in the life of these fads: but it has none the less made its own contribution to our climate.

The same is also true, on an incomparably larger scale, both of Wittgenstein and of Phenomenology. Wittgenstein's doctrine of the essentially social nature of all concepts, and of the as it were terminal authority of speech communities ('forms of life') has precisely the antinomian implications so favoured by the mood in question: all cultures makes their own world, and there can be no other. Wittgenstein is now *vieux jeu* in philosophy: too many people are familiar with the opening moves, so familiarity with them no longer confers any prestige – but they continue to be deployed in fields such as literary studies, where they are still a novelty. Phenomenology also highlights and authenticates the *Lebenswelt*, the lived world. This plays a role similar to a 'form of life' in Wittgenstein. In both cases, there is a tendency to link political correctness to the 'lived' or communal world, and to castigate the use of critical knowledge as 'scientism'.

Can that overall mood, with its variety of social and intellectual origins (which I am sure I have not exhausted) be given a general characterization? Robert Musil, describing the last *fin de siècle*, contented himself with listing the contradictions and contrasting them with the preceding complacent tranquillity. Can we do more? What pervades this mood is an insistence on relativism, subjectivity, intellectual permissiveness, antinomianism and a consequent obscurity. We are in the presence of a conceptual saturnalia, in which the rules are suspended and spurned, and those who cling to them mocked. The violators of the old rules are aggressively self-righteous, and eager to stigmatize those who do follow them morally and politically. Whether it all does much harm is hard to say: carnivals are fun, but carnivals without end may become tedious. Treating all cognitive claims like masks and costumes at a permanent fiesta, optional and free of any factual or logical restraint, all allegedly in the name of intercultural equality, will not do.

There is a highly influential American anthropologist who would have us believe that we have nothing to fear from relativism, and who castigates 'anti-relativists' as men needlessly afraid of something quite innocuous – frightened, it would seem, of their own shadows. He himself, with somewhat self-conscious insouciance and underscored boyish charm, is perfectly at home with the bogey and has no difficulty in domesticating him. It won't bite, not if you show it that you are not afraid.

The truth is quite different. It is only a failure to understand the issues which permits such debonair nonchalance. Cognitive relativism is nonsense, moral relativism is tragic. You cannot understand the human condition if you ignore or deny its total transformation by the success of the scientific revolution. The recognition of the inequality of cognitive claims in no way involves unequal treatment of people – quite the reverse. The accidental initiators of the scientific revolution have no monopoly of it, and are not necessarily its best practitioners. Valid knowledge ignores and does not engender frontiers. One simply cannot understand our shared social condition unless one starts from the indisputable fact that genuine knowledge of nature is possible and has occurred, totally transforming the terms of reference in which human societies operate.

To pretend that the scientific revolution of the seventeenth century, and its eventual application in the later stage of the industrial revolution, have not transformed the world, but are merely changes from one culture to another, is simply an irresponsible affectation. The same is true of the 'social construction of reality', which has been grotesquely exaggerated: it needs to be complemented by *the natural construction of society*. There are limits to the extent to which societies can construct their own worlds, and these limits need to be explored. Our new power to control has also brought a sense of the extent to which we are controlled. It is not true that any old world is possible, and within the range of possible worlds, not all of them are cognitively equal.

At the same time, the great change which brought us understanding and control of nature has also deprived us of the possibility of underwriting our values – something to which large segments of humanity have become accustomed during the age of faith in doctrinal religion. Moral legitimation requires a firm data base, so to speak, for our world, and its rigid linkage to moral assessment. Both kinds of rigidity are destroyed by the very form of knowledge which has also freed us from penury. So our moral crisis is also the fruit of our liberation from want and tyranny. Our predicament is – to work out the social options of our affluent and disenchanted condition. We have no choice in this matter. To pretend otherwise, to claim that the problem does not even arise, but has been replaced by the Permanent Carnival, is absurd. The *fin de millénaire* should have its fireworks, but let it not deprive us of our sense of reality.

Index